MAKING JAZZ FRENCH

American Encounters / Global Interactions

A series edited by Gilbert M. Joseph and Emily S. Rosenberg

This series aims to stimulate critical perspectives and fresh
interpretive frameworks for scholarship on the history of the
imposing global presence of the United States. Its primary concerns
include the deployment and contestation of power, the construction
and deconstruction of cultural and political borders, the fluid
meanings of intercultural encounters, and the complex interplay
between the global and the local. American Encounters seeks to
strengthen dialogue and collaboration between historians of U.S.
international relations and area studies specialists.

The series encourages scholarship based on multiarchival
historical research. At the sa   e
representational character o
critical inquiry into issues of
process, American Encounte
which meanings related to nations, cultures, and political economy
are continually produced, challenged, and reshaped.

D1114601

MAKING JAZZ
FRENCH

Music and Modern Life

in Interwar Paris

JEFFREY H. JACKSON

Duke University Press

Durham & London

2003

© 2003 Duke University Press

All rights reserved

Printed in the United States of America

on acid-free paper ∞

Designed by C. H. Westmoreland

Typeset in Granjon with Monotype

Twentieth Century display

by Keystone Typesetting, Inc.

Library of Congress Cataloging-

in-Publication Data appear on the last

printed page of this book.

To my parents,

Judy and Harold Jackson

CONTENTS

ACKNOWLEDGMENTS

I (unwittingly) began researching this book as a graduate seminar paper. When I found that surprisingly few French historians had written about jazz in the interwar years, I decided to pursue the topic a bit further. This book is the result of that exploration.

Several archives and libraries in Paris provided sources for this research, particularly La Bibliothèque de l'Arsenal. Visits to La Bibliothèque Nationale, La CARAN, La Bibliothèque de l'Opéra, La Bibliothèque Centrale de Radio France, Le Musée de Montmartre, L'Archive de Paris, L'Archive de la Prefecture de Police, and La Bibliothèque Publique d'Information produced additional information in varying quantities. Outside of Paris, the library and archive at La Discothèque Municipale in Villefranche-de-Rouergue—a unique collection of documents about jazz formed from the library of Hugues Panassié—proved quite useful, and the staff was most generous. In the United States, the Institute for Jazz Studies at Rutgers University was a valuable resource, as were the University of Rochester's Rush Rhees and Sibley Music Libraries, and Rhodes College's Burrow Library, and their staffs. The exhibition *Paris in the Jazz Age*, produced by the Smithsonian Institution Traveling Exhibition Service, was on display during the summer of 1997 in Washington, D.C., and it also supplied some additional background material.

First thanks go to Alice Conklin, my adviser at the University of Rochester, who has seen this project grow from an idea into its current state. She guided and encouraged me with her great personal and intellectual generosity through this book's early days, first as a paper, then as a dissertation, with insightful comments and careful, probing questions that helped improve my thinking and writing. Other Rochesterians to whom I am indebted for their assistance and support include the other members of my dissertation committee, Celia Applegate and Ralph Locke, along with William J. McGrath, Daniel Borus, Joan Shelly Rubin, Daniel Albright, Mary Kay Carter, Chuck Brotman, Sean Guerin, and Kathy Kyger, all of whom offered comments and conversations at one point or another along the way. I also want to thank everyone in the Department of History at the University of Rochester—faculty, graduate students, and staff—for providing the kind of stimulating intellectual environment that made this work possible.

In Paris, Anne Legrand at La Bibliothèque Nationale allowed me to have special access to the Fonds Charles Delaunay, which she was still in the process of cataloging, and gave me much important information and wisdom. Ludovic Tournès and I have exchanged ideas and encouragement on both sides of the Atlantic. Michel Fabre graciously invited me into his home in Paris and provided me with information and sources. Christian Senn of Lutry, Switzerland, shared his privately published book on Hugues Panassié with me along with much correspondence and numerous articles on jazz.

Both Tyler Stovall and Charles Rearick have offered valuable advice about sources, archives, approaches, and themes. They have been wonderfully perceptive readers and supporters of this project for a long time. Dan Sherman shared with me *un café*, some expert advice on sources, and a much appreciated critical reading of my *French Historical Studies* article based on this research. Scott Haine, Jim Winders, and Kathy Kyger read the manuscript as it moved along toward final revisions and offered valuable insights. Shanny Peer read the original seminar paper out of which this work emerged and gave me important early criticism. Fellow researchers on the subject of jazz in France, Beth Vihlen and Seth Shulman, shared conversations and ideas with me at conferences. In our collaboration on music and history, Stan Pelkey has helped refine my thinking about the intersection of these two subjects. Jeff Ravel has encouraged me along the way and was the first to tell me how to decipher the "logic" of Parisian archives. Audiences at various conferences and a history department seminar at Vanderbilt University (where I first discovered my love of history as an undergraduate) aided in improving and clarifying my ideas throughout the life of this project.

On the logistical side of things: in France, my thanks to Emmanuelle Gallo for her assistance in finding me a place to stay while conducting the initial research. Isabelle Lehuu provided much appreciated help the second time around. In the United States, my thanks to Ghislaine Radagonde-Eison for her assistance in telephoning and writing to people in France. Both she and my friend and colleague at Rhodes College Sarah Crisler also helped me to translate when my own language skills still fell a bit short. My research assistant at Rhodes College, Robert Edgecombe, aided in getting the footnotes into proper shape. The history department's tireless administrative assistant, Nancy Hunt, helped with the bibliography, the footnotes, and various technical matters (including keeping me laughing and full of candy).

This work was made possible by the financial support of departmental fellowships and awards from the University of Rochester, a National Endowment for the Humanities Summer Stipend, a Bernadotte E. Schmitt Grant from the American Historical Association, and a grant from the Sinfonia Foundation. The dean's office at Rhodes College generously provided funds for reproducing the photographs. Portions of this work have appeared previously as: "Making Jazz French: The Reception of Jazz Music in Paris, 1927–1934," *French Historical Studies* 25 (winter 2002); "Music-Halls and the Assimilation of Jazz in 1920s Paris," *Journal of Popular Culture* 32 (fall 2001); "African-Americans and the French Imagination," book review essay in *Modern and Contemporary France* (August 2000); "Making Enemies: Jazz in Interwar Paris," *French Cultural Studies* 10 (June 1999).

Finally, this work and everything it represents would have been absolutely unthinkable without the loving and gracious support of my entire family, but most especially my parents to whom I dedicate this book.

INTRODUCTION

In 1920, just as France was beginning to recover from a victorious albeit devastating experience in the Great War, one popular song began to proclaim another equally ambiguous kind of triumph: "Jazz-band partout!" (Jazz band everywhere!)—the arrival of jazz in Paris.

> There're jazz bands by day, by night
> There're jazz bands everywhere
> It's all the rage in Paris, it makes men crazy
> It's played in the perfect way
> With flutes, castanets
> Banjo here, bells there
> It's exciting, this little thing
> There're jazz bands by day, by night
> There're jazz bands everywhere
> It's all the rage in Paris, it makes men crazy
> Do the jazz band, girls
> You'll tell me about it
> Here underneath
> In all the holes-in-the-wall
> There're jazz bands
> There're jazz bands, jazz bands everywhere![1]

Lyrics like these are remarkable for several reasons, beginning with the fact that they were written only a short time after a wild, new music known as "jazz" had arrived in France. American bands came to Paris during the war to entertain troops and civilians with upbeat, syncopated music of various sorts, and some of the players had remained behind to perform when the fighting ended. But the suggestion that their novel and often shocking tunes would be "everywhere" so quickly and so thoroughly implied that by 1920, jazz had already become a defining part of life in the postwar age. Although jazz was not yet in every corner of the city, these lines did not entirely overstate the music's success either. All around Paris in 1920, just as the lyricist reported—and even more so in the years that followed—musicians played jazz in music halls (like L'Eldorado, where this song debuted), dance halls, cabarets, nightclubs, bars, and restaurants.

Jazz came into people's living rooms too as recorded dance music and phonograph players became more plentiful and less expensive throughout the 1920s and 1930s. Even the majestic Opéra house, the Second Empire palace of art music, could not escape a jazz performance or two.

The words of "Jazz-Band Partout!" point to more than just the popularity of jazz, though. They also reveal the simultaneous confusion and exhilaration that were common to descriptions of life in the early 1920s. Jazz, the music that "makes men crazy," was already starting to shape the era that some in France would come to call *les années folles*—the crazy years. Jazz was not just music, it seemed. Rather, it marked the onset of a new and challenging age. To all who thought much about it in the postwar years, the arrival of jazz signaled the beginning of a new kind of warfare: a series of battles over music, art, and ultimately what kind of nation France would be in the twentieth century. Like the unclear political and cultural consequences of World War I, to many the conquest of Paris by jazz seemed ambiguous at best.

The first part of this book tries to understand how a song like "Jazz-Band Partout!" could have been written in the first place by describing how jazz music became a prominent and vital part of life in Paris during the 1920s and 1930s. At the end of World War I, Paris erupted into a frenzy of entertainment that almost guaranteed the popularity of jazz, whose upbeat sounds were perfect for the dance craze of the era. Americans and other tourists from around the world along with nouveaux riches French poured money into Parisian show business, helping to make jazz profitable in nightclubs and music halls. Radios, phonographs, and sound film spread the music beyond the city's entertainment districts and, over time, throughout the countryside. French composers also heard the spark of inspiration in its pounding drumbeats and began to blend jazz with their own works.

Many of the early performers of jazz in Paris were small bands that have been lost to historical record keeping. But the history of jazz in interwar Paris is, even more than a record of those who performed it, the story of the listeners who heard it. Parisians struggled to understand what jazz really was, what it meant for this music to be "everywhere," and how they might deal with it. Rather than looking at musicians, except when they worked to affect how audiences perceived jazz, my story focuses on the audiences, their reactions, and the sense that they made out of jazz. In particular, by drawing on a variety of printed sources from the 1920s and 1930s, this book pays attention to the active interpreters of jazz. Some of the voices here are the words of professional music critics, musicologists, composers, and performers, all of whom had a specific interest in music and how it was played, and who frequently wrote about jazz as part of a larger musical context. Many of the interwar era's men of letters, like Michel Leiris and Jean Cocteau, also wrote of their love for jazz. For them, it was less a symbol of musical developments than a sign of broader cultural trends. Other comments are those of a self-conscious community of French jazz fans who eagerly wanted to bring this music to their compatriots. However, most of the words in this story are those of the journalists, commentators, and chroniclers of Parisian life writing in newspapers, periodicals, and books about Paris in the 1920s and 1930s. They did not necessarily speak for the musical profession but rather as more general observers of their times. Although the descriptions and opinions of these writers may not have represented all the ways in which Parisians thought about jazz, they did give voice to a wide range of views. These writers also shaped Parisian attitudes about the music through their analyses and editorials. Despite their diversity, one of the remarkable facts about these authors was their common interest in jazz, a music that while certainly not the only sound in interwar Paris, was nevertheless the one that attracted the attention of so many people because of its power to raise vital cultural questions of the day.

What emerges from among their descriptions, critiques, and commentaries is a series of energetic debates about jazz. Celebrated by its fans, jazz was frequently heralded as a breath of fresh air that would reinvigorate a nation exhausted by war and the constraints of traditional morality. But jazz was not universally welcomed, and its detractors were forceful in their attacks on what the music sounded like as well as what they thought it symbolized. The arguments on both sides of the issue were sometimes about musical qualities, but more often than not, they betrayed a much broader set of hopes and fears about the postwar era. In particular, I would suggest, they revealed a persistent ambivalence about what life would be like in the new century, whose primary feature was now a "total war" that had exaggerated and accelerated dramatic changes begun in the late nineteenth century. The arrival of jazz coincided with the further development of several other aspects of what might be called "modern life" in the 1920s and 1930s, and it came to serve as a convenient symbol for these larger phenomena. By describing jazz as a marker of "modern life," I hope to recreate, from the discussions that surrounded it, a series of themes that critics and commentators themselves believed linked this music to the larger patterns of change that they witnessed in their lives. Together, these transformations constituted some of the ways in which they viewed their experience in what was both a new century and a reconstituted postwar world.[2]

First, the modern life of the 1920s, as it appeared to those who wrote about jazz, meant the increasing ease with which people, ideas, and artistic expressions moved throughout the world. The twentieth century, many interwar authors indicated, would be an era of more intensive and extensive contact between nations and cultures around the globe than in previous times, aided now by the development of transportation and communications technology that increased the speed as well as the quantity of movement and change. Interactions between nations were certainly not new in the early twentieth century, especially in France, which had a long history of global trade, and during the late nineteenth century, a flurry of colonial expansion throughout Africa and Asia. Generations of immigrants to France had already contributed to the country's evolving literary, artistic, and musical traditions. And international exchange in the arts was nothing new to the French since Paris had long been a crossroads at which artists from many countries could meet. But a greater sense of movement, fluidity, and exchange marked off the early twentieth century as something different, according to many, and jazz was a part of that phenomenon. After all, the Jazz Age was also the era of the motion picture, the mass-produced automobile, and Charles Lindbergh's daring transatlantic crossing.[3]

In particular, jazz music symbolized the influence that mobile "foreigners" were thought to be having on France in the years after World War I, especially since musicians from the United States originally played it and many foreign tourists listened to it. But the question of "foreignness" was much more significant in the interwar period than just an issue of fun-loving tourists and raucous musicians. Along with jazz, the Great War had opened the doors to foreign soldiers from Britain, the United States, and the colonies in Africa, and to workers from around the world who came to France in numbers never before seen. By the war's end, the presence of foreign laborers had created enough anxiety among the French to provoke several racial disturbances throughout the country.[4] Although most wartime troops and laborers were sent home by the 1920s, the French government and many businesses had begun to encourage other groups of immigrant workers, mainly from elsewhere in Europe, to come to France and fill jobs left vacant by a generation of young men who had fallen in battle. Doing so, they hoped, would help to rebuild the nation after the ravages of war, but they were also setting the scene for lasting resentments between immigrants and French laborers. Workers were not the only group of newcomers in the early twentieth century. France had also welcomed refugees from Eastern Europe who fled war and revolution after World War I. These new populations set up small immigrant communities, bringing their own food, music, and customs with them.[5] All of these newcomers, sometimes tolerated but often feared, provided evidence for xenophobes who continued to warn against both the impurity and decadence of the era as well as a loss of more traditional French ways of life.[6]

Nor was the musical world immune to the fear of foreigners. As the musicologist Jane Fulcher has shown, the world of French art music had become radically politicized in the wake of the Dreyfus affair with competing music academies that promoted different visions of the nation—one nativist with religious overtones, the other Republican and secular—through their musical philosophies and curricula.[7] In the 1920s and 1930s, many cultural nationalists opposed the presence of jazz musicians as interlopers who were corrupting French artistry. The twentieth-century mobility that brought new music and musicians to France further contributed to what many cultural conservatives saw as a decline in "traditional" French kinds of entertainment. Jazz's wild and crazy noises hardly seemed like the more familiar chansons that told of the exploits of the common French people, for example. Musicians' labor unions, although less concerned with issues of cultural decline, argued that foreign bands, especially the popular jazz bands, were taking French musicians' jobs and salaries, and they sought to regulate or eliminate outsiders for economic reasons.

A second aspect of modern life seen through the lens of writings about jazz builds on the theme of mobility: the growing influence of Americans on Europe, especially France.[8] Although as historians have discussed, the most intensive thrust of *américanisation* did not begin until after World War II, critics in the interwar era had already begun to see the power of American culture and money at work, and they considered the bustling economy of the United States and the mass-produced consumer goods it provided as a measure for life in the modern age. U.S. businesses eagerly invested in war-torn Europe, and American officials believed that U.S. consumer goods would act as a "leavening agent" to help raise Europe's economic activity and quality of life as it rebuilt itself.[9] Americans who traveled to France—whether as tourists, as employees of U.S. firms, or in jazz bands—brought an entire culture with them, according to many French observers. From flashy American-style advertising to discount stores to the "Taylorization" of factories, the United States seemed to be at the forefront of all that was "modern" about the new century.[10] And as the sound of America, jazz also became the sound of the modern age.

A third quality of modern life that was more specific to the Parisian context was the sense of continuing change in urban life that coincided and came to be associated with jazz music. The city of Paris—whose modernization was begun in the 1860s by Baron Georges-Eugène Haussmann—became quieter and more tightly regulated during the war. But afterward, some important changes extended the late-nineteenth-century trends that had made Paris the height of urban living.[11] Electric lights spread further throughout the city, and the steady introduction of automobiles increased traffic and mobility on city streets.[12] Cars rather than horse-drawn carriages now brought people to nightclubs, whose outdoor neon signs lit up the Parisian night sky. Many authors suggested that the character of certain neighborhoods, particularly old artists' haunts, changed dramatically after the war with the influx of tourists and jazz bands. These parts of the city, especially Montmartre and Montparnasse, seemed to illustrate best the effects of the city's transformation into a modern, urban center.

Life in the modern city was also associated with mass consumption and flashy entertainment. With the evolving urban culture came ever more daring spectacles that catered to pleasure-seekers who craved exotic escape. Tourists ready to spend conspicuously and play shamelessly throughout the city appeared, to many commentators, to swell in numbers in the Paris of the modern age. And the city operated more and more on a model of mass consumption, whether in the late-nineteenth-century department stores that remained an important stop for tourists, the relatively new discount *prix uniques* stores, or the studios of artists whose works many Americans came to buy. In this modern, urban setting, jazz was yet another product to consume as part of an evening's leisure.[13]

The theme that underlay all of these interlocking associations between jazz and modern life was a set of persistent questions: What kind of nation would France be in the new century? Was French identity based on a set of deeply rooted traditions, or was it compatible with the cutting-edge changes of the twentieth century? In short, was modern life the opposite of French identity, or was being modern—on the move, open to other cultures, using the latest technology, dancing to the era's new music—a fundamental part of, or at least compatible with, being French?[14]

In the midst of these debates about the nature of modern life and how jazz might affect the future of France, a generation of young jazz devotees began to alter perceptions of the music in ways that brought it into French musical culture. That incorporation—which forms an important set of responses to the challenges that jazz raised as a hallmark of modern life—is the focus of the second part of this book. Some bands composed entirely of French musicians, for example, believed that they had learned to play jazz just as well as the Americans, and they now claimed the glory for French performers. Other musicians played traditional French chansons and folk songs with jazz rhythms and instrumentation, thereby linking a modern style with older French melodies. And during the 1930s, the Hot Club de France, the country's premiere jazz appreciation society, disseminated jazz to new audiences across France. To all of these individuals, and to many in their audiences, jazz was not necessarily foreign because it had become something "French." By altering the performers, musical repertoire, and listenership of jazz, French musicians and fans created their own jazz culture with French songs, personalities, and practices. In doing so, they lived an interpretation of France as a nation that was able to bring new influences into its own tradition and update that tradition for the twentieth century. By the end of World War II, jazz was no longer "away from home," as the jazz historian Chris Goddard has claimed in the title of his book on jazz in England and France in the 1920s.[15] Instead, listeners had given it new homes all across Europe, and especially in France—a fact proven in part by the overwhelming success of jazz during World War II and the continuing present-day popularity of jazz in French entertainment.[16]

In describing this process of "making jazz French," I am not claiming that French musicians transformed jazz as a musical form into something substantially different from what it was in the United States, nor am I suggesting that a musically distinct kind of "French jazz" existed independent of jazz in the United States.[17] Rather, what I aim to show is that this jazz community altered the meaning and perception of jazz in France. They did so by arguing that it was no longer a foreign music, but instead one that could be played by French musicians without threat or hypocrisy. They created a set of institutions that brought jazz into French musical culture because they believed it was something every French person could appreciate. Even more boldly, some contended that jazz echoed various aspects of a presumed French national character. Musicians who played French chansons in a jazz style suggested that jazz was not a break with the past but merely a way to update France's heritage while simultaneously remaining true to it.

This image of a vital and growing jazz community that was able to adapt new influences to a dynamic vision of their nation also says something about the "culture wars" of the 1920s and 1930s. Some historians have chosen to depict the *entre-deux-guerres* as largely "hollow years," to borrow Eugen Weber's phrase about the 1930s, in which the impending Vichy regime and its Nazi collaboration loom large.[18] Drawing on Robert O. Paxton's interpretation of Pétain's conservative political-cultural revolution as the outgrowth of conflicts from the previous decades, historians like Herman Lebovics have portrayed this era as the moment in which cultural politicians on the Right successfully constructed the idea that the authentic and "true" French nation emerged only from the French soil.[19] Lebovics concludes that Republicans and the Left, while maintaining their own definition of the nation, bought into the Right's vision enough to make it the most powerful by the end of the Third Republic.[20] Art historian Romy Golan extends the argument about the power of cultural conservatism to the realm of creative activity by connecting the French artistic community that was devastated by World War I with the cultural politics of Vichy. The depiction of the French people and landscape in interwar painting, Golan suggests, made Pétain's revolution not only thinkable but acceptable in people's minds by showing the nation as "rural, feudalized, 'feminized,' and victimized" in the art of the period, thus leading to "France's craving for self-infantilization during the years of Vichy."[21] In Golan's account, France was weakened beyond salvation, and Vichy, whose path French artists had helped to prepare, was the logical consequence. Likewise, Martha Hanna sees France's intellectual and academic community succumbing to "intellectual nationalism" in the post–World War I era, and a more open, Republican vision of France falling by the wayside.[22] These historians have provided a useful map of conservative responses to the changes that war, Republicanism, mobility, and foreigners wrought in France, and have demonstrated the powerful reaction against modern life in the 1920s and 1930s—a view consistent with many denunciations of jazz from that time.

But other historians have stressed the more flexible and adaptive capacity of France during the 1920s and 1930s, indicating that a variety of creative endeavors remained crucial to people in the interwar years—from the changing literary images of women that Mary Louise Roberts describes to the daring tales found in spy literature that Michael Miller examines. As Miller puts it, "The French possessed greater self-assuredness than we have been inclined to see in these years."[23] Such self-assuredness has come through in the many ways in which the French people adapted themselves to the new era of the 1920s and 1930s. Shanny Peer illustrates, for example, how France negotiated between tradition and modernity at the 1937 World's Fair and, simultaneously, blended visions of a "true France" with américanisation and modern technology to create a new France for the twentieth century. Marjorie Beale and Stephen L. Harp both demonstrate how elites accommodated American methods of management, advertising, and mass production to fashion an updated French business leadership style that still retained treasured qualities of the past.[24] Charles Rearick's examination of popular culture during the interwar years highlights the recurring literary and cinematic image of the *débrouillard*, the resourceful, heroic "little guy" who overcomes the challenges all around him with aplomb and vigor.[25] As described by these historians, the processes of adaptation taking place during the 1920s and 1930s helped France to navigate between the extremes of the immediate past and fears of the impending future to craft a livable present in the midst of profound change. The future and modern age were just as much a part of the understanding of many interwar French people, these authors contend, as the past and tradition were for those who Lebovics and others depict. Such works serve as a reminder that in describing the potency of the Vichy regime, one of Paxton's points was that definitions of the French nation, sparked in part by changes in modern life, were still very much up for grabs in the 1920s and 1930s. The Vichy culture warriors felt the need to settle the issue definitively precisely because there was still a viable alternative to their own.

The story of jazz's integration into French entertainment is another example of the many imaginative ways in which some of the French people dealt with the challenges of life in the new century, and it offers another vision of the contest to define what France would be in the post–World War I era. Amid the xenophobia of the time, which often made jazz a target of attack because of its foreign origins, many French jazz musicians illustrated the more flexible and open side of French culture. Not all parts of the French artistic community were disillusioned by the war, nor were all discussions of culture traditionalist ones. Analyses of the age, like that of Romy Golan's, frequently turn on the conservative overtones of words like *nostalgia*, by arguing that France was "driven toward the restoration of what had been *before* the war."[26] But by playing French chansons in a jazz style, for instance, some musicians used a nostalgia for French music as a way of rooting a modern sound in the French heritage without losing the best qualities of either. To be sure, many players often did seek to keep foreign musicians out of Paris for economic reasons, and they sometimes spoke out against the broader effects of imported music into France. Yet most did not want to eliminate jazz altogether, as if somehow perceiving it as a threat to their sense of national culture like many conservatives did. Instead, French musicians simply wanted to be able to play jazz themselves—as Frenchmen—and to be acknowledged by audiences for their talent.

A final musical note: What, more precisely, did French audiences hear, and what did French musicians play? There was a wide variety of opinion in France (as in the United States) about what actually constituted "jazz" from the moment that American musicians and their syncopated rhythms arrived. Most French listeners and critics agreed that it had been created by black Americans and therefore reflected something of their history. Most agreed that it was noisy, it emphasized rhythm, it was upbeat, and that one could dance to it. Beyond these basics, what people meant when they used the term *jazz* depended on who was using it—just as in the United States, where the term was also being used to describe a wide variety of dance music.[27] For my purposes, music talked about, labeled, and marketed as jazz, regardless of who played it (or whether it meets today's definitions), was part of this phenomenon, and so was the wide variety of dance music that was called jazz in the 1920s, since jazz was usually seen first and foremost as something for dancing. Dance tunes were often labeled more specifically by their steps—such as fox-trots, two-steps, or Charlestons—but they were so frequently talked about in the same sentence as jazz and so often described as subsets of jazz that they can fit into a broader definition here. Bands and orchestras that performed jazz-influenced orchestral pieces like George Gershwin's *Rhapsody in Blue* fall into the category because they often called themselves jazz orchestras. And one must certainly include the music considered to be jazz by today's scholars. What all of these sounds had in common to listeners was the fact that they were new, sometimes shocking, and signaled a change in the way people thought about music and culture more broadly. The word *jazz* applied to any sound marked it as something different. But listeners could make unique things out of their experiences with jazz, including redefining it as something French. Because of its flexible definition, its meaning could be readily shaped. In that sense, this book is not about jazz, in the strictly musical sense meaning the notes that musicians played. Rather, it is about France, about what the arrival of a music that was being called jazz meant to people in the turbulent interwar period, and about how they used the concept of jazz to understand and remake their age.

1

THE

ARRIVAL

OF JAZZ

Parisians were already accustomed to the presence of Americans in their city by the time of the Great War. Throughout the preceding century, Paris had been an important educational and cultural destination for intellectuals, artists, and wealthy travelers from the United States who admired its history, sophistication, and opportunities for recreation. By the century's end, that contact had expanded, and the growing personal familiarity with Americans added to French curiosity about the young, dynamic United States that authors like Alexis de Tocqueville and many others had fueled with their reports on American life throughout the 1800s.[1]

Regardless of these previous connections, however, World War I represented a watershed in the relationship between France and the United States. The influx of some two million U.S. soldiers into the European theater of battle meant that thousands of French and Americans experienced an unprecedented level of contact with one another—now as individuals, not merely as abstractions. And this interaction occurred not only in Paris but in towns and villages in the countryside. Unlike the earlier generations of Americans in France, the soldiers were generally neither wealthy nor highly educated. Instead, they offered the French people a much more representative cross-section of U.S. society, including its racial diversity. Black Americans had traveled to France before, but never in such large numbers (around two hundred thousand). Although most French villagers had never seen a black person, either from the United States or one of France's African colonies, many had the chance to do so by the war's end.

These new wartime contacts begin to explain how French listeners first came to hear jazz music. The Americans brought jazz to the troops and Parisians for entertainment and morale boosting. At first, the French were not quite clear how to evaluate this new music or what impact it would have. In fact, they sometimes had difficulty defining it. During the 1920s, musicians, critics, and audiences alike worked to make sense of the new sound, trying to decide whether it portended good or ill for the future of French entertainment. But common to their assessments was the belief that jazz represented something transformative—above all, something modern. Jazz was a sign of the times because it challenged previous musical norms. It seemed "noisy" and "mechanical." To those who heard bombs and explosions in jazz, the music soon extended the wartime chaos into the postwar age.[2] Furthermore, it represented culture in motion. Jazz was an American music, but it quickly gained widespread popularity in France, Britain, Germany, Italy, and elsewhere. Jazz posed a crucial challenge to many in France by suggesting the arrival of an era when old national boundaries and artistic categories were far more porous than before.

FRANCE, THE UNITED STATES, AND THE GREAT WAR

The Great War created an intimate contact between the French people and Americans that has lasted ever since, but that relationship was ambivalent from the beginning. By 1917, the war-weary French welcomed the Americans coming to fight on their behalf. French merchants were also happy to take U.S. dollars from soldiers who seemed quite wealthy given their comparatively better pay.[3] "America equals innocence plus gold," one French soldier summed it up.[4] Yet appreciation was mixed with confusion as French civilians and soldiers sometimes marveled at the strange ways of their American visitors. One U.S. chronicler of the war remarked, for example, that "the newcomers were regarded by the French as mad, incomprehensible persons—*rigolo*, in their phrase."[5] Misunderstanding and tension went both ways, often arising out of the different styles of working toward their common wartime goals. "They find us dumb at mathematics," recalled one U.S. soldier. "We find them impractical, wasting time on non-essentials. Humor and exasperation on both sides."[6] The Americans were "Janus personified," according to one Frenchman trying to reconcile seeming contradictions. "One of his faces is called idealism, the other positivism."[7]

People in towns that the soldiers visited made the acquaintance of Americans, but Paris was the main place for consistent contact. The many U.S. officers and volunteers who gathered there during the war used their valuable dollars to purchase the pleasures that the City of Light still had to offer. And at the war's end, a loosening of the restrictions that had previously kept enlisted men out of the city now allowed an even greater number to visit. Elated by victory, U.S. soldiers enjoyed the abundance of wine and prostitutes, as well as the city's art and monuments. The continuing strength of U.S. currency relative to the franc allowed the American Doughboys to entertain themselves so thoroughly that the songwriters Sam M. Lewis and "Mighty" Joe Young captured the excitement of those days in the lyrics of the popular U.S. song "How 'Ya Gonna Keep 'Em Down on the Farm (After They've Seen Paree)?"[8] Would U.S. soldiers even want to return home to their farms and hard work, the song mused, now that they had experienced the exhilaration and temptations of Paris? Meanwhile, many Parisians soon began to resent the Americans and their display of wealth in the postwar frenzy. Before 1918, U.S. soldiers had been warned not to spend too much money for fear of alienating their Parisian hosts. Now after the war, some of the city's residents came to believe that the influx of dollars was contributing to the postwar inflation sapping the French people's pocketbooks. That same inflation made the Americans wonder bitterly whether the French were trying to gouge them to make up for lost wartime revenues.[9] The Americans also brought trouble to neighborhoods in Paris. Both officers and enlisted men frequently started fights, openly wielded guns, and sometimes robbed merchants or people on the street. They were often publicly drunk and rowdy to the disdain of Parisian onlookers, and the French authorities had no recourse in such cases but to turn the ruffians over to the U.S. military police. Such a short time after defeating the German invaders, many Parisians soon became wary of this new group of intruders from the United States.[10]

In many ways, however, the arrival of American entertainment and popular culture—particularly film—was far more memorable to Parisians than their encounters with individual soldiers, although again the impressions were mixed. During the war, American films had become more widely available and popular than French productions, in part because U.S. motion pictures brought a refreshing change to Parisian entertainment. "For three years we have lived in an increasing shadow," wrote the Parisian novelist and socialite Colette about life during the war. "Artificial light, dimmer every day, no longer inundates the stages or our private homes. . . . What is left for the public? Where can it bathe itself in decorative illusion, adventure and romance, high life, society, inexhaustible splendor? At the cinema."[11] For Colette and others, American movies enabled Parisians to bask in a kind of luxury that the war had made impossible. Unlike French wartime films, which were often based on historical or patriotic themes designed to serve the war effort, American productions were escapist fantasies.[12] American film companies reaped the rewards bestowed on them by French audiences while the French houses suffered from the competition. According to one tally, the number of meters of French film produced each week accounted for 38 percent of the supply of films in 1913, but by 1916, that figure had dropped to 18 percent.[13] As a result, despite the popularity of American films at the box office, resentment toward the United States and its motion pictures began to surface among French film critics and politicians. The trend toward showing more American films persisted throughout the 1920s, providing a point of increasing tension between Americans and those in France who feared that their nation was being invaded by a cultural import at the expense of their own cinematic artisanship.[14]

THE GREAT WAR BRINGS JAZZ

If World War I opened up many questions about Americans and their culture for the French, one of the clear conclusions that many in France drew during the war was that not all Americans were the same. In particular, the war introduced African Americans to a greater number of French people than ever before, often to the delight of black soldiers, who felt more warmly accepted in France than in their own country. French civilians were, to be sure, happy to meet anyone willing to fight on their behalf, but their reactions to African Americans were especially positive. Many French officers disdained the U.S. regulations that kept whites and blacks in separate units, criticizing the hypocrisy of an army that was supposedly "making the world safe for democracy," in the words of President Woodrow Wilson. French generals who failed to understand such segregation sometimes destroyed American literature that advocated racial discrimination.[15]

These kinds of French actions added to the long-standing belief among African Americans that France was a color-blind country truly practicing the equality that the United States only preached. Previous generations of black American writers, intellectuals, and entertainers who had visited France brought back stories of a nation that was open and racially tolerant compared to the United States. Many black Americans, urged by leaders who continued to describe France in these terms, joined the U.S. army in order to fight for France as the true land of liberty.[16] And contact between African Americans and French civilians reinforced many of these notions. In one oft-quoted story, the mayor of a French village complained when white troops arrived, saying, "Take back these soldiers and send us some real Americans, black Americans."[17] In fact, though, the French army did not treat its own sub-Saharan African troops and laborers or colonial subjects in Africa with the same kind of generosity, and the contradiction between French words and actions on this issue was beginning to make some African American intellectuals, like W. E. B. Du Bois and Claude McKay, doubt the truth of France's claims to racial tolerance.[18] Furthermore, not everyone in France welcomed black American visitors to Paris, as the debates over jazz would soon reveal. But in spite of an evolving understanding of French attitudes toward race in the early twentieth century, the generally positive wartime experience of African American soldiers set the stage for many others, including jazz musicians, to thrive in Paris afterward.[19]

Even if such a large number of black Americans was new to many Parisians, their music was not entirely unknown. By the time jazz players arrived, black American musicians and white musicians playing black music had already been entertaining French audiences with minstrel songs, ragtime, and cakewalks, the latter having been wildly popular as a dance craze around 1900.[20] But the war did provide an opportunity for Parisians to hear black musicians in greater numbers than ever before. One of the central figures in bringing jazz to France during the war was James Reese Europe and the military orchestra that he conducted. By the time he went to France, Europe was already a well-established popularizer of black American music.[21] As a famous New York bandleader in the 1910s, Europe had helped to organize his fellow black musicians to ensure that they could find performing jobs. Touring around the United States with the popular white dancers Vernon and Irene Castle, Europe introduced many white audiences to the rapidly developing sounds of ragtime and early jazz. World War I provided yet another occasion for Europe to employ his talents as a disseminator of black American music, but this time he did so across the Atlantic as an army lieutenant. In 1917, Europe's commanding officer asked him to recruit "the best damn band in the United States Army."[22] Advertisements in black newspapers and personal persuasion enabled Europe to create an orchestra that included the composer Noble Sissle along with the dancer Bill "Bojangles" Robinson as the ensemble's drum major.[23] The band was known as the Hellfighters and originally traveled with the 369th United States Army Infantry Regiment, whose nickname they took. They were later attached to a French army unit.[24] Europe's band toured throughout wartime France to boost the morale of the troops and civilians.

The uniqueness of James Reese Europe's music frequently took the French by surprise. Since his orchestra played many tunes already familiar to audiences, the novelty was not what Europe performed but how he and his band played. Europe noted the distinction between his performance and that of the French when a Parisian bandleader asked him for a copy of his musical score. The French band could not replicate the sound, with its "jazz effects," Europe reported. Some of the French musicians "felt sure that my band had used special instruments."[25] On one occasion, Europe's band performed a rendition of the French national anthem, "La Marseillaise," that confused many French listeners since the sound of its rhythm and the arrangement were so unusual.[26] But the effects of "filling France full of jazz," as one wartime reporter described Europe's accomplishments, were astounding.[27] Along with several other bands, Europe's orchestra performed at a concert at the Tuileries garden near the end of the war. Europe quickly overshadowed the others, and the crowd turned its full attention to his musicians. "We played for 50,000 people, at least," he marveled, "and, had we wished it, we might be playing yet."[28] Noble Sissle recalled that, at another concert, "the audience could stand it no longer; the 'Jazz germ' hit them and it seemed to find the vital spot, loosening all muscles and causing what is known in America as an 'Eagle Rocking Fit.'"[29]

Europe was not the only African American to bring his music to France during these years. While his orchestra was entertaining on behalf of the war effort, the drummer Louis Mitchell and his band played at the music hall Le Casino de Paris and also made a few records.[30] Mitchell had already performed elsewhere in Europe, including in London in 1914 and again in 1915, according to the Belgian jazz critic Robert Goffin, who spent much time in Paris. In 1917, Mitchell was drumming at Le Casino de Paris when the management sent him back to New York to recruit a jazz band, suggesting that they believed the venture to be a potentially profitable one. Goffin remembered their 1917 group called Mitchell's Jazz Kings as the first black jazz band he ever heard, seconding the description of one U.S. observer of Mitchell at the time: "The big attraction at the Casino Theater here and the big attraction for every Parisian theater that can bid enough for his services, is Louis A. Mitchell, who just drummed his way to Paris and into the hearts of Parisians."[31] Goffin also noted the financial rewards for such affection by Parisian audiences. "Paris, at the end of the war was a wide-open and exciting place," he proclaimed. "Louis Mitchell earned money hand over fist. He received seven thousand francs for a week's engagement, or just about ten times the salary of a Cabinet member."[32]

From the start, French audiences identified jazz as an American music—particularly a black American music—but musicians from the United States were not the only ones involved in bringing jazz to France. Some French performers quickly recognized the power of American popular music (much of which they called jazz regardless of its actual musical traits) to reinvigorate shows for wartime and postwar audiences, and they incorporated it into their acts. Most important, in the view of several observers of the Parisian music scene (including composer Darius Milhaud, writer Jean Cocteau, and the music hall producer Jacques-Charles) were the French music hall star Gaby Deslys and her Hungarian American husband, Harry Pilcer.[33] Deslys had starred in musical variety shows in New York, where she met and married Pilcer. During her time there, Deslys also learned much about American music and dancing. On their return to Paris, Deslys and Pilcer starred in the 1917 Casino de Paris music hall production *Laisse-les tomber!* (Let them fall!), a title that mocked the German bombs that rained on Paris. Because of their training in the United States Deslys and Pilcer offered French audiences a show with more thoroughly American musical and dance styles.[34] The show employed a mixture of genres in its fifty tableaux, many of which were specifically American—including songs called "Stars and Stripes" and "Hello My Dearie!" To these, it added French tunes and various "exotic" numbers, including several with Chinese themes. The featured band, led by Harry Pilcer's brother and called Murray Pilcer's American Sherbo Band, was situated in one of the theater's loges. A picture in the show's program offered audience members a close-up view of the tuxedoed musicians and their array of instruments—banjos, saxophone, piano, violin, drums complete with cowbell, horns, triangle, and (what appeared to be) a frying pan. One commentator, expressing the newness of this musical mixture, described the band that "lets out cries, whistles, sings, grunts, howls, while its musicians deafen us by slapping, blowing, pulling out of their bizarre instruments a tempest of appalling, enervating, cramped, crushed sounds. . . . It's a party, a big party, an exceedingly joyful parade."[35] Carrying such language further, and employing some dramatic wartime imagery to link the context of the performance with the shocking power of this music, the avant-garde author Jean Cocteau described the scene this way:

M. Pilcer, in full-dress suit, gaunt and well rouged, and Mademoiselle Gaby Deslys, a great ventriloquist's doll with porcelain face, corn-colored hair, and ostrich-feathered gown, danced through this tornado of drum and rhythm, a sort of domesticated catastrophe which left them, intoxicated and myopic, beneath a shower of six anti-aircraft searchlights.[36]

A slightly less enthusiastic observer wrote of the band's "infernal noise" as it played during the intermission: "Ah! Be careful, be careful, people of Paris, you will wake the dead."[37] Deslys traveled back to New York in 1919, returning to Paris later that same year, once again bringing more American ideas with her. Even after Deslys's death in 1920, Pilcer continued to entertain in music halls and opened a Montmartre nightclub. And in the following years, Le Casino de Paris, where Deslys and Pilcer performed, offered more of this new music in shows like *Ouf!* (1919) and *Pa-ri-ki Danse* (1919), both of which featured black American bands.[38]

EARLY FRENCH BANDS

When jazz musicians and audiences from the United States started arriving in Paris in the late 1910s and early 1920s, French musicians immediately took notice and often started playing in the new style. Sometimes they joined with American bands, but they also listened and then copied on their own what they heard. The repertoires of these early French bands were frequently combinations of older dance tunes and French chansons that were now infused with new, syncopated techniques. French bands like the Orchestre Symphonique du Palais Royal, Marcel's Jazz Band des Folies Bergères, Hot Boys Band, and Orchestra Sticklen performed and recorded songs like "Barnyard Blues," "For Me and My Gal," "Salt Your Sugar," and "Suzett' Blues" in the music's early days.[39] An accounting of such early bands is difficult, in part because there were so many musicians playing around the city that to know them all would be nearly impossible. The histories of many were also lost to the fluid and temporary nature of show business. Nevertheless, a few examples can help to illustrate how jazz began to influence French musicians in the years just after World War I.[40]

Some French performers came across jazz by accident. Edouard Marguliès (or Margouliès), who later called himself Doudou, returned home after the war to his brother's pleading: the brother wanted Edouard to replace him in a band. Replying that he had no idea how to play this new music called jazz, Marguliès's brother told him, "There's a drum, some tin pans, some bells, a tambourine. . . . Above all make lots of noise and laugh a lot."[41] Four months later, with a group of musicians more experienced in the new sounds, Doudou formed a band called the Merry Makers that played successfully in French clubs throughout the 1920s. Another musician, Julien Porret, first heard jazz during the war when he was sent to San Francisco with the French army band of which he was a part. When he got back home, he wanted to spread jazz and began to play the music around France with other musicians.[42]

If some came to jazz by chance, many other professional musicians adapted themselves to the sounds of the times. Fred Melé was one of the most important early French jazz bandleaders and a practitioner of what would come to be referred to as an "orchestral" style of jazz; one newspaper article dubbed him "our [Paul] Whiteman," after the popular American jazz orchestra leader of the day.[43] Melé led a band called the Syncopators and became the musical director at Le Casino de Paris, where he worked with French music hall stars like Mistinguett and Maurice Chevalier. He later conducted at other music halls around Paris, "blending jazz and *la musique de variété* with some good humor," according to the music hall historian Jacques Hélian.[44] Likewise, Lud Gluskin, a U.S. musician, organized a half-American, half-French band called Lud Gluskin and His Versatile Juniors that incorporated many of the up-and-coming young French players of the day.[45]

Léo Vauchant, another influential early jazz player, began playing drums in 1918 at the age of fourteen in the Marigny Theater, where Louis Mitchell's Jazz Kings were also performing (by his own account, Vauchant was a professional musician since the age of eight). Listening to Mitchell, Vauchant began to decipher how the black American musicians played the improvisational style of jazz. "I learned jazz more or less on my own," Vauchant recalled. "I started analyzing a bit what those Mitchell guys were doing—just by hearing them play. I didn't have the records. I knew the tunes they were playing."[46] Vauchant had studied at the conservatory in Lyon, but his true teachers were the musicians he encountered in various bands throughout his youth, whether jazz bands, tango orchestras, or other sorts of musical groups, and he often finished up the evening in the Montmartre nightclubs with other players. "The most enjoyable thing for me," Vauchant remembered, "would be nine [P.M.] till five [A.M.] at the Perroquet, playing jazz. It was the freedom."[47] Well versed in a variety of instruments including the trombone, for which he was most famous, Vauchant was in great demand by the late 1920s and played with a variety of bands. Soon, he left France altogether to make his way in Hollywood as a musical director for motion picture studios.[48]

THE JOURNEYS OF JAZZ

One of the remarkable facts about the introduction of jazz to France— borne by such individuals as Europe, Mitchell, Deslys, Pilcer, and many others—is that it happened not very long after jazz itself had emerged as a distinct musical form in the United States. Blues, Creole music, and rag- time were just beginning to blend into what New Orleans musicians were labeling jazz shortly before World War I. And like French listeners, many Americans, both white and black, were only starting to learn about the music around the time of the war. New Orleans musicians left the city as part of a generation of African Americans who traveled northward in the early twentieth century. Like other African Americans who participated in this "great migration," they were searching for better lives and greater economic opportunity in the North. Between 1908 and 1922, some of the key innovators of jazz, including Jelly Roll Morton, Sidney Bechet, King Oliver, and Louis Armstrong, left New Orleans, often ending up in north- ern cities with larger audiences.[49] In Chicago, jazz musicians began to alter their music in order to catch the attention of listeners. Musicians needed to distinguish themselves from the many other acts on stage in the demand- ing and competitive atmosphere of the city's South Side nightclubs. To do so, New Orleans group improvisation gave way to an emphasis on solo performance, and players developed a greater technical proficiency, in- cluding the ability to make their instruments seemingly laugh or cry.[50] Adapting jazz to different audiences was a critical element of the art from the beginning.

Part of this adaptation, however, centered less on the musical than the racial component. White New Orleans musicians who learned how to play early jazz from blacks had the advantage in breaking into the commercial recording business in the United States since the music industry took them more seriously, at least until record companies discovered the "race record" market of music by and for black audiences.[51] One of the first beneficiaries of the move to the North and the recording contracts that followed was the all-white Original Dixieland Jazz Band (ODJB). The ODJB was the first band to record music in the United States using the name jazz, but as historians have pointed out, they were relative latecomers to the music. Their significance, as jazz historian Chris Goddard puts it, "was not that they were new but that they were timely."[52] Beginning with performances in 1916 in Chicago and 1917 in New York, these New Orleans–born white musicians, who had learned the music of black performers, now made it accessible to larger American audiences by taking it to venues throughout the United States where other whites could hear it. They also skillfully used publicity to heighten their popularity. For example, a lack of musical training and an inability to read music were qualities that the band made well-known because they supposedly made the act more novel. The band caught the attention of show business insiders during a performance at Reisenweber's Restaurant in New York, and they soon began to make popular records.[53] The band's commercial success demonstrated this music's wide appeal, and it allowed the ODJB to start promoting and spreading a music called jazz to a broad American public. Their recordings also proved to be quite influential as other bands began to imitate them and music students dissected the strains of the ODJB's playing measure by measure in order to understand it.[54]

Just as many Americans, and shortly afterward the French, were becoming acquainted with jazz during the first years of the twentieth century, so were people in other nations. From its earliest days, jazz quickly became a global music.[55] Carried by the commercial success of traveling bands and phonograph records initially—both were in demand because of a European-wide postwar dance craze—and then by radio broadcasts and sound film, jazz music became one of the first popular musics with a claim to being worldwide in scope. The music gained listeners in Britain, Germany, Italy, Eastern Europe, the Soviet Union, and beyond. Cosmopolitan Berlin, for instance, was one noteworthy site of jazz performance following the economic stabilization in 1924.[56] When Sam Wooding took his Chocolate Kiddies band on tour there, he remembered that when they opened at the Admirals Palast, "the Germans 'ate it up.' In roars of applause the audiences on the first night started shouting 'Noch'mal,' 'Bis,' 'Hoch,' and 'Bravo.' "[57] German composers like Kurt Weill and Ernst Krenek brought jazz respectability and acclaim by incorporating it into their musicals *The Threepenny Opera* and *Jonny spielt auf*, respectively.[58] And from European cities, jazz often made its way even further, including to the colonies and beyond. In a 1935 article, one bandleader described his orchestra's trip to the Middle East: "We arrived in Bagdad [*sic*] at 6 o'clock in the afternoon. . . . [Our hosts] knew that we were tired and in need of sleep, but the Arabs had learned that the jazz band had arrived, so they came into the café, demanded jazz music and they got it." He also noted the brisk business that an "Arab friend" had "selling jazz phonograph records."[59]

Stories about early jazz in England spotlight the influential performances of two groups: the ODJB and the Southern Syncopated Orchestra. Neither is really credited with introducing jazz music to Britain, but rather with energizing audiences for the new sounds that were already coming to be called jazz and assuring the music's future success there. According to some historians, the ODJB's trip to England in 1919 was jazz's most important early appearance in Europe because it helped to associate most clearly the use of the term jazz with a particular set of musical sounds, especially syncopated rhythm.[60] By the time of their 1919 shows in Britain, other bands were already performing music labeled jazz as a kind of novelty act, as so many of the early jazz bands always remained.[61] But the ODJB heightened interest in this music among British audiences. Coming to Britain at the peak of their popularity, the ODJB appeared at the Hippodrome in London and then at the opening of the Hammersmith Palais de Dance, where over five thousand people heard them play.[62]

Shortly after the ODJB, Will Marion Cook's Southern Syncopated Orchestra debuted in England. Cook, a well-known black American composer and bandleader, took his orchestra across the Atlantic in 1919 on a tour that included a command performance at Buckingham Palace. Although he did not call his music jazz, many critics did. The trumpeter Arthur Briggs recalled that the orchestra "played the classics—Brahms, Grieg and so on—and also quite a few of Cook's own compositions. Also, we played what we called 'Plantation Melodies.' We didn't play jazz, we played ragtime—numbers like 'Russian Rag.' "[63] Another musician did, however, point to the band's use of improvisation, including on the classical pieces they played.[64]

On that trip to England, the Southern Syncopated Orchestra caught the ear of the Swiss conductor Ernst-Alexandre Ansermet, who published an important review of the orchestra in the francophone journal *Revue romande*. Historians of jazz often refer to Ansermet's article as the first critical analysis of the music in Europe, and in many ways, it set the tone for the kind of commentary that followed in the 1920s and 1930s. He began by noting the popularity of ragtime music, which "we dance to . . . under the name of jazz in all our cities," pointing to an ongoing confusion in musical terms and definitions. He observed the influence that these sounds had already produced on "learned music" in the compositions of Igor Stravinsky and Claude Debussy.[65] But above all, Ansermet's praise for

Cook and his band—particularly the clarinet of Sidney Bechet—centered on the "blackness" of their playing. They drew their songs from a wide variety of traditions, few of which were their own, he stated, but "it is not the material that makes Negro music, it is the spirit."[66] Ansermet's description of the show confirms that the Southern Syncopated Orchestra played an array of songs including black spirituals, tunes inspired by English ballads, and European dances. By listing their songs, Ansermet crystallized something that people had already begun to realize: jazz was not really about what one played but how one played it. And like many commentators after him, Ansermet linked that way of playing to race. "We have shown," he wrote,

> that syncopation itself is but the effect of an expressive need, the manifestation in the field of rhythm of a particular taste, in a word, the genius of the race. This genius demonstrates itself in all the musical elements, it transfigures everything in the music it appropriates. The Negro takes a trombone, and he has a knack of vibrating each note by a continual quivering of the slide, and a sense of glissando, and a taste for muted notes which make it a new instrument; he takes a clarinet or saxophone and he has a way of hitting the notes . . . , he discovers a whole series of effects produced by the lips alone, which make it a new instrument. There is a Negro way of playing the violin, a Negro way of singing.[67]

For Ansermet, African Americans brought an innate musical knowledge to their performance that made a new musical sound, and they could even transform old songs and instruments in the process.

DEFINING "JAZZ"

Ansermet's connection between race and musical style became a central way of thinking about jazz music during the 1920s and 1930s in France, and he was not alone in portraying it in racialized terms from the moment of its arrival. Indeed, nearly any music called jazz was also believed to be black in origin, and the term quickly came to encompass almost any music performed by black musicians. For example, one 1929 newspaper article titled "A Famous Jazz in 1844" described the performance of four nineteenth-century black minstrels from Virginia who appeared before "an impatient public that pushed its way to the théâtre du Palais-Royal" to hear them sing and play instruments.[68] Another article detailed a sixteenth-century image on display at a Paris museum that contained, according to the author, "a *jazz-nègre*," shown as five musicians, "participating in the celebration of a marriage."[69] Labeling events that far predated the music of the 1920s with the term jazz simply because they depicted black musicians demonstrated a notion that jazz was a racial expression. It also revealed just how deeply many people believed the black roots of jazz could be traced. Jazz was somehow ancient, and its black essence was present long before the 1920s, many writers suggested.

Furthermore, a truly authentic jazz band was, in most cases, presumed to consist only of musicians with dark skin. In 1924, for instance, the director of the Empire music hall sued a jazz band that was supposed to be composed of five black musicians. When four black players arrived at the show with a white colleague to round out the band, the music hall claimed a breach of contract. Four years later, when the trial was resolved, the court found in favor of the Empire.[70] The financial rewards for black musicians were often enhanced because their music was in demand thanks to their skin color. One observer told of white musicians receiving seventy-five francs a night while black players got five hundred.[71] A Senegalese musician, named Alphonse "Wali" Kane, asserted the racial connotations of jazz when he established a band called "Jazz William's" [*sic*] with an intentionally American name so that people would notice him. He had realized that his skin color was far more important to many listeners than the fact that he was neither a jazz player nor from the United States.[72] And since black musicians were almost automatically expected to play jazz, African Americans who performed songs that did not fit audience expectations were quite surprising. In the late 1920s, the choir of the Hampton Institute toured Europe performing more traditional kinds of music that did not incorporate the new rhythms of jazz, such as spirituals and folk songs. The choir's director, R. Nathaniel Dett, noted that one of the most frequent questions his student singers received in Europe was why, since they were black, the Hampton Choir did not sing jazz. Such an incongruity seemed unthinkable to many audiences.

This focus on race can be set against the backdrop of an early-twentieth-century Parisian fascination with *l'art nègre*—especially African art and sculpture, which had gained much attention from artists and collectors. Ethnographic exhibits, like those at the Musée Ethnographique des Missions Scientifiques that had opened at the Palais Trocadéro in the 1870s and later the Colonial Exposition of 1931, gave Parisians the chance to see a very different style of artistic expression than their own. By the early decades of the twentieth century, many began to take it seriously. Pablo Picasso's inspiration by African masks on a visit to the Musée Ethnographique in 1907 and his incorporation of those forms in paintings such as *Les Demoiselles d'Avignon* is well-known. The parallel growth of a market for l'art nègre spurred private collections and gallery displays, bringing African art to a broader public.[73] Explaining much of the fascination with l'art nègre and its ability to bring new insights to the creative process, the art collector and dealer Paul Guillaume argued precisely on behalf of African art being given its proper consideration. "The intelligence of modern man (or woman)," he said, "must be Negro."[74] Not only in painting but in literature too did l'art nègre gain more than a small measure of respectability when in 1922, the Martinique-born novelist René Maran's book about colonial Africa titled *Batouala: véritable roman nègre* won the prestigious Prix Goncourt.[75] All of these forms of l'art nègre—art, literature, and also music—were often linked together by observers as expressing parts of a single "black consciousness."[76]

The attraction to l'art nègre was complicated, and the taste for things African was often as much about fashion as anything. But the examples of non-Western culture nevertheless brought to Paris both a new conception of art and a new way of viewing peoples of color. Many in France were drawn to this kind of expression precisely because of its novelty.[77] In depicting unfamiliar people and places, l'art nègre not only represented something foreign but also offered an alternative to Western values in the aftermath of a war that had called those values into question because of its brutality. "A public convinced of the excellence of its own culture," the writer and critic André Salmon maintained, "is at a loss to understand the anguish which drove modern artists to seek lessons from barbarian image-makers."[78] African art provided a kind of exotic vision and sense of transport to another place that promised renewal or a search for something better. In his classic study of l'art nègre, art historian Jean Laude put it well when he argued that it "increasingly became used as a theory to promote non-European, archaic solutions" that "could no longer honestly identify [Western] civilization with Civilization itself."[79]

Race was one of the most important ways in which French observers defined jazz, but there were other ways in which to talk about the music as well. Jazz in France was, almost exclusively, a music produced by men. Some women sang and danced with jazz bands, yet more often than not, women were primarily consumers of this music rather than its producers.[80] Indeed, jazz music provided women with new opportunities to consume things other than music, including outfits for dancing or face powder that allowed them to "answer the call of jazz" while remaining fresh and feminine.[81] Inspired by Josephine Baker, many women purchased Bakerfix, a product that permitted them to shape their hair like that of the famous dancer's. The limits of femininity and sexuality seemed to be up for debate in the 1920s, and jazz was believed by many to be a sound that released sexual energy, thus challenging older moral codes for women. Fears that women would be carried away by the new dance steps to heights of passion were not uncommon, nor were concerns that they would neglect their duties as wives and mothers in favor of frivolity.[82] Jazz was part of a larger series of debates over the "modern woman" and a new, more general sense of sexual liberation in a post-Freudian world.

Commentators on jazz in Paris did not dwell excessively on the music's sexual content, though, since there were many other remarkable things about it. In fact, music halls had already been sexualized before jazz arrived. Nude entertainment had been a part of the repertoire for several years, and jazz musicians were simply providing a new sound to which the dancers moved. In these venues, any sexuality generated by jazz was still a spectacle confined to the stage. Josephine Baker's dancing is sometimes remarked on by scholars to demonstrate the sexual potential of jazz, and many commentators certainly responded to her eroticism, but much of her sexuality derived from the double taboo of mixing race and sex. The dance floors of Paris offered women the clearest opportunity to participate in movements that, many feared, unleashed or even simulated sex, although sensual dances like the tango had been clearly present in Paris long before jazz. But as Mary Louise Roberts has pointed out, women's fashions were not always as liberating on the dance floor as they seemed, and often provided the appearance of mobility far more than the actual ability to move.[83] Moreover, not all dresses were recommended for dancing since some did not flatter the wearer while in motion.[84] With such caveats in mind, one can conclude that although concerns about gender relations and changes in sexual behavior predated the arrival of jazz, the music undoubtedly heightened those worries by offering what many saw as a new hedonism and the further erosion of proper ladylike self-restraint.

Other than examining race and gender, most early attempts to define jazz in France revealed a widespread musical confusion, particularly with what tunes could be placed into this musical category. Often any upbeat, danceable sound, or any music with a bit of syncopation in its rhythm, received the name. Sometimes musical sound effects—whistles, "wah-wah" sounds, or kazoos—were enough to warrant the term. Misunderstanding also came from the multiple uses of the word *jazz*.[85] In France, *un jazz* could refer to the music, the performance, or the band itself. Sometimes the word merely invoked the spirit of modern entertainment as in the magazines titled *Jazz: l'actualité intellectuelle*—a magazine of arts, culture, and entertainment—or *Jazz: le magazine du music hall*, which actually contained very few articles on the music during its short run in the late 1920s.[86] In another instance of the varied uses of the term, one manufacturer of player pianos marketed three sizes of its product as "Le Little Jazz-Band," "L'Unic Jazz-Band," and "Le Jazz-Band Rex," hoping to capitalize on the popularity of the music to make a sale.[87] In short, what people meant when they said "jazz" varied depending on who used the term. Irving Schwerké, an American journalist and music critic living in Paris, expressed his frustration over the problem of definition when he wrote in 1926:

> Of late, both in America and Europe, it has become especially noticeable that people do not mean what they think they mean when they speak of jazz. Nine times out of ten, when the word "jazz" is used, "rag-time" is meant instead. The two dwell in confusion, and it is high time that a little housecleaning were done to set things in order.[88]

When describing the musical style of jazz, commentators frequently remarked on what seemed to be its unusual sounds and the techniques used to produce them. Jazz was "a collection of melodic dust, a puzzle of minute imitations, of audacious anticipations, of farcical *glissandos*, of deafening timbres or of pinching tones," as Lionel de la Laurencie, president of the Société de Musicologie, put it.[89] Another observer spoke of "incongruous glissandos, blasts of sardonic whistling, its rumblings of the saxophone and clarinet."[90] Such comments reflected the common feeling of surprise and wonder at the musical sounds associated with jazz as well as the wide vocabulary used to capture it.

Despite the confusion during these early days, there was at least one common musical meaning when people in France invoked the term *jazz*: it meant rhythm and the instruments used to make it. Above all, the drums—*la batterie*—were not only the most prominent instrument but their mere presence, many believed, made any band into a jazz band. Léo Vauchant, one of the few French musicians who quickly learned to play jazz as the Americans did, told of how theaters in Paris scrambled to get jazz bands together just after the war in order to take advantage of their popularity. "But right away, there were French orchestras going all over who didn't know what they were doing," Vauchant remembered. "They were just awful—but they played. When that thing [the jazz craze] started all the little theaters had to have a jazz band. The jazz band meant the drummer. . . . They didn't know that jazz band meant an orchestra."[91] "The 'drums' are its principal organ of expression," recognized music critic Émile Vuillermoz in a 1918 article. "They underline the beats and make them even more irresistible."[92] Ethnographer and jazz enthusiast Michel Leiris heard the beat in many instruments as "banjos and bass fiddle . . . strummed out the rhythm," but in the end, the "deafening drums" were the overwhelming sound he recalled.[93] "How can one not profit at all," claimed Maurice Brillant, a critic and art historian, "from this rhythm at once so precise and so simple, so imperious, so rich, so nuanced."[94] Jacques Heugel, editor of the musical journal Le Ménestrel, noted that "jazz as such is nothing but rhythm," thereby reducing jazz to one of its most basic characteristics.[95] His conclusion was not unique. For many, rhythm was precisely the reason behind jazz's wonderful success as a dance music that caused people "to take part in a sort of danse macabre, where human reflexes that nature tends to harmonize, are on the contrary exaggerated in a spinal trepidation, and, finally, escapes all reasonable control."[96] Sem, one chronicler of the age, wrote that "this frenzy is contagious, because all the dancers sing or whistle to the beat. . . . A joyful seizure breaks out."[97] But to the skeptic, such a loss of control could be part of the music's danger, producing a "crushing and dull crowd that turns, turns, turns without stopping to the obsessive rhythm of jazz."[98] The rhythms of jazz could easily become the music of the mob.

Early confusion about what jazz really was often led to a quest for novelty by what, on reflection later, would seem to be going to absurd ends. The pianist Jean Wiéner reported that "people understood almost too well that jazz was improvisation—but they didn't understand how to do it. So you got jazz bands whose only purpose was to make as much noise as possible—bells, klaxons, drums, revolvers, etc."[99] Cocteau remembered a "barman of noises" in the band at Le Casino de Paris "under a gilt pergola loaded with bells, triangles, boards, and motor-cycle horns. With these he fabricated cocktails, adding from time to time a dash of cymbals, all the while rising from his seat, posturing and smiling vacuously."[100] The music business trade journal Musique et instruments ran a brief account under the heading "Le jazz du peuple" (The people's jazz) of a noisy one-man band who performed every Sunday at the Porte de Clignancourt, complete with accordion, cymbals, and drums.[101]

Other jazz instruments in Paris, as elsewhere, also included saxophones, clarinets, pianos, and trumpets. Some, like the banjo, were recognized not only for their addition to the rhythm but also their unique timbre. If the sound of the saxophone made jazz stand out to many listeners, so did its French origins. Created in 1855 by the Belgian-born though longtime French resident Adolphe Sax, the saxophone found new life in the 1920s as one of the primary instruments for jazz musicians—to the surprise of some. "Jazz is a French invention!" began one newspaper article, hoping to catch its readers' attention. By the end of the piece, primarily an interview with Sax's son, the author tempered his view by reminding the reader that "if jazz is not French, the saxophone, its principal instrument, is."[102] His and others' interest in pointing out the French connection to jazz revealed an underlying fascination with the music, often to the point of wanting to claim at least a bit of the credit for its invention. Even a German critic interviewed for a French newspaper article argued forcefully that "jazz is hardly an American invention" precisely because the saxophone was a French creation.[103] This musical reductionism was common among many writers for whom the surprise of the instruments was part of the shock of jazz music. But even traditional instruments could be put to new uses so that with jazz, according to one critic, the violin "can be renewed."[104]

For many, however, defining jazz as "music" was something of an intellectual and aesthetic stretch because it seemed to signal a shift in thinking about what music meant in the modern age. It symbolized a new aesthetic that one observer believed was "stronger than politics" or other issues of the day.[105] With rhythm predominating and an often unfamiliar instrumentation—including the occasional use of a saw—many simply equated jazz with "noise."[106] In this way, the musical value of jazz could be called into question altogether: it had no sense, just sound. Bands in the early years of the music, in fact, frequently did little else but make loud, clashing sounds, as if jazz should express musically some of the chaos of the immediate postwar era.

More broadly, noise could not only mean disorder but also the intonations of the growing presence of machines in the early twentieth century and the changes that the machine culture created. "Certain rhythms of jazz," wrote Lionel de la Laurencie, "entrusted to the banjo, go on and on with an inflexible rigor like the rhythm of motors."[107] In the view of writer and critic André Warnod, "The jazz band is the panting of the machine, the trepidation of the automobile, the train that squeaks on the rails, the tramway that passes shaking the clock."[108] One author offered an exhaustive list of offensive sounds, saying,

To the clamor of sirens, the humming of *gothas*, responded all of a sudden an astonishing organized racket, a pinching, a squeaking, a scraping, a trembling, the crackling of sticks, the rolling of drums, the cries of trumpets and of klaxons, the chiming of metallic timbres, the noise of chains, of rods and gongs, brass bells, all an ingeniously complicated mechanical sound.[109]

In its association with and reliance on new technology like phonographs and radio, jazz also seemed to be on the cutting edge of modern life—"the contemporary musical aesthetic," as one critic put it.[110] Still, this kind of noise might also have a harmful psychological impact on audiences. A doctor in Toulouse, among others, maintained that while symphonic music could have good effects on listeners, "a noisy music can only have bad ones; and when it is a matter not of symphonic music but of JAZZ . . . , one can expect the worst repercussions on the nervous system."[111] French strings were pleasing to the ear, wrote another critic, but jazz "disconcerts our senses and overexcites them."[112] Some heard wildness in such a mechanical uproar, while others found a mechanized monotony. The conservative critic Jacques Janin contended that jazz bands all sounded too much alike, and that "the problem of originality is not resolved with the clucking of the saxophone and a rumbling of the trombone." All that set jazz bands apart was "the quantity of mustard they put in their sauce."[113]

Jazz was not just a sign of modern times, many argued, but it would ultimately influence the future shape of European music, although observers disagreed on the extent to which it would do so and whether those effects would be permanent. Again, rhythm was an important focus. Many remarked that jazz would add a dimension to European music that was previously lacking. This music offered a "rhythmic renaissance," according to one author, writing in the respected musicology journal *La Revue musicale*, that brought "a vital ferment from which the musicians of our generation will learn the lesson of rhythm."[114] Jazz could also influence European music, many argued, if the saxophone and other modern instruments could find their way into more orchestras—the possibility of which increased with jazz's popularity. The composers Darius Milhaud and Reynaldo Hahn saw jazz becoming a "classical" form of music. Others felt that the impact would only be fleeting, and once the fashion had passed, so would jazz.[115] Some, however, worried about what shape jazz-influenced music might take in the future. Young composers had latched onto it, one critic observed, "a little too quickly, perhaps, and without having completely digested this sonorous food."[116] Henri Christiné, a composer of well-known *chansonnettes* from the *café-concerts* of Paris, remarked sarcastically, "Why are the Opéra and the Opéra-Comique waiting to modernize and economize? . . . Tell me about 'Pelléas' and 'L'Or du Rhin,' played by saxophones, banjos, ukuleles, and don't forget the xylophone, car horn, the klaxon, and the coconuts!"[117]

The influence of jazz seemed certain to many shortly after its arrival, but whether it was for good or ill was not clear in the early 1920s. Music critics and cultural observers of jazz made their cases for and against it, yet both sides agreed that this music was not traditionally French—in spite of the presence of the saxophone. Rather, jazz reflected something of the changing, modern age in which the French found themselves in contact with new influences from beyond their borders. "The war of 1870 came," one author noted, "and then the Great War, wiping the slate clean of all our romantic memories and replacing them with a frightening modernism of which the jazz band is the most vivid expression."[118] Now, the rhythms, timbres, and instruments were often unfamiliar, and even well-known instruments such as the saxophone produced surprising and different sounds in this brave, new musical world.

2

THE

SPREAD

OF JAZZ

As Paris settled back into civilian life after the war, jazz musicians struck up their rhythms in venues all over the city. Audiences heard it in cabarets, nightclubs, dance halls, restaurants, and theaters. Many music halls first presented jazz during the regular show's intermission, but they soon moved it to the main program. In cafés, owners often decided to take advantage of the music's growing popularity and hired jazz bands to lure customers into their establishments. These kinds of commercial concerns were crucial motivations in introducing jazz to Paris. As the story, recounted earlier, of Louis Mitchell being sent back to the United States to recruit a band suggests, many theater owners were already sensitive to the moneymaking potential of jazz. And during the 1920s, the spread of jazz increased as that potential became reality. Jazz musicians, as a result, soon seemed to many to be everywhere. As one author put it, "The clamor of the jazz bands has replaced, even in the furthest provinces, the old orchestras and instruments."[1]

Just as jazz musicians were fanning out across Paris, important changes in the city's entertainment culture were also underway to accommodate the new tastes of audiences. The evolution was particularly striking in one of the favorite gathering places of the 1920s, the dance hall. The "dance craze" of the postwar years provided a business incentive to revamp old venues into flashy and fashionable hot spots so that they could provide space to do the latest steps. Many critics believed that not only was the music different in these places because of the introduction of jazz, they were also beginning to lose their traditional character. Some came to see the growing presence of jazz throughout the city along with the ways in which it altered where and how Parisians enjoyed themselves as an indication of the changing nature of modern life more generally. And talking about jazz was one way of debating what those changes meant.

Another modern development, the new media that were created or improved in the early twentieth century, allowed the sounds of jazz to be carried across great distances. Indeed, perceptions about jazz music cannot be separated from the technology—especially phonographs and radios—from which it roared. Being connected with such devices further equated jazz with the cutting edge of cultural developments. Easily linking jazz to other innovations of the day, one French observer captured the range of overlapping associations between the music and spirit of the age when he wrote: "I like modern dances because I live in 1924, because I have seen the theater, music, the arts, dance evolve, because we live in the century of radio, of the jazz-band, of electricity, of thermal rays, and of negro-mania . . . because I live in my century."[2]

JAZZ AS SHOW BUSINESS

Although the rapid spread of jazz surprised some Parisians, in many ways it was only a continuation of recent trends in French show business. In the late nineteenth century, performers and cabaret owners began to realize that they could make quite a bit of money from the leisure activities of an expanding bourgeoisie. Thus, the economic interests of entertainment became of much greater concern to everyone involved. By 1903, for example, the singer Yvette Guilbert earned one thousand francs a night at the Olympia music hall, and the famous performer Félix Mayol garnered up to two thousand. The money sometimes appeared to be at least as important as artistic concerns when entertainers and cabaret owners became embroiled in costly lawsuits to secure their financial interests.[3]

One of the most famous moneymaking entertainments in the fin de siècle was the Chat Noir cabaret in Montmartre, founded in 1881. The owner, Rodolphe Salis, was something of a publicity genius. He constantly advertised the establishment through a series of attention-grabbing stunts—including, at one point, staging his own funeral procession through the streets of the neighborhood. The cabaret published a newspaper to keep its name in the minds of potential customers and draw as large a crowd as possible. The Chat Noir had begun as a gathering place for poor poets, but as middle-class Parisians came slumming in this artists' haven, Salis expanded his venue's commercial potential by catering to these new patrons and raising drink prices. Setting the tone for Montmartre, other cabaret owners soon followed the Chat Noir's lead.[4] To many observers, this kind of crass commercialism betrayed the neighborhood's reputation for placing a higher value on artistic expression. As a result, many believed that an ethos of "art for sale" was replacing a supposedly more traditional notion of "art for art's sake." The change prompted Montmartre resident and artist Willette, for one, to produce a stained-glass window depicting the worship of a golden calf in Paris to illustrate his distaste for the way that art, like that of Salis's Chat Noir, pandered to the marketplace.[5]

Many other entrepreneurs besides Salis worked feverishly to keep up with the demand for novelty in late-nineteenth-century Paris, turning out new songs, acrobatic acts, and vibrant revues as part of an expanding entertainment industry. In the process of satisfying what they believed to be the public's thirst for new diversions, the aesthetics of that entertainment were also already changing in order to attract the broadest possible audience. Subdued and intimate café-concert or *cabaret artistique* performances, which often featured poetry, songs, or other verbal expressions, were giving way to the luxurious and sumptuous music halls that relied on bright lights, flashy costumes, and seminude dancers to draw the audience's eyes.[6]

When jazz came onto the scene in the late 1910s and 1920s, it fit quite easily with the growth of new, startling, and dazzling entertainment that would attract an audience's attention and raise box office receipts. Many of the successful early jazz bands performing in music halls used visual tricks similar to those already employed in these venues. For example, they passed their instruments among the musicians, included dancers in their acts, or featured bandleaders who jerked around the stage while conducting. With familiar elements like these, jazz performances were not always presented as something entirely new. The music may have been different, and even shocking, but the act as a whole fit into patterns that audiences could recognize.

Jazz may have been especially attractive to theater owners and managers because it promised to continue late-nineteenth-century show business trends, but circumstances specific to the 1920s made jazz almost a necessity. Theaters and other spectacles had closed at the outbreak of the war, then reopened in 1916 once Paris settled into a wartime routine. Because the city's lights were dimmed at night in order to prevent enemy attacks, troops on leave and civilians soon crowded into afternoon shows to watch the increasingly popular genre of musical comedy. "They had no taste for vicarious carnage," remembered author Jules Bertaut. "They wanted singing, dancing, light comedy or even crude farce, and the stimulant of a perpetual rhythm to beat down consciousness."[7] Calling on the industry to play its part in the war effort, the government levied a 5 percent tax on the gross receipts of theaters. Taxes grew after the war in order to help France's postwar reconstruction, thereby altering the economics of Parisian show business. Beginning in 1920, taxes on theaters rose to 16 percent. Ten percent of the revenue assisted the poor, and the rest went to the state. But from the popular music halls, the government required more of their profits: 10 percent of their gross receipts to the poor and 10 percent to the state.[8] The taxes climbed for cinemas, places to dance, and other spectacles, and even those who received complimentary tickets were required to pay the tax on the ticket's value.[9]

In 1917, the taxes collected totaled 10 million francs, and the revenues rapidly rose: 37 million in 1920, 70 million in 1924 when taxes rose again, 80 million in 1925, a slight drop to 77 million in the economically troubled year of 1926, and 105 million francs in 1927.[10] Newer entertainments came under the tax regime too. By 1920, gramophone players and recordings were already being taxed 25 percent.[11] In her memoirs, American expatriate nightclub owner Ada "Bricktop" Smith recounted a story of her mother smuggling phonograph records through French customs in order to avoid the taxes that made them so expensive.[12] And the tax regime changed constantly throughout these years, varying from one entertainment to another as well as between Paris and the provinces.[13] Paris was in somewhat better shape than other cities where, aside from resort towns like Deauville, foreign tourists were not present to swell box office receipts and additional local taxes made the situation more difficult for theater owners. Outside Paris, the French government levied a special tax to make up for the difference between revenues collected from shows in the capital and those elsewhere.[14]

The taxes of the early 1920s caused a great deal of unrest among entertainers. In July 1920, for instance, cafés and restaurants had no musicians to perform. Owners had laid them off because of enormous tax rates that claimed 50 percent of gross receipts (25 percent going to public assistance) when music accompanied a meal.[15] After winning some relief, one union leader still bristled at the thought of what might lie ahead. The secretary of the Fédération du Spectacle argued that "to kill an industry (as the new form of taxes on music would undoubtedly do) is to kill the employer, but it likewise kills the worker. If you suppress the theatres and musical halls, the amusements of the capital, you suppress Paris, the artistic capital of the world."[16] Music hall performers organized and filed a salary scale that same month for all employers to follow, thus placing further demands on the economic success of shows.[17]

Because taxes imposed financial burdens that had to be met, they also created the need for shows that would make a profit. Unless a theater could produce a hit, the owners could hardly expect to pay the taxes and reap the monetary rewards of the business. Under these conditions, jazz was able to provide part of the solution. "Everyone in France is in a shambles," asserted one author, describing the craze for jazz, "but jazz records sell like little loaves of bread without the buyer ever seeming to care if his purchase is good or not."[18] And the popularity of jazz not only sold records but put people in theater seats on a regular basis. Already, by 1917, the Gaby Deslys review *Laisse-les tomber!* had taken in a record-setting 187,085 francs worth of taxes alone during its first hundred shows.[19]

The drawback to such success was that jazz risked being seen as nothing but commercial entertainment with no real artistic merit and a money-making scheme that was being pumped into Parisian ears by businessmen eager only to turn a profit. One critic charged that the quality of shows in general had declined because producers sought only acts that would bring in big profits. "The intellectual level of dramatic production lowers every day," he remarked, because of the drive for revenues.[20] Although this author was writing more specifically about theatrical plays, the logic clearly extended to the music halls and other spectacles whose tax burdens he also made a point of discussing. The U.S. entertainment trade paper *Variety* also noted the struggle in France between the proponents and opponents of powerful show business interests. As one article noted, "Legislation insisted on by the respectable French . . . comes to nothing because of this trust which owns theatres, hotels, dance halls and questionable places of amusement and wants them kept wide open."[21] Charges of excessive profit seeking and pandering to audiences for money haunted jazz throughout its early days in Paris.

Moneymaking in entertainment was certainly not unique to the 1920s, as the case of the Chat Noir and other such venues demonstrates, nor were the attacks on it. But the postwar commercialism struck many observers as different, particularly where jazz was concerned, because it seemed so much more intense and troubling in the midst of the difficult economic times after the war. One leader of the orchestral music community in Paris, Gabriel Pierné, spoke of the comparative advantage that popular bands had in recruiting musicians in the 1920s compared to more traditional orchestras: "Now the restaurants, the cinemas, the dancings and the jazz bands assure performers daily salaries that sometimes reach one hundred francs."[22] Tastes were changing, he and others implied, and they increasingly seemed to be driven by commerce.

Parisian audiences who had more money to spend often helped to create such high salaries through their demand for jazz performances. Nouveaux riches French, who had gained fortunes as war profiteers, armaments manufacturers, financiers, or entrepreneurs with goods and services that fit a crucial niche during and after the war, were among the most conspicuous consumers in these years. They constituted an important part of the early French audience for jazz. "They were possessed by a mad desire to enjoy life," noted Bertaut of these economic arrivistes, "which they could only translate in terms of money. They lived in a perpetual whirl of feasting and dissipation which was remarkable even in the post-war rout."[23] Of course, while many Parisians moved up the social ladder, there were those whose status declined in the postwar years; just as there were nouveaux riches, there were also *nouveaux pauvres*, those bourgeois who had lost money in the economic upheaval and currency crises during and after the war.[24] But many accounts speak of this time, for all its complexity, as one of luxury and leisure for many Parisians, and jazz quickly became a crucial pleasure commodity.[25]

The U.S. tourists who came to postwar Paris in large numbers also comprised a big part of the audience for jazz. Many traveled to the city because it was a center of European heritage in art, architecture, and history. Others passed through on their way to see the scarred landscape of the French battlefields. Tourist bureaus and the Michelin guidebooks were happy to oblige these visitors as a way of expanding foreign trade that would inject money directly into the recovering French economy.[26] But Paris was also a pleasure capital where nearly every kind of entertainment could be purchased. Like the nouveaux riches, Americans could afford the cost of entertainment, in their case thanks to the continued strength of the U.S. dollar in the 1920s. To many French observers, both American musicians and audience members symbolized a new kind of postwar commercialism since the United States had become famous to the French as a culture based on mass consumption. As American-style retailing innovations, like the prix uniques discount stores and bold advertising, became a larger part of the postwar French landscape, Americans and their ways could signal new and more powerful economic forces at work in 1920s Paris.[27] For cabaret and theater owners, however, U.S. tourists meant further profits, and offering jazz became a way of attracting them.

This combination of ingredients in the postwar economy—enthusiastic music hall producers and cabaret owners, a series of taxes that made the most popular kinds of entertainment also the most economically necessary, and French and American consumers willing to pay for an evening's revelry—all helped to spread jazz in the early 1920s. And one of the most significant sites in which these trends merged was the dance hall. Perhaps more than any other activity at that time, an evening's fashionable entertainment in Paris meant dancing. Of course, Parisians had danced a variety of steps before the war, including many from overseas—the cakewalk and the Boston from the United States, the Mattchiche from Brazil, and polkas and other dances from around Europe.[28] The tango, brought by Argentine expatriates in the late nineteenth century, was especially popular before 1914, and it had evoked a wide range of reactions among audiences, from pleasure to scorn to nostalgia.[29] With restrictions on public gatherings during the war, dancers had gone underground to clandestine dance clubs, some of which were run by entrepreneurs who later opened important Montmartre nightclubs in the 1920s.

When the war and its restrictions ended, a dance craze exploded across Europe and especially Paris. Some of the older dance halls from before the war came back to life, and people resurrected dances like the tango. Many cabarets and restaurants now made room for dancing on their premises to keep up with the fashion. "Nobody wanted to do anything but dance, dance, and keep on dancing," recalled Jules Bertaut. "Dancing at all the receptions, dancing at home, dancing in the hundreds of dance halls that had sprung up on every side."[30] One company, sensing a burgeoning market, sold a face powder for women who wanted to "answer the call of jazz" wherever it might occur, yet who nevertheless wished to remain fresh and elegant.[31] Dancing could be done by everyone, as an article in the magazine *La Danse* demonstrated by offering an easy, step-by-step guide to doing the shimmy, one of the era's many new dances.[32] Modern dancing even became the entertainment among the highest social circles on at least one occasion in 1925 when the Bal Franco-Américain, hosted by French prime minister Gaston Doumergue and attended by the American ambassador, featured fox-trotting and "La Marseillaise" played in a jazz style.[33]

Although there was a wide variety of dances, this amusement seemed to take on a particularly American cast in 1920s Paris since many of the popular steps were from the United States. The French musician Jean

Laporte remembered the plethora of dance steps in the early years after the war. As he mentioned in his autobiography, "The presence of Americans, their music too, contributed greatly to maintaining an atmosphere of craziness, with jazz, the Charleston, the Black Bottom."[34] "All modern dance moves eastward," remarked one French journalist. "All modern dance begins in America, arrives in England after six months, takes six more months to get to France."[35] An American observer agreed with the idea of a West-to-East stream of dance, writing that "all of Europe gets its dance tunes and its dance orchestras from the U.S.A. We still import directors on a small scale—for symphony orchestras; but we are exporting music and musicians as never before."[36] And for bands from the United States, the European interest in dancing was good news and good for business, as the bandleader Paul Specht noted: "I find Europeans even more enthusiastic about our dance music than Americans themselves. . . . Europe will furnish employment for hundreds of really good dance musicians who play 'rhythmic, symphonic syncopation.' "[37]

Not only were new dance steps and bands often from the United States, so was the term used to describe the places where one could dance. The Americanized term *un dancing* referred to bars, nightclubs, and cabarets of varying sizes as well as to dance halls themselves. Un dancing, it seemed, required little more than upbeat music and a bit of room to move. Someone's home could be converted into an impromptu dancing thanks to phonograph records. Even fine restaurants bent to fashion by blending music and food in the *diner-dansant*, often to the consternation of the restaurant staff and chef. "We hope and believe that the mania will pass," reported one maître d'hôtel at a distinguished Paris restaurant, according to restaurant critic Julian Street, "and we would close rather than yield to it."[38] The maître d' ruefully pointed out to Street that a "fine chef . . . has the pride of an artist; he carefully prepares a dish and sends it fragrant and steaming to the table, but as the waiter serves it the jazz strikes up and everyone rushes to the floor."[39]

As Street's maître d' noted, jazz and dancing were almost completely wrapped together in many people's minds during these years because jazz bands were thought of as dance bands above all else. "The *jazz band*," Bertaut commented, looking back on this period, "will certainly be, along with the word *dancing* the symbolic terms that will characterize the dancing furor of the last few years."[40] "All that they [dancers] need," claimed another writer, "is a good dance floor and a good orchestra (a good jazz-band orchestra). Nothing else matters."[41] The blending of jazz and dance could even directly include the musicians. Jazzmen sometimes left the stage to dance among the couples on the floor, bandleaders frequently danced around the stage as part of their performance, and orchestras often added dancers onstage as part of the act.[42] Furthermore, the word jazz was commonly just another term for the dances—like the Charleston, black bottom, shimmy, and various one- and two-steps—that people did to upbeat music. Listings of records and songs from the era casually mingled the terms or used them interchangeably. One of the first periodicals to discuss jazz music on a regular basis was called *Jazz-Tango*, emphasizing that what united these two styles of dance music was more important than what distinguished them. And dance bands of various types were sometimes referred to as *un jazz-band*, or more simply *un jazz*, regardless of the style of music they actually performed.

The new term *dancing*, along with the music and movements that accompanied it, arrived at the same time as significant changes in many of the older dancing establishments, and these alterations influenced people's views of jazz. As critic André Warnod suggested in *Les Bals de Paris* (1922), a book that chronicled entertainment immediately after the war, there were three kinds of dancings: "palaces and great halls," "small, new *dancings*," and "places that changed themselves to follow fashion."[43] In this last category, Warnod described many of the older establishments whose owners adapted them to accommodate the new trends, including introducing jazz. In Montmartre, according to Warnod, one could visit Le Moulin de la Chanson or Les Quat'z'Arts in order to see former traditional cabarets artistiques that had been converted into dancing establishments and now always made sure to employ a banjo, one of the typical instruments of a jazz band.[44] The old-style dance hall Le Moulin de la Galette, which Warnod called "the most complete expression of the real face of [traditional] Montmartre," installed a jazz band for its dancers. "A jazz band at the Galette!" he remarked with astonishment. "This is something that one could not have foreseen."[45] Even larger dance halls from earlier years, like L'Apollo, now offered dancers two fashionable, modern orchestras and lots of gimmicks such as costume and fashion dances to draw crowds in the afternoon.[46] The new, flashy music hall aesthetic of the age impressed itself on these places, too. According to one British writer, Le Perroquet on the rue Blanche, where two "strident bands, one of them composed of negroes, play in turn," was strewn with brightly colored parrots.[47] Another Montmartre dancing called Florida catered to Americans with its "glass floor illuminated with different coloured lights from below."[48]

For numerous critics, the modernization of many places was quite lamentable. With origins dating back to the 1840s, for example, Le Bal Bullier, on the border between Montparnasse and the Latin Quarter, had become a student dance hall by the early 1900s. Amid what British journalist Sisley Huddleston called the "mock-Oriental appearance, its polished floors, its gardens, its festoons of lights, its alcoves," students went to dance, but also to stand around and talk.[49] Casual visitors and *flâneurs* were not uncommon before the war, and dance critic Léon Werth observed that "those who did not dance were not out of place."[50] The dancing girls "lifted their legs up to the height of their faces and did the splits. The lace on their skirts and their pants created a complicated flower under the lights."[51] During the war, Le Bullier had been converted into a military store, but it reopened afterward and seemed to return quickly to its old self. But by 1921, the atmosphere was starting to change, according to Warnod, who described it in *Les Bals de Paris*. Le Bal Bullier had always been flashy and fashionable, yet after the war, patrons dressed differently and "more luxuriously," he reported, wearing "silk dresses, embroidery, feather hats . . . shorter dresses." And among the various bands providing music, "the jazz band begins to swing and the dancers never stop."[52] Casual visitors were now out of place amid the constant motion. By 1925, Werth reported that "the Bullier is a vast dancing room and nothing else. Its legend and its character have disappeared with the old character and legend of the Latin Quarter." New music was an important part of the problem, he argued, as "the tangos of Bullier are indistinct and its foxes are dismal."[53]

Dancing had an air of fantasy and exoticism about it in the 1920s, but perhaps its transformative power was nowhere more clear than at Le Bal Nègre on the rue Blomet in Montparnasse.[54] This dance hall began as a weekly gathering of immigrants from Martinique and grew into a popular dancing spot for other black people in Paris, both from the colonies and the United States, "consisting mostly of domestics, automobile drivers, office workers, musicians and soldiers," in the words of one American observer.[55] Some of the regular guests provided the music on a piano, piccolo, and banjo. Soon afterward, the Bal's organizer added a saxophone, drums, traps, and "shaker," which one writer described as "a tube of tin, 14 inches long, peppered with small holes and filled with fine gravel. And the way he shakes it, oh boy!"[56] Another depicted the unusual sounds he heard: "The tambourine and the xylophone mark the measure, with a bizarre cylindrical instrument."[57] Eventually, the white patrons of the nearby cafés found out about the place and turned it into one of the city's fashionable night-spots. Michel Leiris remembered it as one of the "snobbish, high society places," but he and his friends went "to bask in the exotic ambiance, to listen to West Indian music, and to watch the other dancers."[58] Color was not a barrier to having fun at Le Bal Nègre but rather a catalyst, and when they danced together, explained one journalist, "blacks and blacks, whites and blacks, blacks and whites possessed the same frenetic rhythms."[59] Reveling in such racial exoticism was an essential ingredient for whites in a place like Le Bal Nègre because it made the experience all the more exciting and unique. As one reporter put it, "Here is all that is primitive in man under the glaring lights of a Paris night," and whites and blacks experienced it equally.[60] Le Bal Nègre was certainly a place to dance. For many, it was also a place to hear jazz, not because of any particular songs but because the music was performed by black musicians.

The places where people danced were wide-ranging in style as well since some were newly opened or remodeled while others still retained something of the flavor of prewar Paris. Different dancings also attracted different crowds. Indeed, the diversity of dancers throughout the city makes drawing a detailed portrait of them difficult. Yet because so many of the dancings required spending a substantial amount of money, whether done in elegant dance halls or small though chic clubs, dancing was often an elite affair. Many of the fashionable and expensive dancings catered to tourists and wealthy Parisians. "An evening of dancing," stated Warnod, "was extremely expensive; the champagne which one had to drink, eighty or one hundred francs a bottle; and this was nothing compared to the considerably more expensive outfits," of which a woman felt compelled to have a different one every time she went out.[61]

But high costs at trendy dance halls did not keep lower-middle- and working-class people off the dance floor, either in Paris or the new industrial suburbs like Saint-Denis, which already had some twenty dance halls by the 1880s.[62] In the 1920s, Warnod described reading about dancing classes offered "at a very modest price," and then seeing a poster for a modern dancing class "in a working-class neighborhood that was very far away; but I didn't mind the trip."[63] When he arrived, he encountered Mme François, "*professeur de tango économique*," with her class.[64] The students, she reported,

> are the children of all the businessmen in the neighborhood. This little blonde is the daughter of a dairyman who put a little money aside; she

wants to be a young lady and I'm sure she will be. That big boy gives me lots of trouble; but I hope to make him a gentleman, as his father, an important grocer, wants him to be. What do you want? One must live in one's century.[65]

Warnod's anecdote suggested that dancing could serve as a means of social mobility, or at least provide the fantasy of rising up the social scale. A dancer could change himself or herself just as the venues in which he or she danced were also being transformed. In an age when the nouveaux riches spent their money visibly, dancing offered a forum in which to demonstrate their newly found wealth.

At the same time, the longtime Paris resident Sisley Huddleston maintained that social climbing was not as important in the 1920s as a new kind of social mingling. Agreeing with an artist friend, Huddleston referred to this era as the "cocktail epoch." Not only were people fascinated by new alcoholic drinks, like the gin fizz, but everything in postwar Paris was mixed together as in a cocktail, including people of all social classes. Traditional distinctions were attenuated in this modern culture, especially as members of an older aristocracy no longer felt ashamed to associate with people of lesser status or manners, he argued.[66] The glass in which this social—and in the case of Le Bal Nègre, racial—cocktail could be mixed was frequently the modern dancing. Werth called one dance hall a place with "the power to gather and unify diverse groups. Dance is stronger than caste."[67] The interwar chronicler Sem imagined the power of jazz through the story of a lady and gentleman of high social rank who, when a jazz band struck up its music, let go of their status and began to dance: "At the first crash of the cymbals, as if by magic, these slaves are set free, exorcised of the demon of pride, and here they are just like little innocent children."[68] For many, social pretensions seemed to disappear under the spell of jazz.

Jazz was not the only dance music in Paris, but it was so closely identified with the dance craze of the 1920s that the two went hand in hand. Most Parisians probably first heard jazz in the context of dancing, whether at a dance hall, restaurant, or elsewhere, and associated the two throughout the era. But jazz could also be linked with—and seemed to contribute to—a series of changes in these venues as older characteristics gave way to those of more modern sites where social and racial mixing occurred openly. The "*dancings* of today," claimed one observer, "with their black dances, completely change the countenance of Parisian dance halls."[69] And by helping to frame such changes with its new presence, jazz also became associated with them. For better or worse, a dance hall could not be considered complete—or completely modern—without a jazz band.

THE TECHNOLOGY OF JAZZ

Although dance halls were changing, they were still familiar to Parisians. They presented jazz musicians with stages and audiences that were already in place by the time the performers arrived. But listeners also discovered jazz through new media: radio, records, and the cinema. Jazz appeared just as the technologies that could spread it quickly were being created, improved, or put into wider use. Consequently, jazz reached audiences that might not venture into a nightclub, including people outside Paris. Jazz was not only a symbol of the modern age because it was new. It was also modern because many people heard it thanks to the latest technological innovations.

Recording technology was not entirely unheard of by the 1920s, having been invented more or less simultaneously in the late 1870s in both France by Charles Cros and the United States by Thomas Edison. Edison's more marketable version did not begin to catch on until the 1880s, following a series of technical improvements. But by the 1890s, the number of phonograph machines and recordings was still small, if growing steadily. Advertising and an ever larger number of recordings by famous singers helped to move sales forward, although poor sound quality and high prices still kept them at moderate levels. Eventually, through further refinements and the production of cheaper models, phonograph and gramophone machines were becoming an established part of the entertainment life of Americans and Europeans.[70] Demonstrations of the improved device at the Académie des Sciences in Paris and the Royal Institution in London introduced it to Europe and captivated audiences, particularly the French. Edison's agents promoted the machine heavily throughout the continent, even arranging a demonstration at which German chancellor Otto von Bismarck made a recording.

Most of Europe relied on imported phonograph technology until 1894, when the Pathé brothers of Paris, who had been attracting customers to their bar in the Place Pigalle with a phonograph, decided to make the machines themselves. Opening a factory in Paris to produce phonograph players and another plant just outside the city to make cylinder blanks, the Pathés could barely keep up with the orders by the end of the century. Their headquarters on the rue de Richelieu doubled as a recording studio, where beginning in 1896, singers from the Opéra and Opéra-Comique made recordings. At the time, Pathé cylinders cost between 1.25 and 2 francs, and by 1899, their catalog boasted 1,500 titles. The record industry in Britain and Germany, and other French ventures such as the Compagnie Française du Gramophone, followed not far behind. Nevertheless, the United States retained an important influence on recorded music in Europe. The trade journal *Musique et instruments* reported that by 1929, nearly half of U.S. records were made explicitly for export, whereas by comparison, French companies only exported 15 percent of their records.[71] U.S. corporations also worked through their subsidiaries in European countries to disseminate music made in the United States.[72]

Recordings spread quickly and became a part of Parisian entertainment in several ways. Pathé Frères maintained a Salon du Phonographe on the Boulevard des Italiens that one historian has described as "a palatial emporium, beautified by thick carpeting, red plush, and polished mahogany, in which top-hatted *boulevardiers* could be found day and night sampling the latest tunes." A patron sat in one of the comfortable armchairs, inserted fifteen centimes into a coin slot, and made his or her selection on a dial. While he or she placed the listening tubes into the ears, a worker below ground rushed to find the desired recording and play it—supposedly not to take more than ten seconds from the time of selection.[73] In addition to the Pathé salon, large audiences attended phonograph concerts that various record companies arranged, often in halls like Le Théâtre des Champs-Elysées or La Salle Pleyel, to introduce their latest releases.[74] People could also purchase phonographs and recordings in stores throughout the city, or by placing requests with record shops or record companies by mail order.

The ability of audiences to find jazz records grew as part of this more general interest in recorded music. According to the magazine *Musique et instruments* in 1926, "music sellers who do not sell phonographs are becoming more and more rare."[75] And many record shops offered jazz music among their selections. Ultimately, stores that specialized in jazz like La Maison du Jazz or La Boîte à Musique could promise quick delivery from the United States of any titles not already on hand. For many devoted purchasers, the label jazz was enough to guarantee a sale in spite of the taxes that elevated prices. "The jazz records sell like little loaves of bread," one magazine article claimed, "the purchaser never seeming to be worried about knowing whether his purchase is interesting or not."[76] In this way, members of a jazz public began to grow through records whether they heard the sounds in the listening salon, concert hall, or at home.

Specialized magazines and newspapers surfaced during the 1920s to keep growing phonograph audiences informed about the latest recordings, including *Musique et instruments*, one of the leading trade magazines for the music business. Beginning in 1919, it included a special section called "La revue des machines parlantes" (The review of talking machines) that eventually split off to become a separate publication. There, one could find articles about the latest technological advances in records and record players, the music business, and musical production. *Arts phonetiques* and *Le Phono* were among some of the several French titles devoted specifically to recorded music.[77] These publications frequently included long lists of all the new records that had just become available so that phonophiles could stay current, and they usually discussed the newest jazz releases. Like the music trade press, musicological journals also began to review records, and most of the titles that offered record reviews to their readers included comments on jazz records as well. For example, Henry Prunières, one of the editors of the respected *La Revue musicale*, regularly wrote reviews praising the jazz records that he found enjoyable. In major Parisian newspapers and other periodicals, the French press wrote much about this new recording technology and the variety of music that it made available, including jazz.

Film provided another crucial setting for recorded sound. In the mid-1920s, even before the advent of sound film, several specialized cinemas in Paris incorporated recorded music into their film programs. At the Montmartre theater Studio 28, according to one report, "The music issues from recesses in the right wall of the auditorium," coming from two gramophones and an electric piano, the latter used "for variety." At the Ciné-Latin, "an electromagnetic Melodium is operated behind a folding screen to the left forecorner of the movie screen, but the music issues from a loudspeaker placed behind the movie screen."[78] But by the late 1920s, films themselves—following in the wake of *The Jazz Singer* (1927), the first sound film—incorporated sound so that it did not need to be added in the theater. Popular musical styles like jazz were part of sound film from its earliest days. Concert films like *King of Jazz* (1930) by American bandleader Paul Whiteman, which came to France in 1931, featured jazz musicians and songs. At the Cinéma Falguière in 1933, films of jazz performances were shown to audiences eager to hear the music.[79] The French production *Minuit Place Pigalle* (1934 remake), based on Maurice Dekobra's novel, featured jazz music provided by the Frenchman Ray Ventura as part of the setting.

French versions of two imported films of the 1920s, the German production retitled *Mon Cœur est un Jazz-Band* (1929) and the Spanish movie now named *Le Danseur du Jazz* (1928), suggest something of how filmmakers and promoters across Europe linked the spirit of jazz to contemporary productions, and they give insight into how jazz was presented to French audiences in motion pictures. *Mon Cœur est un Jazz-Band* (My Heart is a Jazz Band) offered French viewers the story of a London innkeeper's daughter who performed for her father's guests and eventually became the star dancing girl for a large orchestra. This modern woman, "simple, likable, audacious, full of spirit, of guts, of energy," as one French reviewer portrayed her, saved a would-be lover from being framed for a jewel heist by his scoundrel associates.[80] If this film demonstrated some of the modern values associated with jazz in the persona of its dancing protagonist, *Le Danseur du Jazz* (The Jazz Dancer) presented a more tragic tale. It told the story of a doomed interracial romance between a famous "danseur *nègre*" and a European woman who, in spite of her affection for the dancer, was "tested by her repulsion for those of his race," as one French review put it.[81] Such films traded on the term *jazz* to increase their popularity, regardless of what the movie's music was actually like, and they offered themes that viewers might associate with jazz's impact on French culture—from the modern woman to the mingling of races.

Radio was another new medium that helped to spread jazz. In the early part of the decade, French radio was a combination of state- and privately owned stations that brought many sorts of music into people's homes. By the end of the 1920s, there were some five hundred thousand radios throughout France.[82] Initially, jazz bands performed live on the radio. Once the technology to transmit recorded sound was available by the late 1920s, phonograph records were broadcast as well. The historian of French radio Cécile Méadel has noted the difficulty in discerning the actual content of radio programming for this period given the fluid categories used in the documentation that described the music being broadcast. The amount of jazz is particularly hard to estimate since the word meant so many things and could be easily interchanged with terms like *musique de danse*.[83] But reflecting the patterns of performance in other venues, jazz music soon became part of regular broadcasts as orchestras performed various kinds of dance music. On occasion, entire radio programs would be devoted to jazz, but in other cases, the music was mixed together with several genres.[84]

Part of what made jazz so remarkable as a music in the new century was its close connection to the modern technology of phonographs, radios, and film. Yet the influence of so-called mechanical music, of which jazz was a part, sparked debate about the impact of technology on the musical arts. Many critics recognized the potential for the technology to make great music more widely available and to educate listeners about music, but others worried about the potential effects of these new devices on what audiences heard and how people listened to music. Records might preserve a piece of music across time and space with precision, but what would be the quality of such mass-produced music? they wondered. New media could democratize music by spreading it more broadly, but in aiming to reach the largest audience, standards might decline. "There is a real danger that the directors of the radio are often preoccupied with satisfying everyone," argued music critic René Dumesnil, "that is to say the majority of incompetent listeners. It is useless to pretend to educate and at the same time to try to follow the advice of those who have no education." The masses would prefer "a broadcast of *chansonnettes* or accordion music"—or jazz—to symphonies.[85] Listeners would cease to know what a truly good performance should sound like, other critics claimed, because they would not have as much good music available to them. The quality of mechanical music was also in danger from the forces of the mass marketplace that some also believed would diminish the quality of performances. "One cannot," contended critic Etienne Royer, "let an instrument as powerful for broadcasting and education [as the radio] fall into the hands of unscrupulous businessmen, or mediocre people in search of publicity." Great musicians must support and participate in the new medium, he pleaded, lest radio become the preserve of "composers and performers of an inferior quality."[86] In the forefront of the "rationalization" of music that recorded sound implied, critic Lionel Landry alleged that Americans—as the producers of large numbers of phonograph records for export—would decrease the number of orchestras, "leaving only enough to assure the diffusion of works over the entire surface of the globe" through recorded music. The few remaining bands would lead to U.S. dominance of the recorded-music industry, he feared.[87] Finally, with the spread of technology, people might not learn to play music for themselves but instead listen only to what was broadcast or purchased on records. Remarked one observer: "The sound that I make when I take up an instrument is the fruit of my own tree," but music from the new technology was merely "the commonplace fruit bought at the grocery store."[88] The new technology with which jazz was associated offered promise yet also problems, as these critics noted.

Not only the sounds of jazz but the new ways in which people heard it seemed threatening to French musical culture.

Common to the ways in which observers discussed how jazz spread—whether as a moneymaking endeavor, through the modernized dance halls, or via new technology—was the fear that France was continuing to evolve into a "mass culture" where distinctions would be blended together in a homogenized blandness.[89] Catering to market forces and standardizing musical works by recording them often seemed to reduce music to a formula and audiences to a uniform body with no taste. And as one of the most prominent forms of mechanical music, jazz appeared to be at the forefront of creating a mass culture. Yet the case of jazz also demonstrates that although new media such as radio, records, and films were capable of bringing a new music to large numbers of people all at once, not every audience member was willing to listen. Even those who did listen to jazz often heard something quite different than their neighbors. Rather than seeing a homogenized mass audience, it might be more accurate to see a fragmented set of Parisian audiences who reacted to the music differently. The result of such division was a vigorous series of debates about what jazz meant and what it was doing to French culture. Audiences actively engaged with different messages by interpreting and assigning meaning to them. As a result, the audiences who did appreciate the music played an important role in the process of making jazz French as they responded positively to it—but not without a struggle.[90]

3

JAZZ
AND THE
CITY OF
PARIS

Almost immediately after jazz musicians arrived in Paris, they began to gather in two of the city's most important creative neighborhoods: Montmartre and Montparnasse, respectively the Right and Left Bank haunts of artists, intellectuals, poets, and musicians since the late nineteenth century. Performing in these high-profile and popular entertainment districts could give an advantage to jazz musicians because Parisians and tourists already knew to go there when they wanted to spend a night out on the town. As hubs of artistic imagination and experimentation, Montmartre and Montparnasse therefore attracted the kinds of audiences that might appreciate the new and thrilling sounds of jazz. For many listeners, these locations leant the music something of their own exciting aura, and the early success of jazz in Paris probably had at least as much to do with musicians playing there as did other factors.

In spite of their similarities, however, by the 1920s these neighborhoods were on two very different paths, each representing competing visions of what France could become after the war. And the reactions to jazz in each place became important markers of the difference between the two areas and visions. Montmartre was legendary as the late-nineteenth-century capital of "bohemian Paris," where French artists had gathered and cabaret songs had filled the air.[1] In its heyday, Montmartre was one of the centers of popular entertainment, and its artists prided themselves on flying in the face of respectable middle-class values. But by the 1920s, Montmartre represented an established artistic tradition, not the challenge to bourgeois life that it had been at the fin de siècle. Entertainment culture was rapidly changing both in substance and style in the postwar era, and a desire for new sounds, including foreign music and exotic art, was quickly replacing the love for the cabarets' French chansons. Jazz was not entirely to blame for such changes, of course. Commercial pressures, especially the rapidly growing tourist trade, eroded the popularity of old Montmartre cabarets, which were not always able to compete with the newer music halls and dance halls. Yet jazz bore much of the criticism from those who saw the changes in Montmartre as the death of French popular entertainment. Montparnasse, on the other hand, was the face of a modern Paris. It was the international crossroads where an ever changing mixture of people celebrated, rather than lamented, cosmopolitanism and exoticism in all its forms, especially in jazz bands. These different attitudes within the entertainment districts and their institutions reflected the impact of the broader trends at work in Paris—the influx of foreign populations, for example, or the advent of cars and electricity on city streets as indicators of modern technology—and the possible consequences for French culture. Jazz was at the confluence of these trends, and it became a convenient symbol for the struggle they represented.

BOHEMIAS OLD AND NEW

Montmartre was the *quartier* that had become famous in the late nineteenth century as the home to painters, poets, and singers. By the beginning of the twentieth century, it was the established emblem of an authentically French artistic and popular entertainment tradition, both in practice and reputation. People had gone there to live outside the regular rules of society as well as to unite life and art. From the hill on which this community sat in the northern part of Paris, a resident could look down onto the rest of the capital and the conventions he or she had left behind. The area was one of quaint, steep streets filled with lively activity. Impressionist painters had found the place and its inhabitants such inspiring subjects that they often painted scenes from the cafés and sidewalks to illustrate the everyday life of the neighborhood.[2]

The cabaret was the chief place where people—young artists, writers, painters, and musicians, along with their hangers-on and admirers—gathered to escape from the bourgeois culture of the city below and celebrate their art.[3] The most famous cabaret of all, the Chat Noir, became the model for many later establishments. Owned by one of Montmartre's most colorful characters, Rodolphe Salis, the Chat Noir opened in the early 1880s when Salis lured a group of poets who called themselves the Hydropathes to his establishment. Soon it became a gathering place for artists of all sorts. Salis decorated the cabaret in a mock–Louis XIII style—a humorous junkyard pastiche of cheap antiques and fanciful artwork—but this decor, along with most other aspects of the place, was completely tongue-in-cheek. Waiters wore the robes of the French Academy in high irony as Salis mockingly greeted guests as "Your Excellency."

Music was central to the cabaret atmosphere, and these institutions became venues for young musicians to pay their dues in the profession. Composers like Erik Satie and Claude Debussy, for example, played in cabarets early in their careers. On a visit, one could hear singers like Yvette Guilbert or Aristide Bruant perform the sometimes rowdy, sometimes mournful chansons that had been a mainstay of popular entertainment for much of the nineteenth century and were now enshrined in the cabaret.[4] Chansons, a song style with roots in medieval times, reveled in the details of everyday life, and took up themes and images from society and politics to describe various aspects of French life in their lyrics.[5] Until the creation of a cabaret culture in Montmartre, chansons could be found in the many café-concerts and other shows around Paris, especially on the city's grand boulevards. By the 1870s they were wearing thin, having been reduced to overly sentimental or vulgar tunes. Chansons, however, underwent a revival in the 1880s and 1890s thanks to the Montmartre cabarets and the singers who performed there. These fin de siècle chansons in particular were imbued with deep social and political concerns, often exposing the unglamorous side of Parisian life in gritty detail by depicting the lives of prostitutes or the poor, for instance. With Paris and all its people for their subjects, the new singer-songwriters of this era chronicled life with both humor and pathos. The *chansonnier* Xanrof portrayed the lives of the musicians themselves, and the other artists of the Montmartre cabarets, in his song "Les Bohèmes":

> In cafés decorated in strange style,
> The dropouts and unruly
> Draped in fringe topcoats
> Speak ill of their friends;
> Or composing bohemian verses
> Stare at the bottom of their beer mugs.[6]

As chansons like Xanrof's and those of other composers often described in their lyrics, late-nineteenth-century Montmartre was not just an escape from Paris but also a voyage to a strange and exciting locale. Prostitutes, criminals, drug users and dealers, and the poor called this place home alongside the artists. *Apaches*—young hoodlums—roamed through the quartier looking for trouble or an easy victim to rob. Precisely because it was a bit dangerous and seedy, the respectable bourgeoisie in Paris frequently went to Montmartre to "slum" and take in the sights and sounds of wilder living not too far from home. A significant part of the cabaret experience for the late-nineteenth-century bourgeoisie was being able to hear themselves mocked and insulted. Full of pithy satire, Aristide Bruant aimed denigrating comments at middle-class visitors when they entered the door of his famous cabaret, Le Mirliton. "You shall take me to the Chamber of Horrors—eh?" spoke one of the wealthy characters in Émile Zola's novel *Paris* of a fictionalized Montmartre cabaret based on Le Mirliton. When one of her companions objected that dressed as she was in an evening gown and jewels, she would be ridiculed, she replied, "Pooh, it will be all the more amusing if they do jeer at us!"[7] Zola's description of the cabaret was "a suffocating place, narrow, irregular, with all sorts of twists, turns, and secluded nooks, and a low and smoky ceiling. . . . The walls had simply been placarded with posters of violent hues, some of the crudest character, showing the barest of female figures."[8]

During World War I, laws that regulated public gatherings and dimmed the city's lights at dark also shut down much of the entertainment in Montmartre. As the neighborhood awakened again in the 1920s, so did its nightlife. "After the sun went down," singer and American expatriate club owner Bricktop remembered, "Paris did become the City of Light, and Montmartre changed from a sleepy little village to a jumpin' hot town."[9] Similarly, writer and Montmartre habitué Pierre MacOrlan recalled that "when the Place Pigalle and the rue Pigalle light up around midnight, we forget everything that we learned," as the red and purple lights shone on the people below like a "new sun."[10]

But observers also began to notice important changes in the character of the quartier. The bourgeoisie again came to this part of Paris, but now, far from being the source of ridicule, evening dress was expected or even required as people rolled up to the clubs in limousines or the taxicabs that were replacing the horse-drawn carriages on the city's streets after the war. Montmartre in those days, with champagne flowing in all the night spots, was for many "a party every night," according to one chronicler. Rather than being a gathering of poor poets, he continued, "this is not only a marvelous orgy, it is a magnificent exaltation of the bourgeois who finally takes off his mask, . . . of the *nouveaux riches* who want to regain the times they lost when they were broke."[11] These revelers were fascinated by jazz music's very modernity—its newness, energy, and sense of drive—and musicians could always find an audience among them. Like the electric lights that now illuminated Montmartre, jazz quickly became a symbol of the twentieth century.

Jazz found a home in Montmartre partly because many black Americans had moved there after World War I.[12] Drawn both to the cabarets where they could hear familiar music and the cheaper apartments at a time when housing was scarce throughout Paris, black American musicians continued to find Montmartre a friendly environment throughout the interwar era. The entertainment business and its growing tourist base provided many opportunities for work either as a musician or in other jobs. Washing dishes in the club Le Grand Duc, poet Langston Hughes listened to the music that flowed through the place. "Blues in the rue Pigalle," Hughes wrote in his memoir, *The Big Sea*, "Black and laughing, heart-breaking blues in the Paris dawn, pounding like a pulse-beat, moving the Mississippi."[13] The neighborhood provided a point of transition between the United States and Paris for many black Americans. Soon, jazz became a central part of Montmartre's culture thanks to African American club owners like Ada "Bricktop" Smith and former boxer Gene Bullard, both of whom hired black jazz musicians to play in their clubs.[14] As a familiar part of African American culture, jazz music united the black American community in Paris.[15] The jazz clarinetist Sidney Bechet recalled, for example, that he could not walk home at night without running into friends all along the way.[16]

The presence of such an artistic community in Montmartre was part of the neighborhood's heritage, even though now many of the artists, like Bechet, were foreigners. For some white visitors, the black residents and musicians of Montmartre added to the exotic flair that they had already come to expect from this neighborhood since before the war, and there was a certain continuity between the strange sounds of jazz and Montmartre's reputation as the city's artistically provocative quartier. More generally, as a new and experimental art form, jazz made sense in this neighborhood that was famous for cradling artists and providing a haven for challenges to bourgeois propriety—precisely what jazz, with its explosive sounds, seemed to be doing.

But even though jazz could be seen as continuing the Montmartre tradition of shocking audiences, not everyone welcomed it because of what the music symbolized about changes in Parisian entertainment culture. Jazz threatened to erode a uniquely French bohemian culture centered in and symbolized by Montmartre. The cabarets artistiques that had built Montmartre's reputation in the late nineteenth century had already been growing more and more elaborate during the 1880s and 1890s to include, for instance, shadow theater and puppet shows. At the fin de siècle, the Divon Japonais introduced an Asian influence to the neighborhood with Japanese artwork for the walls and costumes for the staff. New forms of entertainment like the showy music hall—with its bright lighting, elaborate costumes, and large orchestras—continued the trend.[17] Yet the music halls of the 1920s took this new kind of entertainment to greater extremes. Cabarets had typically remained small, with the performers and audience in close proximity, but the music hall could seat hundreds. Cabarets primarily offered verbal entertainment in the form of poetry or songs, but music halls were overwhelmingly visual. Historian Charles Rearick has captured the vividness of the postwar music hall by describing it as "a dream factory full of behind-the-scenes machinery and lighting systems, a technological complex producing the magical succession of scenes and bathing them in rainbow hues and bright whites."[18] And music halls quickly became an important venue for jazz throughout the 1920s, where it started as entertainment during an intermission, but became one of the headlining acts as it grew in popularity.

Musically, jazz was a challenge to the French chanson, which had been at the heart of cabaret entertainment in Montmartre. The chanson was certainly not dead, but by the 1920s the growing presence of jazz posed a question: Would this foreign music with a new, syncopated rhythm replace the French chanson?[19] And this sort of change taking place in Montmartre seemed to foreshadow broader developments to come. For example, one critic leveled a series of charges against foreign music in a 1926 article titled "Is This the Agony of the French Chanson?" in the entertainment trade journal *Comœdia*. As he put it, "It's a fact: melody is dead, sentimentality is no more, music as well as modern life must be hectic." Two of every ten songs performed in France were foreign, he estimated, and the demand for "authentic" music kept French composers out of competition with others. "According to the editor [at a music company], a tango can only be composed well by a Spaniard or an Argentine, a 'blue' only by an Italian; a shimmy only by an American and a waltz only by a German." The result was that foreign composers reaped the rewards. "It's money that leaves France," the critic concluded, linking economic and cultural success, "it's the slow but sure death of the French *chanson*."[20] Poet and chansonnier Georges Millandy agreed: "The violins have left and jazz is king! . . . The French *chanson* is truly very sick . . . could it die?"[21] Theatrical producer

Gabriel Astruc recalled that the French productions he mounted could find only small audiences. For a Festival de musique française, he noted, "the French did not want it." Toward a production of French composer Gabriel Fauré's *Pénélope*, he remarked, "Paris remained unmoved."[22] As the lyrics of the song "Ah! La Musique Américaine" already said by 1913, "Ah! American music is charming, it's much more elegant than Parisian music."[23] And the popularity of jazz suggested that this kind of music would continue.

Not only were the artists and their art changing in Montmartre, so were the audiences. Foreigners were not new there, but their larger numbers were. Tourists had started coming to Montmartre in the early 1900s, claimed American travel writer Robert Forrest Wilson, and "it was the end of Montmartre's bohemia."[24] They had long visited the cabarets artistiques and provided much of the impetus for the increasing reliance on new kinds of spectacles and higher drink prices.[25] But after the war, people from around the world descended on Montmartre like never before. Some were refugees from Russia and Eastern Europe, who established their own nightclubs—like Shéhérazade and Cazenova, both of which featured Russian music—as part of their expatriate communities in Paris.[26] In the quartier, though, the constant international flow of tourists was the most significant foreign influence, and their presence was especially critical in changing the tenor of postwar Montmartre. "Strangers from all nations of the world flooded in" to Montmartre, according to author Jules Gravigny in his book *Montmartre en 1925*.[27] Visitors from many countries soon filled the nightclubs in this neighborhood, particularly those around the Place Pigalle, in search of their fun, and they often found jazz to be their chief entertainment. As one chronicler of Paris put it, "To the strain of jazz bands, French, Czecho-Slovacs, Russians, Indians, Cubans, Brazilians, eat and drink and dance as publicly as possible."[28] In Montmartre, critic Jean Émile-Bayard nostalgically lamented, "after midnight, one speaks every language except French."[29]

The presence of visitors from the United States, something that people all over Europe were confronting given a wave of postwar American travel, was especially remarkable to many French commentators.[30] Some had gone to France to tour the battle sites from the war, while others went to absorb the art and culture. Many just wanted to be entertained in the pleasure capital for which Paris had gained a reputation, and they often found their way to Montmartre. Soldiers who liked listening to music from home as well as other Americans traveling abroad on the strength of the dollar began to create an audience for music that had crossed the Atlantic during the war, including jazz. Many observers, including Americans themselves, noticed the Americanization of entertainment in Montmartre, fueled in part by the demands of transatlantic travel. "At every hour of the day," Wilson noted, "the Parisians find themselves in contact with things American. . . . They name restaurants and cafés after us and drinks that we in our wettest days [before Prohibition] never knew. They prefer our movies to their own, and during the intermissions they eat our Eskimo Pies." And, he remarked, "They dance to our jazz."[31]

Not just the encounter with U.S. culture but also its seeming dominance over France, especially in music, stood out to some. In particular, American influence and tourism often meant growing commercial concerns, and many believed that the invasion of business into art was destroying Montmartre's heritage as an artist's colony. In reality, advertising, publicity, and commercialism were nothing new to this part of Paris. Comments about this supposed change are thus ironic given the neighborhood's moneymaking past. As we have seen, the Chat Noir's Salis was famous for his skill in publicizing his cabaret. Yet many critics believed that commercial concerns were more intense in the postwar era and often linked them to an American way of living. Given the money that American tourists were spending thanks to the strong U.S. dollar in the 1920s, perhaps this connection is not surprising. Many critics underscored the new reliance on artistic commerce, fearing that it had corrupted the old values of art for art's sake that presumably had been part of Montmartre's character—or at least was now a part of how it was remembered.

The geography of the neighborhood itself reflected the changes in entertainment. The older face of Montmartre still existed on the upper portion of the hill, and the new tourist areas remained largely on the boulevards around Place Clichy and Place Pigalle at the bottom. Commentators frequently called these different areas of the neighborhood the "two Montmartres" because they seemed to have little or no relation to one another. Some were afraid that the new style of entertainment would slowly creep its way uphill, demolishing what was left of the old artists' haunts, and that lower Montmartre would engulf the remnants of the "true" Montmartre that had managed to survive. "Lower Montmartre," wrote MacOrlan, "differs little from all the great crossroads of the world where the women, jazz, and the neon go together finally resulting in identical spectacles."[32] As MacOrlan suggested, jazz alone did not appear to be eating away at Montmartre. But it was one powerful symbol as well as a source of the larger changes in modern life that were transforming a semirural village famous for its windmills (and that had been annexed to the city only in 1860) into part of the greater urban conglomeration of Paris. "As business extended its salient up the hill," remarked Robert Forrest Wilson, "art stubbornly retreated ahead of it."[33]

Much of the postwar image of prewar Montmartre was a myth. Indeed, an entire generation of writers including MacOrlan, André Salmon, and Francis Carco made their reputations recalling just how different the old Montmartre was from the new. In the end, many writers believed, the Montmartre of the 1920s was no longer French. "I see Montmartre, not as it was then," wrote Carco, "but as it is now, with its high buildings and its *guinguettes* full of foreigners. I feel as if I had lived a dream, and I don't know where I am."[34] Writer André Warnod recognized the ambiguity in these changes, arguing that even though prewar Montmartre was gone, a new kind of life had emerged in the area. Still, he wrote with a sense of longing for times past that could not be recovered by the light and noise of the new century.[35] Many of the changes these writers chronicled were only perceptions—as was the image of old Montmartre that was now thoroughly wrapped in a nostalgic glow with certain elements of that past conveniently forgotten. There had always been exotic and foreign music, for instance, and tourists had long visited old Montmartre to soak up its atmosphere just as they did in the 1920s. But the memory of the prewar days and the feeling that the neighborhood was dying were powerful interpretations that influenced how many French observers responded to jazz. Amusements that had seemed to be more truly artistic and French appeared to be passing away at the hands of those that emphasized glamor, the exotic, and escape rather than, for example, the realism and social concern of the late-nineteenth-century chansons.

Many cabaret poets and musicians, whose tastes were for smaller and more intimate shows, continued to leave the hillside for other places in the city like Montparnasse or the Latin Quarter on the Left Bank. Montmartre, as one writer put it, "had already become too old and was being crushed under the weight of the wit of the Cabaret of the Chat Noir, totally out of date."[36] Not everyone was so quick to give up the fight. In 1920, a group of artists declared Montmartre, somewhat comically, but with an underlying bitterness at the transformations taking place around it, an independent Free Commune. One of the stated goals of this separation from the rest of Paris was to keep Montmartre's artistic heritage alive and guard the neighborhood as a refuge for the more traditional sort of French entertainment. The Free Commune was full of festivals and old-fashioned celebrations that brought the neighborhood together. The rituals of this newly imagined community featured French revolutionary dress and symbolism; they included a competition for young girls to represent the figure of Marianne, the icon of the Republic.[37] But despite such attempts to preserve something of the past, in the battle between the flashy, jazzy tourist haunts and quaint cabarets, the former seemed to have more to offer in the new century while the latter were remnants of the century that had just finished passing away in the war.

Montparnasse on the Left Bank was the other prominent home of jazz in Paris. Centered around the Boulevards Montparnasse and Raspail, Montparnasse had been a quiet artists' neighborhood before the war. It had remained largely unknown other than by artists themselves, many of whom had already begun to move there in the early 1900s to escape the growing tourist and commercial influence in Montmartre. By 1914, according to Guillaume Apollinaire, who helped lead the move of artists across the river, Montparnasse was "for painters and poets what Montmartre was fifteen years ago."[38] Filled with Cubists, Surrealists, American expatriate writers, the Japanese artist Foujita, famous personalities like the model Kiki, and others, Montparnasse in the 1920s soon took over from Montmartre as the city's artistic headquarters. It was also an unmistakable international crossroads and the heart of cosmopolitan Paris. Perhaps even more than in Montmartre, people from all over the world filled the streets, clubs, bars, and restaurants of Montparnasse. Longtime Paris resident and literary critic Paul Cohen-Portheim provided a wonderful description of the diverse community that Montparnasse became:

It really is, however, a centre where all peoples, nations and languages meet. Here you find American and African negroes proclaiming the Coming of the Negro (the superiority of the black races is an article of faith in Montparnasse); Indians who want to free themselves, and the Chinese too, from English oppression, and Englishmen with the same ambition; Americans who hate America, lament the Americanisation of Paris (while contributing to it) because they do not know Berlin, and leave mechanical progress to the admiration of Europeans; innumerable Scandinavians, fair-haired and fine-looking or surprisingly dark like the pair of dancers known as the Rocky Twins; a lot of Germans—daughters of the Kurfürstendamm who think everything much too *bourgeois* and make a show of being tremendously wicked, which is *vieux-jeu* [old-fashioned]; a lot of painters, journalists and writers; Spaniards, both genuine and transatlantic; and anti-Fascists—besides the innumerable people from every country who come to look at them.[39]

One French journalist appropriately called the quartier the "crossroads of the world."[40]

Drawn to the cutting-edge artists and entertainments in the neighborhood—and to the alcohol prohibited at home—Americans often made Montparnasse their first stop on a trip to Paris. "Montparnasse may properly be regarded as the forty-ninth State," asserted one observer. "It is a State which includes all the other forty-eight States of the United States. Here is the microcosm of America."[41] An American in Montparnasse during the 1920s did not feel too far from home in this hub of the "American colony" with U.S. newspapers, shops, consumer goods, movies, and music. Nearby in St-Germain-des-Près, Sylvia Beach's famous bookstore and library, Shakespeare and Company, provided a meeting place for American intellectuals.[42] Gertrude Stein also helped many American writers find their footing in Paris when they visited her apartment not far away near the Jardin du Luxembourg.

Montparnasse was not normally described with the same kind of nostalgia as Montmartre, although a few people did lament the invasion of this artists' neighborhood by foreigners. For some, new trends like Surrealism hardly measured up to the memory of what Montparnasse's artists used to produce. As in Montmartre, a "false" Montparnasse was emerging, in the view of writer Jean Émile-Bayard. An international, rather than a uniquely French crowd amused itself nightly in the clubs and the "American bars"—where one ordered and sat at a counter rather than at tables as in a café—that had sprung up after the war, he argued. "For those who are in contact with all the nations of the Universe, the Montparnassian risks forgetting his own language" amid the new people and new styles of art, Émile-Bayard wrote.[43] The changes in the neighborhood inspired the chansonnier Georges Millandy to write the poem "Nuits de Montparnasse" (Nights of Montparnasse), which longed for a different city:

Montparnasse! Montparnasse!
What are you hiding under your grimace?
What nightmares . . . and what remorse?
Who knows whether the dead,
Whose corpses you awaken,
Might not rise up howling to the chords

Of jazz, under the gold of your fancy hotels?
Montparnasse! Montparnasse![44]

"To sing French songs in the heart of cosmopolitan Montparnasse," concluded Millandy in his memoirs, "that's a challenge."[45]

Despite the voices speaking out on behalf of an authentic artistic culture being corroded by foreign influences, many visitors to Montparnasse appreciated the mixing of peoples that added to the neighborhood's creative spirit. "Montparnasse," claimed André Warnod, "is a neighborhood without monuments, with the exception of the little old church Notre-Dame-des-Champs. It's a new neighborhood [*un quartier neuf*]."[46] And jazz supplied one of the most important entertainments for the nightly reveling there. Amid the "chatter, jabbering, the sound of saucers and spoons, the clash of glasses on the tables, the calls to the waiters, the brouhaha of a thousand conversations," there were, according to Warnod, "the notes of the jazz band, the cries of the guitar, the moan of the accordion."[47] On one occasion, in 1927, Paris police prefect Jean Chiappe decreed that the quartier was, in fact, too noisy and ordered all bands to stop playing. Claiming that many of the cafés and clubs were not licensed for music, the police went so far as to lock up pianos in some cases.[48]

Montparnasse and Montmartre were the playgrounds of the interwar years for people of all types: French and foreign, artist and tourist, bohemian and bourgeois. Yet these two areas of the city expressed different sides of Parisian culture. In the late nineteenth century, a trip to Montmartre for a middle-class visitor had meant slumming among the impoverished residents of the quartier, reinforcing the rank of wealth and status by contrast. But the old Montmartre bohemia was dying while the lower part of Montmartre and Montparnasse were on the rise. These two places had more in common with one another through their reliance on tourist-oriented entertainments and foreign visitors than with the old Montmartre that remained higher up on the hill above Paris. Montparnasse "was at once highbrow and jazzy," British journalist Sisley Huddleston remarked, and slumming was not as easily done.[49] Montparnasse had its share of strange characters and poverty to be sure, but since the early twentieth century, it had been at the center of artistic commerce that brought plenty of money into the neighborhood. Wealthy Americans and newly rich French bought the modernist works of Montparnasse artists. "Many of them drew substantial sums from the picture-dealers," explained Jules Bertaut, "to whom they had sold the whole of their future output."[50]

Like so many things in the years after the war, Bertaut believed, art had been openly reduced to commerce. As Huddleston noted, "Bohemia is so attractive for the wealthy idler that one enterprising company has arranged visits to the studios of real artists."[51] Bohemianism in postwar Montparnasse meant sharing the same nightclub space with fashionable, up-and-coming artists rather than sinking temporarily to the level of poor poets.[52] These kinds of changes in artistic bohemianism in many ways served as an index of just how much had changed since the war. Bohemian and bourgeois values, rather than standing as opposites, merged even more fully into an amalgamation of experimentation, commerce, and art than they had before the war.[53]

More important, these changing neighborhoods offered two contrasting interpretations of French culture. One was the nostalgic vision of the late nineteenth century in which art was created for art's sake and performers drew on the city around them or the past for their chansons or poems. The other was a France that not only welcomed but reveled in a modern, foreign music and new kinds of entertainments. Although many of these transformations were often perceived rather than real, such perceptions were crucial in shaping how many Parisians thought about their city in the years after World War I and how they heard jazz. In Montparnasse and lower Montmartre, the fashion for jazz was part of the neighborhood's success, while for the older section of Montmartre, jazz brought the sort of decline that inspired tributes to the cabarets of old or the celebrations of a Free Commune. Jazz reminded people just how much had changed in the last few years. Such tales of decadence, decay, nostalgia, and the "remembrance of things past" were just as prevalent in 1920s Paris as modernist experimentation.

Which of these visions of Paris would triumph was one of the burning cultural questions of the day, and discussing jazz often became a way for many Parisians in the 1920s to articulate their attitudes toward the direction their city was taking. Writing in *Les Annales politiques et littéraires* in 1925, one author penned an imaginary account of someone returning to Montmartre after a thirty-year absence. When the protagonist steps into a cabaret, he sees just how much the entertainment of the neighborhood has been altered:

> A jazz band, in the corner of the room, struck up a fox-trot. Except for the leader, who was white and played the violin remarkably, the orchestra offered all the shades of skin-tone of people of color. A mulato stretched an accordion. An ebony colored man from Martinique played the melancholy

notes of a saxophone like velvet while a frenetic Cafre rattled, in his immense arms, the ten pieces of his drums. Finally, a pensive Madagascan pulled a slide-whistle with metallic whines, while a Hawaiian alternated between a banjo and a little nickel whistle that imitated the chirping of birds.[54]

Putting it more simply, another Parisian spoke of the changes that he witnessed and distinguished them from his own restaurant in an older part of the city when he said, "*There* are jazz bands and American music—*here* is calm and poetry."[55]

Fans and detractors agreed that jazz meant change, but whereas for fans it was something good, for detractors it was to be decried. Paris was becoming the cosmopolitan capital of a modern age symbolized by jazz and other imported music. France seemed to be joining an international culture by blending itself and its art much more thoroughly with peoples from around the world, and many of its artists were now drawing inspiration from abroad rather than at home. But, many observers wondered, did this mean losing what was French as symbolized by the old Montmartre cabarets? Was the fate of France one in which the chanson would give way to the shimmy?

JAZZ IN THE POSTWAR CABARETS

Despite their differences, Montmartre and Montparnasse were linked by the new cabaret culture. The nightclubs and bars in these two neighborhoods ranged from the cramped to the spacious, from the dingy to the luxurious. But whatever their appearance and atmosphere, these places were nearly always fashionable. Like the dance halls, each establishment had its own character and charm, although to skeptics such places seemed to have all too much in common. As a U.S. writer cynically observed,

> One cabaret is like another—a pink silk sort of place, rows of tables around the walls, open dancing floor in the middle, orchestra platform at one end, hat bandits, uniformed doormen and waiters at the other. . . . Mirrors and lights to dazzle them, jazz to excite them, hot and smoky air to make them thirsty—and they will buy plenty of champagne.[56]

Cabarets used the sounds of jazz and a flow of alcohol to lure patrons inside and keep them entertained. Alcohol, forbidden by Prohibition at home, attracted Americans and added to Paris's reputation as a pleasure capital. Going out in the evenings to a club with jazz usually meant a night of drinking, a potentially expensive endeavor. Champagne was often the beverage of choice, sometimes with a required minimum purchase. "Booze has a very big B and Art a very small a on the Boulevard Montparnasse," one commentator put it, but his observation could suffice for much of fashionable nightlife in Paris.[57] A hostess, who sang, visited with guests, and kept order in the sometimes rowdy Montmartre places, often tended the cabarets. And going to any particular nightclub was usually only one stop on a nightlong round of Paris club hopping. Tired of one place or hearing of a great jazz band in another location, groups of revelers would head off to another establishment. Jazz musicians were also mobile in the Parisian night. Finishing their work at their usual venue, they went to various other clubs where they could gather and talk with other musicians, and they often jammed together into the early hours of the morning.

Besides being places to hear jazz, clubs and cabarets were also important spheres of U.S. influence. American bars served newly fashionable cocktails from the United States, and catered to tourists and expatriates. But Americans were not only the customers. They also owned many of the clubs in Paris and led the way in featuring the jazz that their clients enjoyed. One of the most popular destinations in Montmartre, especially for Americans, was Zelli's, run by the "King of the Cabaret-Keepers" Joe Zelli. He had opened his first club on the rue Caumartin in secret during the war because public dancing was illegal and remained so until a few months after the armistice.[58] A visitor needed a membership card to enter the underground dance hall, but Zelli's remained a popular spot in spite of this imposition and several police raids. Once police lifted the ban, Zelli closed this club and moved to Montmartre. The boîte he opened on the rue Fontaine was, according to one travel writer, "a big, oblong hall lined with tables, which in turn are lined with girls."[59] "More than thirty girls work in Zelli's as dancers," who served as partners for male customers who arrived unaccompanied, reported another patron.[60] In the Montmartre cabaret tradition, Zelli greeted people at the door. Unlike some of his nineteenth-century counterparts who mocked their clientele, Zelli treated his guests quite well. According to travel writer Basil Woon, Zelli bought "the best available lot in St. Ouen cemetery" and paid other expenses when the U.S. entertainer Charley MacCarthy died in Paris.[61] With such generosity and the atmosphere he created for his customers, including alternating bands that played black American jazz and tangos, Zelli's became one of the most beloved stops in Montmartre.[62]

Another prominent American in the neighborhood was Jed Kiley, who "vaccinated Paris with jazz and the one-step," in Woon's words.[63] Woon credits Kiley with bringing jazz to the continent when a "soldier orchestra, later to become known as the 'White Lyres,'" led by Bill Henley—the self-proclaimed "jazz missionary" who also performed in Turkey and Egypt—played in one of the clandestine dance clubs that Kiley opened just after the war. All but one of the original band members continued to perform in Paris.[64] Police ignored Kiley at first because his dances catered only to U.S. soldiers. When British and French officers and civilians began to attend, however, the authorities chased Kiley from one arrondissement to another on a regular basis, but the crowds still followed. After dances became legal again, Kiley tried the ice-cream business instead and succeeded until the weather turned cold. He then went back to entertaining, opening a club in Montmartre called Kiley's Place, which the Prince of Wales and other members of the British aristocracy visited along with many rich Americans until Kiley was forced out of business for legal reasons.[65]

Bricktop's was one of the most important clubs in Montmartre not only because it was a famous destination for hearing jazz but also because it served as a cultural hub for black jazz musicians in 1920s Paris. After playing in other clubs or dancings, African American musicians gathered there to talk and jam with one another as well as to enjoy the hospitality of the club's owner. Born Ada Louise Smith, but nicknamed after her red hair, Bricktop went to Paris in 1924 to replace the singer Florence Jones at the club Le Grand Duc. Disappointed and tearful at the sight of the club's small size, Bricktop nevertheless soon settled into a performer's life in Montmartre. The white U.S. film star Fannie Ward discovered Bricktop's performances and brought her friends to hear the singer perform. Two years later, Bricktop opened her own club, the Music Box, attracting luminaries like F. Scott and Zelda Fitzgerald and Cole Porter. The Prince of Wales threw a private party in the club before it had officially opened to the public. Legal problems put her out of business, but she returned a year later, this time with a place called Bricktop's.[66]

Bricktop's became one of the best places to hear jazz performed by black American musicians as well as to dance and drink. Bricktop herself often performed, and she made sure to keep order when things got a little rough.[67] This club was also a center for the black community that formed in postwar Paris, as historian Tyler Stovall has described. Blacks and whites could mingle there without racial divides. As Stovall put it, "Bricktop's was at the same time a refuge from the burdens of racism, for both black and white Americans, and a celebration of a uniquely African American art form."[68] And Bricktop made sure to keep up with the latest musical styles from the United States. When her mother came to visit, Bricktop recalled, "the opening of Mama's trunks was an event we'd all looked forward to as much as seeing Mama" because of the things she had smuggled past customs. In addition to the whiskey, hair straightener, cigarettes, and aspirin, she brought "Fletcher Henderson and Duke Ellington records [which] were pure gold in Paris; you could buy them, but once the tax had been slapped on them, you had to pay an outrageous price."[69] Bricktop kept her audiences up to date on the latest dances, too, doing the Charleston in her club and teaching it at "Charleston parties" that Cole Porter threw in his home for various celebrities and royalty.[70]

Montmartre was full of other such clubs where one could enjoy jazz. The Americans Harry Pilcer, Louis Mitchell, and Palmer and Florence Jones all had clubs there, as did Josephine Baker. Bricktop got her start at Le Grand Duc, which was owned by the black American boxer and former Zelli's performer-turned-*cabaretier* Gene Bullard.[71] Several places used American names to attract visitors, like Teddy, So Different, and Maurice's Club.[72] Some of the cabarets of the older type, like Le Ciel (Heaven) and L'Enfer (Hell), continued to dress their waiters in costumes as the Chat Noir had done and to "give a sort of weird entertainment in a dim irreligious light."[73] These places also saw some U.S. and other tourists who visited not for the modernism but for the romanticized atmosphere of the "old Montmartre." But despite these remnants, in the 1920s the new sounds of jazz predominated in the neighborhood.

Meanwhile, across the river, Montparnasse—what Huddleston called the "Transatlantic Terminus"—also had its remarkable gathering spots, most famously the cafés called Le Dôme and La Rotonde, which sat opposite one another on the carrefour Vavin, along with the nearby La Coupole and Le Sélect.[74] Peopled by artists, writers, intellectuals, and those who sought their company, these places were among the most popular in all of Paris. Among them was also a small, dark, smoky, crowded nightspot called the Jockey, where customers had to squeeze past each other to find a few inches at the bar.[75] Despite its lack of comfort, it was nevertheless one of the most fashionable destinations in Montparnasse. Named for the occupation of one of its first proprietors, the Jockey featured "bizarre posters and other weird decorations" on the walls and ceilings along with paintings of "cowboys and Indians" by painter Hilaire Hiler, who occasionally played piano.[76] Sometimes, poetry and lectures accompanied the various musical entertainers, who passed the hat to collect tips. One could find a Russian, who performed his national dances, and Chiffon, who was known for climbing on the tables and doing a Charleston. According to the well-known model and Montparnasse personality Kiki, Chiffon was "full of life, but is always a little crazy behind the piano, which drives the orchestra crazy."[77] Francis Carco described a black jazz band at the Jockey "situated on a trestle, blaring and backfiring."[78] "The place became a 'night joint,'" recalled Huddleston, "and despite its eccentric appearance, its exiguity of space, its intolerable atmosphere, its negroes and jazz-band, was and is, as I write [in 1931] the most fashionable rendezvous of Montparnasse," with cars lined up outside this bohemian boîte, and men and women from all over the world in evening dress inside.[79] One of the Jockey's main competitors was a club called the Jungle, which according to Paul Cohen-Portheim, "looks tremendously hot, highly coloured and African."[80] The place was famous for its black dancers, who were, for another critic, "perfectly supple and perfectly savage."[81]

Wild or chic, large or small, nightclubs and cabarets provided a central home for jazz in 1920s Paris, but they were not the same as the old cabarets of the nineteenth century as new influences encroached on these Parisian institutions and often altered their character. Whether owned by Americans, like many of the trendy Montmartre nightspots, or incorporating images of cowboys and Native Americans as in the Jockey, U.S. culture was part of the scene, and jazz was one of the most obvious symbols of the United States in these locations. These clubs may have borne some similarities to the older establishments of the fin de siècle, but they were filled with foreigners and pleasure-seekers for whom jazz was a crucial element of the clubs' atmospheres.

The city of Paris itself reflected one critical aspect in the debate over jazz: whether France would welcome music from abroad or continue to look inward for its culture. Although the division was clearest in the artistic neighborhoods of Montparnasse and Montmartre, jazz was quickly spreading throughout the city. Establishments on and around the Avenue des Champs-Elysées, like the Lido—a music hall famous for its fountains—and Place de la Madeleine, with the nearby L'Olympia music hall, were just a few of the many other places around the city where jazz of one sort or another became a fixture. Harry's New York Bar and Ciro's (both near the Opéra) as well as the Ritz (Place Vendôme) were internationally famous too, often attracting a wealthy clientele. And as in Montmartre and Montparnasse, jazz in these places around the city signified the transformations in postwar Paris. "Pascal's restaurant on the Rue de l'Ecole-de-Médicine," wrote Wilson, "where once the medics themselves and their professors foregathered to listen to classical music and discuss grisly topics, is now a Chinese restaurant with chop-suey and a jazz band"—a juxtaposition that again emphasized the mixing of cultures during the era.[82] Jazz "has taken root a little bit everywhere," commented one author in the entertainment trade journal *Comœdia* in 1926. "It reigns in the music hall from whence it has deigned to come to us. It has become established in the suburb, in the hotels, in the *apéritif-concert*. It dictates the frolicking of the humble and of the more fortunate, throwing its frenzy everywhere, its solid rhythms, its biting and disparate timbres."[83] In truth, jazz was not quite everywhere, but it was in too many places around Paris to be ignored.

4

THE

MEANINGS

OF JAZZ

America, Nègre, and Civilization

Jazz provoked controversy all around Europe. It drew the ire of the British monarchy and the pope, among many others. Italy banned jazz dancing in 1926, and German musicians protested the presence of U.S. musicians.[1] In Paris, the archbishop banned what he believed to be provocative dances.[2] According to the *New York Times*, the rector of the Sorbonne removed three black saxophone players and drummers when they appeared in a dance class not knowing that only the classical Greek style would be taught.[3] Even outside the French capital, police sometimes tried to keep a lid on the music. In 1923, law enforcement officials stopped the performance of a jazz band at a funeral in the town of Udine. The deceased had requested that one of his close friends conduct a jazz band for his funeral procession, but the police, "scandalized at the sight," as the *New York Times* reported, "descended on the band and ordered it to stop playing."[4] After the bandleader pleaded with the officers, they allowed him to continue, but only if he would play at a slower cadence.

If many listeners had difficulty coping with the shock of jazz, the task of the commentators who tried to interpret the music was even more challenging. For them, jazz was problematic because it symbolized much more than just a fad for crazy dancing or a loud, new sound. It also signaled a broader cultural shift. "Knee-length skirts, neck-length hair, women with men's coats and cigarettes," wrote journalist Lucien Farnoux-Reynaud, for example, in his 1926 article "The Epoch of the Jazz-Band,"

> multicolored pullovers and the silk underwear of their companions . . . , crazy virgins . . . race cars . . . , and confusion of the sexes; the anguish of living and the feverishness in everyday pleasure; all of this starts again,

blends itself, with a suspicious cosmopolitan shiver, in the cadences born at the conjunction of a shady bar in Jackson City and an ancestral memory of Tombouctou [*sic*].[5]

Such a statement vividly captured the sense of upheaval that inspired the French to dub the 1920s "the crazy years." It also demonstrated just how easily jazz could be connected to other changes of the post–World War I era.

Farnoux-Reynaud's observations were particularly remarkable because they brought together some of the paradoxical ways in which French commentators described jazz as they tried to make sense of it. Most notably, as Farnoux-Reynaud suggested, jazz had come to represent the "modern" world of the twentieth century and, at the same time, the "primitive" culture of the music's purportedly African origins. Jazz was a fitting sound for an increasingly technological era ("race cars"), even while it recalled the presumed simplicity of the lives of "noble savages" in a nearly forgotten other time (the "ancestral memory of Tombouctou").

These connotations were not random, however, because they stemmed from two important and immediately clear facts: jazz was an American music and simultaneously, as the French called it, *une musique nègre*. In many ways, jazz was one of the best representatives of the often debated américanisation of France that began in the 1920s and then exploded after World War II. By the first decades of the twentieth century, more Americans now traveled and invested throughout the continent than ever before, and Europeans were beginning to buy new mass-produced consumer goods from the United States in larger quantities. With its seemingly endless mechanical rhythms and broad commercial success, jazz reflected the qualities of modern life in the United States that occupied the minds of many French writers and critics in the interwar years. Like other kinds of American consumer culture, especially films, jazz seemed to be pushing aside older types of French entertainment. As a result, it frequently served as a harbinger of life in the new century and signaled to many the loss of a more traditional French culture to the rising Americanism.

At the same time, jazz was une musique nègre whose immediate origins were African American, but whose ultimate roots French writers generally traced to the jungles of Africa. The African sensibilities, French critics stressed, had been preserved in jazz because of the common racial connection between its performers and their ancestors on the so-called Dark Continent. Even when white musicians played jazz, they were believed to be performing a black musical style. At the height of its popularity, jazz music could suggest an "Africanization" of France—an ironic reversal of the colonial project simultaneously underway in sub-Saharan Africa in the 1920s and 1930s. Jazz rested at the intersection of these two powerful and controversial trends, thereby making it all the more meaningful and controversial.

AMERICAN MODERNITY

Americans were already a significant part of entertainment in Paris by the end of the nineteenth century. French circuses, music halls, and cabarets often attracted large crowds with the presence of performers from the United States. Parisian audiences especially appreciated U.S. military band music. In 1878, Patrick Gilmore and the Twenty-second Regiment Band performed one of the first big concerts of military music at the Universal Exposition, putting on thirteen shows in two days.[6] John Philip Sousa took Paris by storm when he played at the Universal Exposition of 1900. "Not an empty chair around the kiosk where the American flags fluttered," reported a Parisian newspaper describing one of Sousa's performances, "and great success as on all the days."[7]

Besides military bands, American dancing and dance music also entertained the French as the century turned. In the years just before and after 1900, Loïe Fuller and Isadora Duncan danced on Parisian stages, becoming famous for the freedom of their movements as they departed from more traditional ballet forms. New dance steps popularized by the team of Vernon and Irene Castle animated Parisians in the 1910s. After struggling at first with an act that did not strike a chord with French audiences, the Castles, who were already well-known in the United States, began to create their own versions of popular American dances based on newspaper clippings that Irene's mother sent to them in Paris. "Vernon decided that if we hadn't seen the 'Grizzly Bear,' the French hadn't either," she wrote, "so they wouldn't know whether we were doing it right or not."[8] The success of these dances turned their floundering Parisian debut at the Olympia music hall into a triumph, all to the tune of "Alexander's Ragtime Band." "The French audience was enthusiastic," Irene Castle wrote in her and her husband's autobiography. "They stomped their feet and clapped their hands and yelled 'Bravo.' They stood up at the end of the number and cried out 'greezly bahr' until we appeared again."[9]

In light of such precedents, the presence of another American music like jazz was not necessarily remarkable to audiences. But jazz's roots assumed a much larger significance against the backdrop of changes in the U.S.-French relationship during the war and in the interwar years, including an influx of Americans and their ways into Paris. For example, although they were still usually outnumbered by British visitors, U.S. tourists were among the most prominent foreigners in 1920s Paris, in large part because of the dollar's strength during these years.[10] Compared to the nineteenth century, not all Americans who traveled to Paris in the 1920s were wealthy, and with the favorable exchange rate they did not have to be.[11] By early 1920, the U.S. dollar was worth nearly eleven francs, and the value quickly rose. In July 1925, the dollar reached just over twenty-two francs, and it attained an interwar high in July 1926 of thirty-six francs in the midst of an economic crisis.[12] With such value, students, teachers, workers, and retirees could save up for a trip to the continent, and with money to spend, they went to Paris for many reasons. Sightseers could ride around the city in "Paris by Night" tour buses or stroll the streets with their Baedeker's guidebook in hand.[13] Many people purchased art, antiques, entertainment, and alcohol. Others traveled for an education at French universities or one of the U.S. schools that opened after the war. The Fontainebleau School, for one, served as a summer institute for American artists and musicians beginning in 1923.[14]

Emboldened by the power of their purses, U.S. tourists often harbored prejudices about themselves and the French that did not always leave their hosts with a favorable impression. American writer Walter White asserted that "far too many Americans who have little but the money necessary to take them to France or England or Germany create . . . the picture of America as being a country of barbarians and snobs." Insensitive to European customs and with a self-important attitude, White noted, many Americans easily offended the French.[15] Because of their economic power, the image of the U.S. tourist became one of wealth and privilege, while the French, by contrast, were recovering from the devastation of war.[16] Despite a somewhat different truth, French writer Paul Morand confirmed the misperception on the part of the French when he argued that only the American elite traveled, "this aristocracy of money, of birth, or of merit."[17]

The tourist-fueled entertainment industry in the 1920s was a visible sign of the increasing economic strength of the United States in Paris. Americans found the continent a hospitable economic environment as well as a pleasant place to visit, and they began to exert a wider range of economic and cultural influences. The Great War had ravaged the European economy, so U.S. companies had a more-than-competitive edge in postwar business. Although the more famous segment of the American presence in Paris consisted of the literary and intellectual figures who inhabited the Left Bank, the Right Bank financial, industrial, and commercial concerns were far more central to the larger U.S. community. As one historian has argued, the American colony in Paris "was the only [expatriate] colony primarily dedicated to business enterprise and promotion."[18] Branches of American banks such as the influential Morgan Bank and various corporations worked with the U.S. Chamber of Commerce in Paris, which had been founded in 1894 to promote business interests, or the Office of the American Commercial Attaché, an arm of the U.S. Department of Commerce.[19] In these years, the United States went from being a debtor to a creditor nation and poured millions of dollars into Europe.

Investments and loans were not the extent of U.S. economic interests. American companies saw the Old World as a vast new marketplace for manufactured goods that were now more abundant because of mass-production technology. The United States had been sending agricultural products and raw materials to Europe, typically cotton, wheat, copper, tobacco, and lumber. In the years before the war, finished manufactures represented only about 16 percent of U.S. exports to Europe, but by 1927 that figure had risen to just over 26 percent and included new products like steam shovels, washing machines, razor blades, cars, and adding machines.[20] In order to remain in service, the new American technology required parts supplied by U.S. factories and American-trained technicians who brought their knowledge from across the Atlantic. If a factory in the United States did not provide such new goods, they could be generated by American subsidiary companies, European businesses that had joined into partnerships with U.S. firms, or European companies that had adopted American methods of production. American business leaders enthusiastically and optimistically described this shift in trade as beneficial for both the U.S. economy and Europeans. Refuting charges that the United States was forcing goods onto foreign markets, James H. Smiley, the Los Angeles district manager of the Bureau of Foreign and Domestic Commerce, argued that "foreign peoples do not buy American merchandise because they have to, but because they contribute to their necessities and well-being."[21]

Many French business leaders had begun to study U.S. industrial practices and adapted them to their own factories. The dynamic French car manufacturer André Citroën, for example, heartily embraced the new innovations in production being developed in the United States. Citroën prided his country on being "a good second" to the United States in the number of cars on the road. He introduced an assembly line into his factory—"chain work," as he called it—and emblazoned his name on the Eiffel Tower as a flashy, American-style advertisement for his cars.[22] The Michelin tire company also adapted U.S. techniques and propagated the ideas of the scientific management theorist Frederick Winslow Taylor in its company publication, *Prosperité*.[23] Representatives from the ceramics, paper, and textile industries organized the Commission Générale de l'Organisation Scientifique du Travail in order to acquaint themselves with U.S. techniques. The secretary of the French Federation of Labor spent a year working and studying in the United States in hopes of learning more about how factories there worked.[24] French companies did not always adopt American ideas wholesale; they frequently modified them to meet particular French circumstances. French economic and technical elites were just as interested in preserving many older aspects of French business culture and protecting the psychological well-being of workers. Nevertheless, the trends in economic development clearly drew much of their inspiration and impetus from the U.S. model of business and industry.[25]

Many French critics, however, were not as excited about these kinds of changes as were Citroën or U.S. trade officials. They frequently objected to such transformations in production techniques as being harmful for French workers and consumers. Moreover, they saw developments in the United States as a warning for what France might become if it continued down such a path of intensive economic and technical evolution. The United States had entrapped itself in a "myth of production," alleged conservative cultural critics and opponents of américanisation Robert Aron and Arnaud Dandieu in *Décadence de la nation française* (1931).[26] Once a bastion of democratic ideals, the United States was developing a more intense form of industrialization that replaced freedom with Fordism—a new slavery to the machine and the assembly line. Taylorization, the reorganization of work according to scientific principles designed to improve efficiency, promised a more rational production method, but as many inquired, at what cost to the workers' moral and spiritual being? People in this kind of society, critics feared, would lose their individuality to the uniformity required and produced by the machine.[27]

Mass production also implied mass consumption, and from some customers' points of view that meant a dreary homogenization. Author André Maurois had great difficulty getting a black cup of coffee in New York, he reported, because it was habitually served with cream. He could not get his typewriter repaired because the company that made the machine insisted that he purchase a new one since such mass-produced products were simply interchangeable.[28] Of American society, Aron and Dandieu complained that "if one produces for the sake of production and not for satisfaction, likewise one consumes for the sake of consumption, not for enjoyment."[29] The United States suffered as economic motives replaced human values, and Aron and Dandieu feared that France might become mired in the same situation. Likewise, many critics saw as threatening the growing popularity of the American-style prix uniques discount stores that seemed to encourage mindless mass consumption of shoddy goods that lacked any sense of taste.[30]

The loss of uniqueness created by the mass production and consumption of goods extended into other aspects of life as well, some argued. Georges Duhamel was a prolific social critic and author of the biting critique of life in the United States titled Scènes de la vie future (1930)—when translated to English, it became America the Menace (1931). On a grisly visit to the Chicago stockyards, he observed other tourists marching "in single file, led by guides in uniform caps, who shouted through a megaphone in order to be heard above the noise of the machinery and of the victims."[31] In the industrial wasteland, individuals had become indistinguishable to him, but his most frightening observation was that "America . . . represents for us the Future."[32]

The economic attraction to Europe, both as a field for investment and a market for new goods, brought individual Americans to the French capital in ever larger numbers. Unlike the tourists, though, these Americans came for a much longer period of time. According to one set of admittedly conservative statistics, the U.S. colony in Paris, which had numbered around five thousand during the Second Empire and eight thousand by 1920, soon reached thirty-two thousand by 1923.[33] U.S. businesses brought executives, office staffs, technicians, and their families to Europe, and provided Americans with a network of business and employment opportunities in Paris. One could move to France with a reasonable assurance of finding a job in one of the U.S. companies or the growing number of service sector enterprises that catered to these expatriates.

But this colony did not simply consist of U.S. citizens residing in Paris. It was also a miniature United States that had grown up within the French capital. One could be born in an American hospital, attend American schools, shop in U.S. stores, and read U.S. newspapers and magazines published in Paris. An American library, churches of various denominations, a YMCA, and organizations such as veterans' groups and women's clubs all connected Americans living abroad to one another and to home. An American could even eat ice cream sodas, buy chewing gum, and receive milk processed the way it was in the United States.[34] Americans were not only bringing goods and money to France but an entire way of life.

Nevertheless, French reactions to Americans and their ways were ambivalent in the 1920s. Americans remained the source of amusement for many Parisians who dressed in their fashions, including sometimes as cowboys.[35] Parisians were famous for hailing the U.S. pilot Charles Lindbergh for his daring crossing of the Atlantic.[36] And the love of jazz was an important part of the French fascination with things American. Yet at the same time, the presence of Americans and their culture could be worrisome. As jazz grew in popularity, it came to represent for some a particularly troubling example of everything that was wrong with the New World. It also threatened to bring those problems to France. In his visit to the United States, Duhamel did not see mechanization and industrial standardization only in workplaces. He also heard these forces in the sounds of jazz because the music could be easily associated with other noises from the era. Duhamel linked the new "modern" music with the age from which it came in a fascinating passage in his diatribe against the decay of American culture:

> The music suddenly burst forth from a corner. It was the falsest, the shrillest, the most explosive of jazz—that breathless uproar which for many years now has staggered to the same syncopation, that shrieks through its nose, weeps, grinds its teeth, and caterwauls throughout the world.[37]

For Duhamel, the "shrieks" and "grinds" of the music were part of the mechanistic world that he deplored. He heard this "explosion" of jazz in a club in Chicago, but to him, the intonations of the machinery that he witnessed at the stockyards possessed a similar quality:

> And all the time the scream continued, ever renewed at the start of the chain—that scream, so strong and so alive that the packers will make something of it some day. It is absurd that that enormous sum of energy should thus evaporate and lose itself in space. They will make music of it, pretty tunes for the jazz band.[38]

Writer and diplomat Paul Claudel echoed Duhamel's sentiments in one of his essays on the United States when he wrote of "the rhythmic pulsation and nervous uniformity of the pistons of a steam engine interrupting the cyclical roaring of the dynamo that one feels across all of American life and of which jazz is the supreme expression."[39] Jazz, maintained one music critic, "is the music of . . . mass-produced men."[40]

Other French listeners rejected jazz because it reflected the encroachment of a more general American way of life that went far beyond the machine culture. "Jazz is not made for us," insisted journalist Jacques Janin. "Everything in us rejects it: spirit and tradition." This U.S. export was not welcome, he concluded sarcastically: "Let us not put up the Monroe Doctrine for discussion. America for the Americans."[41] Others were even more outraged in their responses to an imported music. Stressing its foreignness in an article called "The Infernal Rhythm of Jazz," one essayist ended by calling for the prefect of police to take action. "Will you let the strangers who come to France," he demanded, "import this abominable vision from their countries?"[42]

Jazz was only one part of the changing entertainment trade in the 1920s that included such new phenomena as the flashy, stylized music hall and, more recently, the cinemas that were growing in number as well as popularity. Both of these entertainments partly depended on the presence of Americans in Paris, the former because of tourist dollars and the latter through U.S. film companies. But along with jazz, motion pictures became one of the clearest arenas of struggle over the seeming américanisation of France that began in the 1920s. Financial reasons were just as important in the debate over film as the medium's cultural impact. Audiences for films grew enormously throughout the interwar years, increasing box office receipts from over 85 million francs in 1923 to over 230 million in 1929.[43] The prospect of profit sometimes even persuaded music hall owners to convert their stages into movie screens. The motion picture business also signaled the further spread of industrial methods associated with the United States to which so many objected.

As we have seen, American movies had come to France during the war as an alternative to French patriotic propaganda films, and they met a growing public desire for more lighthearted and entertaining features. After the war, as American films proved to be more and more profitable, theaters showed them in greater numbers than French films. Outraged, French producers lobbied the government to regulate the flow of films from abroad, but to little avail.[44] Movies from the United States—which were created by big studios that had lots of money and were able to produce films quickly for worldwide audiences—threatened to replace the

domestic, small-scale French cinema craft. European pictures had traditionally been the creation of artisan filmmakers working in small studios
making films for narrow audiences. In the 1920s, French filmmakers began to abandon their craft, adopting U.S. methods to compete.[45] As historian Victoria de Grazia has argued, such changes threatened France's
traditional coupling of cultural and political sovereignty—the construction
of a national identity based in part on an artistic tradition that came from
within its borders, and reflecting something essential and important about
its character.[46] And jazz, many feared, could do the same. "An independent jazz music?" asked critic Jacques Heugel. "It exists in America. But
does the whole world have to be American?"[47]

Movies and jazz along with the changes they represented were often
attacked by critics, but they had their defenders and celebrators as well. For
many intellectuals, the modern spirit that these innovations brought to
France were precisely their value. The Surrealist writer Philippe Soupault,
for example, looked to new kinds of entertainment like films and jazz precisely because they were American. Following the suggestion of Guillaume
Apollinaire, who had asserted that "the epic poet would express himself
with a film," Soupault saw in American films and jazz a celebration of
life.[48] Soupault had fought in the war and became disgusted with the
culture for which he was supposed to have been fighting: "Those who in
early youth were witnesses of nothing but death and destruction . . . ,
turned with a kind of fever toward life." He found that life impulse in
modern entertainment. Soupault demonstrated his appreciation for the
pace and style of U.S. culture, particularly in films, in his brief book *The
American Influence in France* (1930). "We rushed into the cinemas, and
realized immediately that everything had changed," he wrote of the era
when films were becoming popular in France. "We were living swiftly,
passionately. It was a very beautiful period."[49] Soupault's swiftness came
through in his writing and living, as the American Matthew Josephson
remembered in his memoir, *Life among the Surrealists*. Soupault sought to
express the modern life he lived, and as Josephson recalled, "Soupault's fast
pace was also related, no doubt, to his having adopted what he regarded as
the 'American tempo'."[50] "The American cinema brought to light all the
beauty of our epoch," Soupault declared, arguing that it influenced French
poetry, theater, and painting.[51]

Soupault was fascinated with the United States, but as Josephson remarked, "Soupault and his Dada friends now wanted to discover the true
America, represented by our common soldiers in Europe, our Negro jazz

bands, and, above all, by our silent cinema."[52] For Soupault, jazz was indeed a crucial part of American culture and a way to get at the more authentic essence of the United States. Jazz "has helped us finally to discover and to understand the United States," he wrote.[53] But for Soupault, to understand the United States and its art was part of his larger intellectual quest of blending art and life. European music had been long divided into "popular music (songs, marches, operettas)" and "highbrow music, that is to say, concert music," Soupault claimed. Yet American music had no such distinctions within it. Instead, he argued, "One of the most definite qualities of the American influence resides in the close relationship between art and life."[54] Like film, jazz expressed something about life that Soupault found irresistible in the wake of the war's destruction—the energy, the breaking down of barriers.

Writer Paul Morand also saw and felt the energy and drive of the United States as the herald of a new age.[55] In his book *New York* (1930), Morand took readers on a tour of Manhattan from one end to the other, commenting on the scenery, people, and customs that he observed. Not everything was praiseworthy for Morand, such as the predilection in the United States for eating quickly and poorly. But his account was filled with wonder and respect for the new power and influence of the United States, and of New York as one of its best representatives. "I like New York," he declared, "because it is the biggest city in the world, and because it is inhabited by the strongest race in the world—the only one which has succeeded in organizing itself since the war; the only one which is not living in its past reputation."[56] Indeed, this newness and sense of motion was one of the things that drew his attention: "To have America, you need only to put the adjective 'New' in front of Rochelle, Jersey, London, Utrecht or Brighton, repaint these old European signs, and add twenty floors."[57] Inventions like the car liberated Americans for the modern age since the "American car spreads out over the world, an instrument of escape, the tool of speed, which after freeing the United States, is shattering Puritanism, volatilizing savings, demolishing the family, reversing the law, leading the world toward catastrophe and the glory of adventure."[58] For Morand, jazz was also part of the landscape of New York, particularly in Harlem. There, he heard a blending of sounds since "jazz is the Negro melody of the South arriving at Pennsylvania Station and suddenly maddened by adorable Manhattan, where everything is noise and light." Jazz reflected the modern mixture of black and white America, of both rural and urban settings. Jazz was "the Mississippi's dream become a nightmare, cut across by motor-horns and sirens."[59]

Morand's mixture of black and white in his description of jazz was not unique. It pointed to the overlapping categories that jazz evoked in many minds, even in its connection with the United States. Soupault saw no real distinction between the blackness of jazz and its Americanness, saying that "I know, of course, that it is said to be not American, but negro. This point of view I refuse to discuss, first because it is silly, and second because it seems to me radically false."[60] Although this statement was unclear and received no further elaboration, it suggested that jazz had become such a fixture of modern life in the United States that to separate the two no longer made sense for Soupault. For others like Morand, jazz was neither purely black nor white, nor was it purely American because it contained something more essentially African, but the two had become intertwined. His depiction of blacks in Harlem was of people "so very un-African, of Negroes in sweaters and woolen helmets, cutting the ice with their swift, dark arabesques."[61] These black people had been "Americanized," Morand maintained, and so had their music. Listening to the music in the African Room of the Harlem Club on Lenox Avenue was somewhat disappointing to him because "for all the syncopated murmurings of the Africano's company, the place was just like all the rest."[62] Jazz had become so much a part of American culture that it had lost something of its purity. Others agreed, suggesting that the United States had robbed jazz of its distinctly primitive qualities and had tamed it, thus making the jazz they heard something less than the "real" thing.[63]

As the sound of the United States, jazz was also the sound of a broader set of cultural changes in the way that people lived, worked, and played in Paris. It could be the sound of the machine or stockyard—frightening and foreign images that suggested the impending brutalization of a French tradition. But the United States was a land of promise and renewal, as people like Soupault and Morand noted, and new kinds of art, like film and jazz, were at the forefront of that hopeful image that was attractive precisely because it was foreign.[64]

AFRICAN PRIMITIVISM

Like music from the United States more generally, African American entertainment was not new to Paris in the 1920s.[65] Black performers had been traveling to France for many decades, and Parisians had become familiar with black choirs, minstrel shows, and especially with the cake-walk and ragtime—respectively, a dance and a music created by African

Americans in the nineteenth century that music historians often describe as the immediate precursors to jazz and jazz dancing in the United States.[66] The cakewalk originated as a strutting dance performed by slaves on U.S. plantations as a way to mock their owners. Not understanding the sarcasm, the owners instead offered a cake to the best dancer. After working its way through black variety shows and vaudeville revues, cakewalking became an enormous hit in the United States by the 1890s, and it inspired popular musicals performed either by blacks or whites in blackface. In high society cakewalk contests, the winner would "take the cake" as a prize. Dancers usually performed to marching tunes, but they sometimes substituted the syncopated beat of ragtime music. Ragtime's popularity grew as the cakewalk's accompaniment, yet it also succeeded in its own right as a dance and marching music. Soon, its enticing rhythms could be purchased as sheet music, on player piano rolls, and eventually on phonograph records.

In France, as in the United States, the terms *cakewalk* and *ragtime* were often interchanged given their close relationship, especially by the American entertainer John Philip Sousa, who popularized them in Paris. Traveling across Europe, Sousa's band played a variety of popular American dance tunes along with the marches that had made him famous, and according to numerous accounts, French audiences listened enthusiastically to these songs.[67] Playing at the 1900 Exposition in Paris, Sousa "bewitched" audiences, in the words of one writer, who were "reveling in the musical message he has brought them."[68] Not only were the cakewalk and ragtime on his playlist, so were other kinds of African American music. In a 1903 concert in Paris, for example, Sousa's final act included what he called "songs from the American plantation," and he was already known for performing " 'coon songs' and his own negro melodies" on various tours of France.[69] Sousa illustrated what would become one of the important facts about jazz in the 1920s and 1930s: white performers were just as likely to succeed with their versions of black American music as black musicians themselves.[70] Nevertheless, French commentators still defined the cakewalk, ragtime, and jazz as something created and best played by black Americans. Early on, some also saw the potential effects that this musique nègre could have. A 1908 article noted that "the cakewalk is a dance of savages: it is made from a savage music. There is nothing that can act more effectively on our civilized souls," thus already expressing the belief that black American music posed the kind of racial challenge to civilization that soon came to be associated with jazz.[71]

Sousa's influence, and the early availability of the cakewalk and ragtime in recordings, fostered a growing popularity of these tunes in Paris around the turn of the century. The theater producer Gabriel Astruc, who (incorrectly) claimed he introduced la musique nègre to France, saw the cakewalk in Chicago at the World's Fair in 1893, and then wrote articles to popularize it and predict its great success in France. Once French musicians applied their "French sauce," to it, he declared, this "exotic dance . . . that persists with its crazy gaity will become established in Paris."[72] One place in which that establishment began to happen was in the show *Joyeux Nègres* (1902), by Le Nouveau Cirque. It presented a variety of scenes including, according to one description, "a burlesque dance, the cakewalk, which is unlike anything we know and which people have demanded to see again."[73] The revue ran for almost a year, and on its hundredth performance, one newspaper reported that when the show came to an end, members of the audience danced the cakewalk for many hours.[74] This kind of music impressed musicians as well as audiences, and French composers adopted some of these styles of music into their own work. Debussy, for example, penned "Golliwog's Cakewalk" (1906–1908, from *The Children's Corner*) and "Le Petit Nègre" (1906). Erik Satie incorporated African American music into the score of his important modernist ballet *Parade* (1917). And the Russian composer Igor Stravinsky, living in Paris, wrote a piece called "Ragtime" (1917).[75]

Other kinds of black American music crossed the Atlantic in the years before and after the war, including choirs that sang spirituals and other songs from the black American folk tradition.[76] Traveling to Paris usually as part of a European tour, choral groups like the Fisk Jubilee Singers went to France in the late nineteenth century and continued to journey there in the 1920s. Black minstrel groups, musical productions, and vaudeville companies also toured the continent, and black performers were often part of otherwise white troupes. Some African American players stayed behind when their companies returned to the United States, and they continued to perform in Europe.[77] Black theater and musical groups that incorporated jazz into their acts followed in this well-established tradition, becoming important to the spread of jazz during the 1920s and 1930s.

The French were not just receptive to black Americans as performers, however, but to African Americans as people. A long-standing belief that France was a color-blind nation led many black Americans to perceive an atmosphere of openness in Paris that they could not find at home. That assumption gained credence during World War I, when many black soldiers felt more at liberty among the French. In the 1920s, that sense of freedom continued since overt racial discrimination was not part of the regular Parisian way of life. "Paris affords to black men," remarked the U.S. writer Robert Forrest Wilson, "an equality of treatment unknown in the United States even in the North. . . . We see black men walking with white girls and white mothers leading mulatto children."[78] This seemingly more generous French attitude played a critical role in encouraging many jazz musicians and other entertainers to relocate across the Atlantic. Josephine Baker described the relative freedom, saying, "Why did I leave America? Because one day I realized that I lived in a country where I was afraid to be black. In Paris, I feel liberated."[79] Henry Crowder, a trumpet player who became the lover of the white, British heiress Nancy Cunard, echoed Baker's sentiment when he wrote of his departure from the United States, "France! No color bar there. No discriminations! Freedom! A chance to live as every other man lived regardless of his color. No taboos. Not a single sigh escaped my being because I was leaving. Only unbounded joy existed."[80] Baker and Crowder were not alone, nor were they unique as performers. Whether opening successful businesses—including Montmartre nightclubs—working as laborers, attending school, or engaged in the arts, blacks from the United States created an exile community in interwar Paris that existed in relative harmony with its French neighbors.[81]

If the French seemed to give black Americans a warm welcome, white Americans in Paris, by contrast, often spread racial intolerance and encouraged discrimination, according to many accounts. The black writer Walter White, who identified both the Americans and South Africans as encouraging prejudice, recounted an incident in a restaurant where he was having lunch with "a distinguished Negro musician and composer, a graduate of the London Conservatory of Music." Shortly after beginning their meal, "above the conversation and the subdued clatter of the dishes I heard the word 'nigger.' Looking in the direction from which this word came I saw a man, obviously an American, who seemed on the verge of apoplexy."[82] Josephine Baker remembered a similar incident when a white patron from the United States in the same restaurant in which she was dining demanded that Baker be ejected. Instead, the management asked the complainant to leave.[83] Although as in Baker's case, the French did not usually go along with such intolerance, U.S. tourists sometimes carried enough clout in entertainment and dining establishments because of their strong dollars to affect the experiences of people of color. In one notorious incident in Montmartre in 1923, white Americans successfully convinced a nightclub to exclude two black men who started to enter the establishment with two white women. Both of the men happened to be princes of Dahomey, and one was a leader of the Pan-African movement in Paris who had recently praised the city for its lack of racial prejudice at the 1919 Pan-African Congress. The nightclub owner eventually faced retribution from the government, including denunciations from President Raymond Poincaré and Prime Minister Aristide Briand, for bending to the wishes of what one report called "his rich and noisy clientele," and his business was shut down.[84] The president declared that the same fate would befall any other bars with racially discriminatory practices.[85]

Still, simply because the French did not discriminate against black Americans in traditional U.S. terms, such as Jim Crow–type laws, did not mean that the French were truly color-blind in the 1920s. Rather, they operated with a range of assumptions about what blacks, including those from the United States, were like. The French understanding of race, especially as it related to jazz, was different than definitions of racial characteristics in the United States. "Blackness," in other words, meant something different on each side of the Atlantic. The French perception of les nègres had been shaped under quite different circumstances than attitudes about blacks in the United States, and that understanding, along with France's own set of racial stereotypes about people of color, influenced views about jazz.

In the United States, jazz emerged from a large domestic black population. But because of the nation's racialized history, many Americans viewed "black culture" as something distinct from "white culture," even though the two had been intertwined since colonial days.[86] Black and white entertainment in the United States had frequently intersected in significant ways throughout the nineteenth century. The cakewalk, as we have seen, emerged as a kind of resistance by blacks against white, southern plantation owners. Moreover, blackface minstrelsy was an important genre of performance that brought black entertainment to white audiences in a more acceptable form—one that historian Eric Lott has described as tinged both with "racial insult and racial envy"—and thus reflected a historically ambiguous relationship between whites and blacks in the United States.[87] Taking another perspective on the relationship between whites and blacks in minstrelsy, historian Michael Rogin has discussed blackface and "blacking up" as a way for Jews to negotiate the transformation from "immigrant" to "American" by embracing a uniquely American style of performance.[88] In other words, as these and other scholars argue, black performance in the United States cannot be separated from domestic cultural politics that includes questions of slavery, racism, and definitions of national identity.

French audiences were certainly familiar with U.S. stereotypes of African Americans, and those views were perpetuated by many of the jazz-accompanied shows of the interwar years. Images of black America, particularly of antebellum plantation life, were not uncommon in interwar Paris, and they served to reinforce a view of African Americans as only partially civilized and working in a "primitive" agricultural setting. For example, *La Revue Nègre*, in which Josephine Baker starred, featured scenes of southern U.S. plantations, and this show was not unique. A 1927 exhibition at the Jardin d'Acclimatation called *Charleston City* even claimed to re-create an authentic southern plantation for display. It "is the exact reconstruction of a black village in the southern United States," proclaimed one newspaper. "We have before our eyes, like words come to life, the life of blacks, we know their customs, their work, their hobbies, and notably their dances. . . . The dancers are those of the Garland troupe made of ten women and four men accompanied by the famous Palm Beach jazz band."[89]

Many French critics translated common stereotypes of African Americans into musical terms, taking note of what they described as a pronounced emotionalism within jazz along with a kind of sadness and melancholy in the music due to the history of black Americans. Critic René Dumesnil, for instance, portrayed black American choirs like the Fisk Jubilee Singers, black "plantation songs," and jazz as all illustrating a characteristically black way of singing or playing music in which the innate emotional qualities of les nègres combined with the tortuous past of African Americans. Born out of oppression, as Dumesnil put it, black American songs "are examples to vanquish the oppressor or reasons to hope for liberation."[90] Playing jazz, observers like Dumesnil argued, offered a form of emotional freedom from the lives that blacks had led in the United States.

Unlike in the United States, however, there was never a very large black (African or American) population in France, even in the 1920s.[91] And French observers were never particularly clear on the distinction between Africans and African Americans, who they often believed had more in common than not.[92] Because many listeners assumed that jazz expressed certain essential racial qualities that transcended specific historical circumstances or experiences, jazz easily turned the minds of French critics from antebellum America to sub-Saharan Africa and the colonial project at its height in the interwar years. For the French, jazz was "jungle music" more often than "plantation music."

As many scholars have pointed out, the French response to Africans was contradictory at best. The image of Africa in the French imagination already had a long and convoluted history by the 1920s, much of it based on misunderstanding.[93] For centuries, ideas about Africa were created through myth, rumor, and legend without much direct contact between the French and Africans. As colonial interests expanded at the end of the nineteenth century along with an increasing attention to economic exploitation, scientific research, and political experimentation on the African continent, knowledge of its people became more widespread, even if that understanding was not always more accurate. Those within France who hoped to exploit Africa for its resources frequently presented Africans as "noble savages" and the Dark Continent as an unspoiled territory waiting to be explored. But this attitude changed in the wake of African resistance to French colonial advances in the late 1800s. Africa soon began to seem like a territory with a vicious race of people that needed to be conquered and controlled.[94]

During World War I, relations between the French and Africans from the colonies became increasingly complicated. France welcomed colonial soldiers to its soil because they were seen as valuable members of a Greater France and were fighting on behalf of the nation and its values. At the same time, though, many French workers feared that laborers from the colonies could threaten their jobs, and the resulting resentment sparked race riots, which themselves helped to bring about more highly politicized perceptions of race in the 1920s.[95] Unrest within the colonies from educated Africans demanding French citizenship after the war added to the French desire to keep a reasonable distance between themselves and their colonial subjects by employing a policy of "association."[96] Also in the wake of World War I, eugenics, social hygiene movements, and pronatalist concerns about declining birthrates all stressed a more clearly biological conception of racial categories, including those in the colonies, and emphasized the need to protect the French "race" by preventing racial decline or dilution.[97] Therefore, by the time of jazz's arrival, foreigners in general, and Africans in particular, could seem at least as dangerous as they were exotic.

The most basic fact about jazz to most French listeners was that even though many white musicians played it, the music was still la musique nègre. Writing in *La Revue musicale*, musicologist Blaise Pesquinne, for example, argued that "in spite of its popularity in Europe and in all the countries of the white race, one must not forget that jazz is, for us, an essentially exotic product. . . . Jazz is by no means an internal phenomenon from within Western music, it is the artistic manifestation of a race that is different from our own."[98] Underlying this common idea of a distinct musique nègre was the notion that it was an expression of a universal category of blackness—an essential set of qualities common to all people of color—that transcended the individual experience of each musician. "*Les peuples nègres* are particularly known for being endowed with a musical aptitude," remarked musicologist Julien Tiersot in the introduction to his collection *Chansons nègres* (1933), which brought together the music of folk tunes from black America, Africa, and Oceania. Even though the musicians from these diverse locations were not "*de race pure*," he argued that "*négritiques ou métissés*, mullato or creole . . . their songs have taken a different shape than those that Europe has produced."[99] La musique nègre, as many French saw it, contained certain special qualities peculiar to all black people because of its beginnings on the Dark Continent. Music critic Émile Vuillermoz put it simply in 1923 when he wrote that "the black race possesses a musical sense of a rare subtlety and an instinct of rhythmic suppleness of which we have the right to be jealous."[100] Many commentators made the music an emanation of the black soul—"*l'âme nègre*," in the words of music critic René Dumesnil and others.[101] The rhythm that distinguished jazz was linked directly to its African past because, some asserted, rhythm was part of life in Africa and therefore ingrained into black musicians throughout the world. The "imitative nature" of Africans was "endowed with a highly sharpened musical sense, sensitive to the least percussion in the middle of a thousand noises in the forest," according to one author, and now this element had seemingly reemerged thousands of miles away in the sounds of jazz music.[102]

One supposed proof of this link with Africa that many French critics offered was the sense of nostalgia that they perceived in jazz, the musical expression of a longing for a world that had been lost. Nostalgia had been, since its conception in the seventeenth century, a medical diagnosis describing a feeling of intense homesickness, but by the nineteenth century, it also came to explain in France a more general "crisis of civilization" that people underwent as their lives changed.[103] Modern technology and the movement of populations from the countryside to cities took people away from home and familiar surroundings and "civilized" them, but it stripped something of their old self in the process. Turning from a peasant into a Frenchman meant giving up an identity that could become the object of nostalgic feeling. Nineteenth-century physicians often claimed that such homesickness for another place and time would be cured by the very processes of modernization that created the condition itself. Railroads and communications technology took people away from their native soil while still allowing them to be psychologically close to home. But for cultures or individuals believed to be caught in the middle of the process, longing for another time and place was seen as common. Nostalgia linked life in the present with a memory of the past.

Depicting jazz as sounding nostalgic often reinforced an understanding of its origins not as distinctively American but African. Having been uprooted from Africa by slavery, American blacks expressed through their music a sadness and longing for an idyllic past before their forced emigration to the United States, in the view of French commentators. Blacks, as Pesquinne put it in his *La Revue musicale* article, for example, were "nostalgic and unhappy in the towns [of the United States and] did exactly what the Russian immigrants did in the various capitals of Europe: they came together to sing."[104] From this point of view, jazz was the music of exiles whose real home was Africa, and depicting jazz as nostalgic emphasized the essential racial nature of the music. Demonstrating the partially civilized state of black Americans, one author stated of jazz: "From this duality, the tam-tam and the fever of the combustion engine, a fantastic humor, sometimes a little monkeylike, alternates with a tragic nostalgia of exiled slaves curiously corresponding to that of an extreme civilization bullied by the machine culture."[105] Black Americans, many French observers concluded, were therefore only partially civilized, so their music retained much of the primitivism of African music.

The most important argument for the deep racial origins of jazz music came in the 1926 book *Jazz* by André Cœuroy, an editor of the journal *La Revue musicale*, and ethnomusicologist André Schaeffner. Cœuroy and Schaeffner's reputation on the subject had been at least partly established by the time of *Jazz*'s publication because elements of their argument had appeared in the musical journals *La Revue musicale* and *Le Ménestrel*. In 1925, they had also surveyed musicians, artists, critics, and intellectuals for their opinions about jazz, printing the results in a running column in the newspaper *Paris-Midi*. Once Cœuroy and Schaeffner's *Jazz* was published, it quickly became a standard citation in later French writings about the music. Their book was a landmark not only because it was the first French text that purported to be about jazz as a musical form but also because it drew together some of the other critical writing on jazz up to that time from articles in France and the United States, and it linked jazz with other musicological discussions.

Yet Cœuroy and Schaeffner did not attempt to explain the musical qualities of jazz as it existed in the 1920s. Rather, they placed jazz at the end of a larger history of la musique nègre and focused on where jazz had come from rather than what it was actually like in their day. Asserting both jazz's African roots and its connection with other kinds of black American music, *Jazz* was more an early ethnomusicological study of a racially based musique nègre than an exploration of jazz. In fact, their book was really not about jazz music at all but rather the musical qualities that nègres, regardless of when or where they lived, possessed. These traits, Cœuroy and Schaeffner asserted, had led up to the modern phenomenon of jazz.

In *Jazz*, Cœuroy and Schaeffner maintained that "at each moment, each people only has one music through which it prays, dreams, or dances," yet there were essential underlying elements that continued across generations.[106] Distinctions between musical genres produced by a single race therefore made little sense since each kind of music only expressed variations of deeper, racially determined qualities. The music of Africans and African Americans should be seen as part of a single black musical continuum of which jazz was simply the latest form, they asserted. "The violent music of Africa to the planting songs of the Antilles or Louisiana, to *spirituals*, finally to *jazz*," were all members of the same musical family.[107] In this scheme, there was no significant difference between black Africans and black Americans, who remained united above all by ancient and ultimately immutable characteristics. Blacks were united in particular by a love of music and dance with a special affinity for rhythm, they suggested. Much of their book traced the development of la musique nègre as a background to jazz, and it cited the observations of seventeenth- and eighteenth-century travelers as evidence of the longevity of a specifically black style of performance. They also followed the history of various instruments, such as the drum and banjo, along with the traditions of song and dance that they believed defined black music.

Cœuroy and Schaeffner's views were not universally held. Readers of *La Revue musicale* were reminded of the importance of the racial basis of their analysis in a brief exchange between Schaeffner and music critic André Hoerée in 1927. Responding to *Jazz*, Hoerée argued that jazz music had emerged from the European dances of the pre–World War I era rather than African roots: "I do not take jazz as an essentially black expression but as a black interpretation of an art of the white race of European origins."[108] Yet by ignoring the longer prehistory of jazz and focusing only on the dance steps that gave jazz its immediate form in the 1920s, Schaeffner countered, Hoerée had missed the larger point. "There is no example in the history of music, as in the history of art, of invention where several individuals, several races did not collaborate," Schaeffner conceded. He and Cœuroy had, indeed, talked about European religious music sung by black Americans as a precursor of jazz. "But," Schaeffner concluded, "the *inventor* is he who places his accent on it."[109] For Schaeffner, despite the contributions of others, jazz remained une musique nègre because it was permanently and indelibly stamped with a black style of playing that had come from the performers themselves.

Many listeners were attracted to jazz precisely because of its perceived blackness, including Belgian poet Robert Goffin, who became an important figure in early jazz criticism in France. By the time Goffin published his first critical book on the music, he had already made a valuable contribution to jazz-inspired literature with a book of poems titled *Jazz-Band* (1920) and articles in the journal *Le Disque vert*. His new book in 1932, *Aux frontières du jazz* (At the borders of jazz) reflected a decade of listening to and thinking about the music. In it, he did not seek to analyze the origins of the music, as Cœuroy and Schaeffner had done, but rather the music as he heard it in the 1920s.

Goffin's earliest experiences with syncopated music came, like those of many other listeners, during the Great War. While serving as an interpreter for a Canadian battalion, "among the soldiers," he remembered, "were some Americans who taught me their songs."[110] Later, as a student, he listened to Belgian, French, and English orchestras perform music that they called jazz, but his real introduction to the music came when he encountered Louis Mitchell in Paris. Inspired by what he heard, Goffin wrote his early articles and poems "possessed immediately by a sort of frenzied lyricism."[111] Goffin took a few lessons from the black trumpeter Arthur Briggs in 1922 while playing in a "humble orchestra which some friends and I formed."[112] Experiences with Mitchell and Briggs confirmed for Goffin that jazz was a black music set apart by its players' unique expression. "How I prefer *les nègres*, the beautiful *nègres* who laugh with all their teeth," he proclaimed in *Le Disque vert* in 1922. By contrast, for Goffin, the music of whites was cold and overly rational.[113] Jazz was about feeling rather than reason, and for him black American musicians were in touch with the more emotional side of human experience.

Unlike Cœuroy and Schaeffner's book, which ended where jazz began, *Aux frontières du jazz* was the first book-length work in French to treat jazz as it actually existed in the 1920s. Goffin explored the general history and character of jazz before offering a series of miniature portraits of the various 1920s performers. He was among the first to praise Louis Armstrong at a time when white bands were experiencing their greatest popularity in Paris, and in doing so, he reemphasized the crucial contribution of black American musicians to jazz.[114] The stress on musicians and the techniques of their performances also distinguished Goffin from other critics. Most French writers referred to jazz as a single musical entity with little distinction between bands or styles. They perhaps wrote about one or two musicians in order to make a larger musical point, but they did not usually recognize nuances within the evolving genre. Goffin, however, discussed an entire range of performers, commenting on their performances not as a general music critic but rather as a jazz critic using a specialized set of criteria to judge and elaborate on the music. Unlike most of those who wrote about jazz casually as amateurs or who saw it as simply one music among many, Goffin was an unabashed aficionado of jazz. He invested much of his time visiting clubs and record stores to study the music he loved. Rather than merely describing the unique use of rhythm, syncopation, or musical instrumentation, Goffin took those elements for granted and wrote instead about how musicians worked within the jazz idiom. "Open your dictionaries because here are the beautiful new words that France accepts as they are instead of translating them," he announced.[115] "Jazz, drummer, lyrics, hot, break, chorus," were some of the new American terms that those who wrote and spoke of the music must use, declared Goffin. In doing so, his book helped to establish an emerging pattern for a specific literature of jazz criticism in France—one that a distinct clique of writers whose sole and serious focus was jazz were creating and would expand during the 1930s.

Jazz also fascinated anthropologist and author Michel Leiris, who, as a young man in Paris in the 1920s, was also cultivating an interest in African art and cultures. As part of the intellectual and literary avant-garde drawn to exploring exotic peoples, Leiris sought to investigate realms outside of traditional Western experience, whether in Africa or within himself. Indeed, the two became closely intertwined in his ethnographic writing in which he cast aside the objectivity of scientific inquiry in favor of an intensively psychological engagement, both with himself and his subjects. Leiris's depictions of jazz blended the richness of an ethnographic study with the confessional self-revelation and "personal ethnography" for which his writing is known, as if the music had penetrated to that deep level as well.[116]

Leiris remembered his first encounter with jazz in 1918 during the intermission of a music hall program at Le Théâtre Caumartin, where one of Louis Mitchell's bands, the Seven Spades, performed. In the following years, as jazz grew in popularity and moved from a music hall intermission to a headlining act, Leiris became an enthusiastic fan. He visited various nightclubs around the city and participated in surprise parties that brought jazz into people's homes. Josephine Baker's performance in *La Revue Nègre* fascinated him, as it did so many French intellectuals, because of its provocative blending of "primitive" images with modern music and themes.[117] Leiris was drawn to jazz as part of his search for something new, disgusted as he was with what Europe had become by the early twentieth century. "What is certain," he recalled in an interview later in life, "is that I enjoyed jazz as something exotic and non-European, as an affront to European music and art."[118] Like many intellectuals and artists in the interwar years, Leiris thought that cultures outside Europe offered the hope of regenerating a seemingly dead Western imagination that had been exhausted in the war.

Goffin and Leiris were not alone, but in spite of the widespread love for music performed by African Americans, many French commentators continued to praise white bands. The role of white musicians seems to raise a contradiction in the racial aspect of the music because jazz often did have a white face in interwar Paris, particularly in the music halls, where many of the famous white U.S. and British bands performed to larger audiences than could crowd into any nightclub. Despite their admiration for jazz because it was une musique nègre, many critics and journalists frequently appear to have preferred, or at least did not withhold compliments from, the jazz performed by U.S. bandleader Paul Whiteman, Briton Jack Hylton, and other white performers. Music hall composer Vincent Scotto, for example, claimed that jazz played by black musicians left him "suspicious," but listening to Whiteman "completely destroyed this apprehension."[119] For one journalist, Hylton's band was "the model, the paragon of jazz bands, the supreme flower of American music."[120] Cœuroy and Schaeffner themselves, in spite of having traced the black roots of jazz, felt Whiteman to be "currently the most complete jazz band."[121] By 1926,

Cocteau claimed disparagingly that "now the elite admire the bland orchestra of Whiteman, academic, official jazz."[122] Hoerée continued to argue for a greater emphasis on the white origins of jazz. Jazz was the product of "several races and crystallizes the contribution of several apparently irreducible aesthetics," he suggested. Given the tremendous blending of styles that had made jazz, Hoerée believed that only the "blues" was really black. Otherwise, he said, "all the production that we know, that which attracts us, not only by its rhythms but also by the suppleness and the unity of its writing, the haunting subtlety of its harmonies, this production is uniquely of the white race."[123] By the middle of the decade, bands like Whiteman's and Hylton's were among the most popular and highly touted, as we will see in the next chapter.

One can begin to account for this seeming paradox between the frequently proclaimed African origins of jazz and appreciation of white musicians by noting that although many writers praised white bands, they still recognized these orchestras' reliance on African American musical forms for their initial inspiration. Because of this background, many white bands were still heard as wild and chaotic. One reviewer called Hylton "a little *nègre*."[124] Hylton himself stressed the blackness of the music he played when he argued that it came from "mysterious Africa."[125] Of course, with black music in vogue, publicizing any sort of jazz as une musique nègre might simply have been good business. Nevertheless, one composer, Raoul Laparra, offered a "hierarchy" of jazz in which Turks, Spaniards, and Parisians did not play jazz as well as white Americans, who were inferior to black Americans, who were themselves not as good as their ancestors. Thus, he reasserted the African roots of jazz while also acknowledging the albeit lesser talents of white musicians.[126]

Whiteness sometimes introduced another racialized issue into the debate over jazz because Jewish composers, such as Irving Berlin and George Gershwin, wrote many of the Tin Pan Alley tunes popular among jazz and dance bands of the 1920s. Many French writers referred to Berlin as the "king of Jazz." But critics also frequently depicted Jews as a special kind of white musician. In a 1932 speech, French writer Gérard Bauer explained that "in these crossroads of the towns of America where blacks expressed their great nostalgia, other melancholy voyagers passed through, capable of understanding the persecution and endless travel: Jews from old Europe who emigrated to the new world."[127] French jazz musician Ray Ventura agreed, arguing that "the two races were oppressed" and hence could understand each other.[128] In other words, Jews were believed able to translate African American feelings into written words and music. Just like black Americans, Jews were between two worlds—the modern world of 1920s Paris and the primitive one of Eastern Europe—and their music captured the same quality.

Although many in France were attracted to the blackness of jazz, for others this quality, drawing on the dangerous aspects of the stereotype about Africans, was precisely the music's problem. La musique nègre was frequently seen as part of a more general l'art nègre that, for some, threatened to turn black everyone around it. "If the 'folie noire' is not stopped soon," declared one critic in an article that rejected everything black including jazz, "in a few months, I won't see any whites!"[129] In a 1930 article titled "Progress toward the Simian," another author argued that because of jazz, "the reign of the Negro is nearly finished. The reign of the monkey is starting again."[130]

Criticisms of the blackness of jazz begin to make sense against the larger backdrop of other concerns in the interwar period, especially fears of racial degeneration. Particularly important during the 1920s were eugenicists' concerns about how the presence of foreigners would effect the "quality" of the French people.[131] Already troubled that an invasion of immigrants in the postwar period might weaken France physically, many French critics also saw jazz as the symptom and a further cause of such degeneration. They cast the music in terms that emphasized its potential for producing nothing but the basest physical responses in listeners. Writing in La Revue musicale, critic André Suarès called jazz "an orchestra of brutes with nonopposable thumbs," saying that it "is all excess." Jazz contained a purely visceral element since it was made, Suarès argued, "from five or six formulas, two that are useless and two [that] make one want to vomit: jazz is the music of the stomach and of all that carry their soul between the liver and the thigh."[132] Playing jazz as the black musicians did, some critics suggested, constituted a step backward and away from civilization toward the jungles, and echoed the fear of "going native" that some observers voiced about the French in their African colonies.[133] "Is one still in Paris?" asked one critic in desperation on hearing the sounds of jazz. "Is one still in a civilized country?"[134]

The case of jazz in Paris helps to clarify and emphasize some French views of blackness in the 1920s and 1930s. Whether or not the French were racist in the interwar years, it is clear that they, along with most Westerners, thought in increasingly racialized terms.[135] And as the history of interaction with colonial subjects indicates, French racial attitudes evolved through a series of often competing responses depending on historical circumstances, perceptions, and the needs of the moment. Jazz could evoke many such racialized reactions depending on whether one heard it as friendly or frightening, especially when linked with colonial Africa. Observers of jazz perceived blackness as a biological category that produced cultural manifestations. Musical qualities like rhythm emanated from supposedly inborn traits, even though the unique history of African Americans had played a role in shaping how jazz developed and sounded. Most important, whether one liked jazz or despised it, the music's blackness—like its Americanness, although for different reasons—made it alien to French traditions.

FRENCH CIVILIZATION

In spite of the apparent differences between these two ways of characterizing jazz—American music linked with economic and cultural influence and la musique nègre based on a racial category—both pointed to still larger challenges. One question centered around the influence that foreigners and foreign cultures were, for better or worse, exercising in postwar France. As a music that blended the symbolism of both the United States and Africa, jazz was doubly foreign and therefore a touchstone of debate about how France interacted with those from beyond its borders. This debate itself was double-sided. Many in France celebrated the seemingly new and refreshing influence of foreigners. Others, however, decried the erosion of what they deemed to be a more traditional French culture by immigrants, feeding the xenophobic nationalism for which the interwar era is already well-known. Those on both sides of the debate about jazz employed the terms *American* and *black* to their own ends.

The issue of jazz's foreignness can be set against the backdrop of a wave of immigration into France that had begun during the Great War and changed Paris dramatically in the 1920s. Most of the foreign laborers and colonial troops that had come to France to assist in the war effort were repatriated, but some Allied soldiers did remain afterward. In the early years of postwar reconstruction, as we have seen, the government and businesses brought in new workers, largely from other European countries, to fill gaps in the labor force and as a way to increase the French population at a time when France feared a further decline in its numbers.[136] France had been especially willing to accept refugees during and after the war, and exiles from the Russian Revolution as well as the political and economic chaos of Eastern Europe soon established their own immigrant communities in the neighborhoods of Paris.[137] Official immigrants to France numbered between 150,000 and 200,000 each year of the 1920s with only three years of the decade falling below these figures. The number of foreigners residing in France more than doubled between 1911 and 1931.[138] Although foreigners were never a large percentage of the population—between approximately 4 and 7 percent from 1921 to 1931, after which the number dropped off somewhat—their increasing presence in the 1920s aroused a wide range of responses, from interest and sympathy to suspicion and fear, and each reaction became intensified as their numbers grew.[139] Immigrants were nothing new to French society, of course, but the influence that foreign populations had during these years seemed more profound than in the past, in part because of the new languages, food, music, and lifestyles that they brought to Paris as visible symbols of their presence.[140] Neither Americans generally nor African Americans more specifically were the most numerous foreigners in postwar Paris, and their numbers were not large compared to the overall population of the city. But because of their economic impact and visibility in the arts, these particular individuals from outside France signaled to many a significant change in the postwar era.

As a foreign music, jazz was also a powerful reminder that in the twentieth century, France would have to exist in a different relationship with other cultures and peoples than it had in the nineteenth century. Distances and differences were shrinking between countries, and the effectiveness of political boundaries to keep national traditions separated was eroding more quickly than ever. Airplanes and automobiles allowed people to travel faster and farther as well as to cross borders easily. Radios facilitated long-distance communication at the same time that films and phonographs could bring music like jazz from one country to another with surprising ease. The war itself had done much to break down boundaries. It expanded the theater of battle across much of Europe and also around the world through espionage and intelligence that took place beyond the belligerent nations themselves.[141] It also brought to the center of the international stage the two powers that would dominate twentieth-century history, the Soviet Union and United States, thereby beginning to shift the international balance of power out of Europe for the first time in the modern age.[142]

Another issue underlay the discussions about foreigners and jazz, however. In particular, the perceived modernity of the United States and the so-called primitivism of la musique nègre both threatened to erase a more traditional notion of French *civilisation*, one important element of how many people in France conceived of their nation. By virtue of their language, their Cartesian heritage, their Enlightenment and revolutionary roots, and their purported clarity of ideas, the French claimed a cultural leadership within Europe. And they had been exporting those values, along with the accompanying idea of "mastery" of self and others coupled with a belief in the moral power of improvement, as part of their "civilizing mission" in the colonies.[143] World War I had been, for many combatants, a struggle on behalf of these traditional conceptions of what civilization meant, but the brutality and shock of the war had also called into question whether those values could continue to survive.[144] Perhaps poet Paul Valéry best captured the postwar sense of despair when he remarked, "We modern civilizations have learned to recognize that we are mortal."[145] And in the 1920s, the perceived modernity and primitivism of jazz music forced many French listeners to ask whether their unique and privileged civilization was again being challenged, this time by foreign influences.

Bringing these ideas together in the 1939 *L'Age d'homme* (Manhood), an exploration of his youth and psyche, Leiris wrote that

> jazz was a sign of allegiance, an orgiastic tribute to the colors of the moment. It functioned magically, and its means of influence can be compared to a kind of possession. It was the element that gave these celebrations their true meaning: a *religious* meaning, with communion by dance, latent or manifest eroticism, and drinks, the most effective means of bridging the gap that separates individuals from each other at any kind of gathering. Swept along by violent bursts of topical energy, jazz still had enough of a "dying civilization" about it, of humanity blindly submitting to The Machine, to express quite completely the state of mind of at least some of that generation: a more or less conscious demoralization born of the war, a naive fascination with the comfort and the latest inventions of progress, a predilection for a contemporary setting whose inanity we nonetheless vaguely anticipated, an abandonment to the animal joy of experiencing the influence of a modern rhythm, an underlying aspiration to a new life in which more room would be made for the impassioned frankness we inarticulately longed for.[146]

This complicated and beautiful passage connects many of the themes in the debate surrounding jazz in the interwar years. Ultimately, it suggests that there was very little difference between the modern, machine-age qualities of jazz and the primitive, Dionysian responses that this music was thought to bring out in people. As he described jazz, "modern rhythm" effortlessly met "animal joy." Leiris also coupled the search for new artistic inspiration in the postwar years with the belief that jazz drew from a timeless and transcendent culture of black people.

Like Leiris, some listeners appreciated the vitality of jazz because of its ability to cut through layers of old art and culture, thereby finding a new inspiration at the beginning of a new century. Even the conservative musicologist Lionel de la Laurencie recognized jazz as "the sound image of an epoch of realism, of brutal simplicity, destructive, and repudiating all romantic sentimentalism."[147] That it also appeared to have non-Western origins was all the better for many as the West seemed to have proved itself bankrupt in the war. In this pairing of the modernity of the twentieth century and primitivism of black Africa, fans of jazz invoked a liberationist fantasy implying that the nineteenth century could be shed by embracing the newest developments where "all that is solid melts into air" and, at the same time, returning to a golden past and the beauty of the noble savage. Writer and artist Sem, for one, put the second half of this formulation plainly when he maintained, "We have been civilized for too long, and this primitive music communicating to us its naïveté gives us once again for a moment the simple souls of children."[148] Both the modern and primitive in jazz promised its fans the ability to rebuild France and start life over in a new, modern world that was also a rediscovered state of nature like the imagined primitive society.

In this, both America and nègre represented modernity and primitivism at the same time. The United States could be both the height of technological advancement and the land where everything was starting anew. Likewise, blackness could represent both the primitive, savage world of Africa and the modern world that promoted change and novelty, that reveled in exoticism. The modern and primitive values that jazz emulated were simultaneous welcome attacks on the venerable institutions of French civilization—the mores, values, and principles on which many aspects of French culture had been built for so long, but that many now found oppressive and antiquated.[149]

But to its enemies, both the modernity and primitivism of jazz were its worst qualities for the very same threat they posed to French civilization. "The last war has abolished the aesthetics as well as the ethics of the past," lamented conservative critic Henry Malherbe in language similar to that of jazz fans. "We have been obliged to return to the beginning of art and civilization," he claimed, and "with its elementary melody" and other qualities, jazz was part of that process.[150] As much as anything, the criticisms of the Americanness of jazz were attacks on the modern, post–World War I world and the kinds of economic as well as cultural changes that France was undergoing. In that respect, jazz was a sign of the times. Jazz "continues its crazy song!" wrote one critic, "Crazy like the age in which we live."[151] Yet the noise of the modern world and its psychological effects were, in the end, not far from what many called primitive; indeed, they were two sides of the same coin. The modern world—in its very desire for progress and renewal in the wake of the war, and as the result of technological change that eroded old ways of seeing the world—had become primitive again, stripping away all the previous morals, values, tastes, and rules to return to a new, and for many frightening, state of nature. And for many critics, jazz was the sound track of this era. Theater critic Gustave Fréjaville likened the effects of jazz to the events in the novel *The Island of Doctor Moreau*. Once familiar instruments, mutated by the effects of jazz, had come to sound like monsters, he claimed.

> One thinks that one hears a painful concert of curses and muffled maledictions, while the executioners, eager at their task, manifest their satanic joy with a savage gesticulation, and while, as it is common during the sacrifices of certain primitive cults, a man with a black face, a fanatic priest of this modern Baal that one calls Pleasure, unleashes an infernal racket by beating on the taut skins and bronze shields to stifle the cries of the victims.[152]

Fréjaville made the link between the primitive and modern worlds, seeing a kind of racial and cultural degeneracy in both.

There were other related issues at stake that stemmed from such fears of jazz as both modern and primitive, as the harbinger of a new cultural order. Some felt, for example, that French taste, itself a significant component of the definition of civilization was in danger of being corrupted by jazz.[153] One author wrote that his good, French taste enabled him to see the truth about jazz, which was an "abominable mixture" that undermined more tasteful musical expressions.[154] "I do not see the slightest relationship between our beautiful art and the more or less black manifestations [of jazz]," argued Guy de Lioncourt, secretary general of the conservative music academy Schola Cantorum.[155] An editor from the south of France remarked that "we are many, very many, my friend, who are too full of jazz . . . [which] invades, deforms art, makes the senses stupid." Jazz, he believed, "is becoming a danger to taste and to public moral health."[156] Another feared that dance music like jazz "cannot justify this complete erasure of our taste and our national personality, taste that had to be developed over the centuries," unlike that of the Americans.[157]

For many others who lamented these developments, the problem went further than taste because gender roles and their supposed moral underpinnings were also in danger. Jazz went against older codes of conduct by encouraging wild dancing and enticing young ladies to go to nightclubs. The music became part of the new "flapper" image, thanks in part to Josephine Baker and others who provided a sometimes sexualized image of jazz music that rejected nineteenth-century morality. One author claimed that jazz "has invaded salons, dancing courses, dance halls where honest women can go," thus implying that only dishonest or corrupt women would enjoy jazz.[158] The threat of jazz to the morality of women became part of a larger political concern during these years as pronatalists, expressing panic over the perceived depopulation of France due to a declining birthrate, often criticized young women who preferred to spend their nights out on the town rather than at home raising children. Jazz, they asserted, was one more lure away from traditional female duties toward the lifestyle of the "modern woman."[159] Victor Margueritte, for one, depicted the erosion of traditional morality in his famous novel of the 1920s, *La Garçonne*. Using jazz to set the scene for the decadent age, he wrote, for example, that "the dance club pulsated deliriously to the savage rhythms of the jazz band."[160] Furthermore, as others suggested, women were not safe in dance halls that were filled with gigolos who sought only to take advantage of them. One critic's calls for police action were based not only on the "infernal rhythm" of jazz that he heard but also the corrupted—and like that of the garçonne—gender-bending lifestyle that he connected with it—one of "shameless ostentation." "All around us," he said of a jazz club, "were only pretty young men with tired gestures, with trailing voices, with eyes made languid by drugs and covered with mascara that waddled with a studied nonchalance. Each of their gestures is a replica or a caricature of women's gestures."[161]

Ironically, the attackers of jazz often used the same language as those who loved it. As a 1926 article began, for instance, "A group of blacks made their instruments howl wildly, giving off a humming sound." It continued to describe the pounding rhythm and "brutal force" of the instruments playing for dancers who were "elevated, driven, hypnotized, driven mad." Overall, the article, titled "C'est un enfer sonore . . . ," argued for the hellishness of the jazz sound and denounced the music as "satanic."[162] But for jazz's proponents, all of these qualities were precisely what constituted the music's great value. Describing the music at a concert at Le Casino de Paris, for example, Cocteau, who throughout much of the 1920s not only enjoyed the music but also occasionally played drums in a Paris nightclub, praised "the brave blacks . . . [who] threw pieces of raw meat to the crowd in the trumpet blasts and the rattling."[163] Like the article that suggested jazz's hellishness, Cocteau invoked the animal, wild, and noisy side of the music, and this terminology was only one set of concepts used to describe it. None of the perceived elements of jazz—its supposed primitivism, its noise and rhythm, the emphasis on dancing, the challenge to older moral codes, or the powerful psychological effects of the music—were as much in dispute as what these qualities meant to listeners. Fans often expected jazz to open new areas of human consciousness and provide new social as well as cultural experiences through the impact it had on the mind and body of the listener. Opponents did not dispute these effects on the audience. Rather, they feared those very effects along with what they believed to be the negative consequences for both individuals and society. In the end, the actual portrait of jazz was not nearly as contested as its potential consequences and the larger issues for which jazz became a symbol.

By the end of the 1920s, France had been filled with jazz, both to the delight and dismay of many. But the situation began to change in the 1930s. Americans and other tourists began to go home with the onset of the depression, and the frivolity that had accompanied jazz in the crazy years began to subside. Jazz did not die out, however. On the contrary, it began to undergo a transformation. For some ten years, this music had been a foreign import, associated with alternatives to traditional French culture, whether nègre or American. French musicians had performed music called jazz, but few seemed to believe that they could play nearly as well as the Americans who were in much greater demand. In the 1930s, though, French musicians began to take this music up as their own, and they made jazz into a French music. In the process of doing so, French musicians had to confront the association of jazz with "America" and "blackness"—how could these defining elements of the music be reconciled with various elements of the French past? They did so in various ways, either blending the cultural symbolism of jazz with French songs or creating new ways of looking at the music. Some musicians replaced the so-called blackness of the music with a "Latin" quality. Others embraced the supposedly black elements as the true essence of jazz, which they believed also reflected something of France.

5

MAKING

JAZZ FAMILIAR

Music Halls and the Avant-Garde

Even while debates raged over the effects of jazz on French culture, some
Parisian musicians and theaters were actively working to alter their audiences' perceptions of the music, sometimes in quite different ways. Many
of the changes they put into place were driven by commercial consider-
ations. As we have seen, jazz could quickly fit within a familiar style of
music hall theatrics and thereby help to sell tickets. To continue expanding
business, many music halls—with some notable exceptions—modified the
public image of this controversial music by de-emphasizing the presumed
blackness of jazz. If jazz was a challenge to French morality and taste
because of its African primitivism, part of making it commercially viable
to the broadest possible audience required selling listeners on a music that
was still fashionable, but more tame and white. In doing so, Parisian jazz
musicians were not necessarily innovators but were copying the successful
white U.S. and British bands who played so-called orchestral or symphonic jazz in Paris by the mid-1920s. Taking a somewhat different approach to expanding the audience for jazz, several prominent Parisian
avant-garde composers worked to incorporate jazz techniques into their
work throughout the 1920s. Doing so, they thought, would help them to
revitalize French music. But unlike music halls, they added a powerful jolt
of modernity and energy to their compositions by reemphasizing the purportedly black qualities of jazz music. Composers like Darius Milhaud
and Jean Wiéner looked to jazz in large part because it was nègre, believing that this quality of the music was one of its most prized aspects, even
while they adapted it for their own purposes.

Despite their different motivations and tactics for changing how Parisians thought about jazz, the effects of music halls and the avant-garde in
adapting jazz to a French context were similar: jazz became further inte-

grated into the French entertainment scene, and a growing number of listeners heard it. Music halls and the avant-garde both offered Parisians interpretations of jazz music that were distinct from what they might hear in the nightclubs and cabarets of Montmartre and Montparnasse. The result of this assimilation was a style of music that critics still called jazz, but it was not believed to be identical to the music created by black Americans that was still popular in cabarets and on records. Music hall and avant-garde jazz seemed musically lighter and less jarring to French ears.[1]

MUSIC HALLS

The music halls of Paris became famous during the 1920s and 1930s for presenting talented stars like Maurice Chevalier and Mistinguett in lavish shows with sumptuous production values. Their aesthetic was brash, bold, and visually as well as musically stunning—a style that the smaller and more verbally oriented cabarets artistiques had not usually employed. Of these qualities and the changes they represented, one writer lamented that "there is nothing left but mise-en-scène. The luxurious decors, the artifices of machinery, the deployment of extras, . . . the false jewels . . . ," and more things that he believed damaged public tastes.[2] These words offered in criticism nevertheless illustrate the vibrancy of the new music hall setting and its powerful effect on audiences.

Music halls emerged in the fin de siècle to supply audiences with this new style of performance. Their immediate predecessor, the café-concerts, featured singers on a stage surrounded by tables. Customers could drink and talk in an informal atmosphere, sing along with the performers, and shout out insults if the show was not good.[3] Many future music hall stars, like Chevalier, got their starts in these places, which always remained small in scale. *Caf'-concs*, as they were sometimes known, began to change into music halls after 1867 when the government removed restrictions that prevented costumes, plays, and dances in such venues, thus allowing their brashness to take shape.[4] Even the buildings themselves reflected something of the evolving style of the show. The novelist Joris-Karl Huysmans described Les Folies-Bergère in 1879 as a crowded and cigar-smoke-filled hall with plaster statues holding gaslights, and a wooden-legged ticket taker. "It is ugly," he wrote, "but it is superb, it exhibits an outrageous and exquisite taste."[5] Commercial interests and potential profits also fueled the music halls' evolution, but they managed to retain much of the café-concerts' diverse audience because of their relatively low admission fees.[6]

In 1879, Les Folies-Bergère attracted around five hundred thousand people and took in approximately one million francs per year—a figure that more than doubled by 1913.[7] By the early twentieth century, one could attend such a performance for between two and seven francs.[8] And by 1934, one observer noted that music hall box office receipts were almost as important as those in theaters. Music halls, he remarked, were contributing to an alarming decline in theater attendance.[9]

By the turn of the twentieth century, bright, flashy costumes, splendid decorations, and more elaborate sets were quickly replacing the venue's simpler, less embellished, and more informal café-concerts origins. As Jules Bertaut put it, music halls "began to ascend that mounting curve of spectacles, more and more lavish, more and more extensive and more and more undressed."[10] Baedeker's guidebook for Paris advised readers that in the café-concerts, "the music and singing at these establishments are never of a high class," but that the music halls were "very popular."[11] Small performance spaces were abandoned for larger ones, especially since the new acrobatic acts frequently required more room. Seating was now arranged in rows, rather than as a jumble of tables and chairs, to focus the audience's attention on the stage. As critic Pierre Bost portrayed the change, "the [music hall] audience exists by itself, independent of the show, face to face with the artist, like a judge and no longer as a collaborator."[12] Nevertheless, viewers still moved about quite a bit during a music hall performance to purchase drinks, look for friends, or simply come and go during the sometimes four-hour performances.[13]

With such changes in the setting and the larger shows that they enabled, music halls entered their golden age in the interwar years, the era of stars like Mistinguett, Chevalier, Deslys and Pilcer, and Baker, all of whom helped to make the major music halls of Paris famous.[14] "A mixture of the café-concert, the circus, the operetta, and the pantomime, the music hall takes some ingredients from all these while actually resembling none of them, Bertaut commented.[15] Shows featured jugglers and gymnasts, dancers and cyclists, marionettes and magicians, in addition to a wide range of musical acts and glittering, feather-covered costumes.[16] Often presenting between ten and twenty acts during a show in which the main performances lasted for no more than ten minutes, productions sometimes connected several scenes together to tell a story with sketches, musical tableaux, and a plotline. At other times, they offered a variety revue with one act following another.[17]

As soon as jazz arrived, it became a regular fixture of the music hall repertoire and continued to expand throughout the 1920s. Several music halls offered Parisians the chance to hear jazz, particularly Les Ambassadeurs, located just off the Champs-Elysées. Begun in 1764 as an open-air café, it became a *café-chantant* in 1840, and the music hall format appeared there in 1867. A series of producers quickly built up the reputation of Les Ambassadeurs, and in 1929, the music hall began calling itself a theater and moved to a new building. Over the years, Les Ambassadeurs was home to many famous entertainers, such as singers Yvette Guilbert and Aristide Bruant, who came down from Montmartre to perform. But the 1920s was increasingly an era of U.S. reviews. *Broadway à Paris* in 1927 featured French and American musical numbers and performers. The orchestral jazz sounds of Fred Waring and His Pennsylvanians accompanied *Show of 1928*, of which one reviewer remarked, "Not a word of understandable French; not a measure of European music . . . [in this] spectacle for rich Americans." Les Ambassadeurs was also home to the African American revue *Blackbirds*, with its star Florence Mills.[18] A publicity brochure from 1926 trumpeted the continuing presence of American entertainment when it said proudly, "You will also see the most famous jazz that comes to us from America."[19]

Likewise, Le Casino de Paris was another significant venue for jazz. Opening in 1890 on the rue de Clichy, this music hall gained fame thanks to the revues created by well-known producers like Jacques-Charles, who gave audiences *Laisse-les tomber!* in 1917, starring Gaby Deslys. Jacques-Charles claimed that the band for this show was the first jazz in France. "One called these orchestras *ragtime bands*, a name given by the Americans," but soon came the name jazz, he remembered.[20] The American-inspired music at Le Casino continued in shows like *Paris Qui Danse* (1919), featuring dances that had been fashionable from the 1870s to the period right before World War I, *Cach' Ton Piano* (1920), and *Paris Qui Jazz* (1920–1921), which included a variety of foreign acts such as a Hawaiian orchestra, Spanish dancing, Japanese-themed tableaux, and music by Gershwin.[21]

Indeed, as this last example indicates, exotic and foreign entertainment was an integral part of the music hall show. Throughout the 1920s, these performances exhibited an international character, offering listeners the chance to hear polkas, South American tangos, Russian folk music, Spanish songs, music from Asia, and popular songs from the United States, including jazz music.[22] "The music hall had already become a vast international factory for the mass production of pleasure," recalled Bertaut.

"Every season its impresarios combed the earth and racked fantasy to produce more and more sumptuous spectacles, colossal casts, dazzling costumes, and original sensations."[23] In the music halls, author Pierre MacOrlan described how one could see "Gauchos on trampolines, Spaniards who sing six sunny 'slices of life,' English clowns . . . stocky middle-aged Japanese fumbling on the end of a pole balanced by two short arms."[24] Music halls had established a cosmopolitan musical context that was familiar to audiences, and jazz could fit easily into it.

Trying to reach as broad an audience as possible, music halls also made special efforts to target the next generation of listeners. The *Boîte à Joujoux*, a children's variety revue, began at Les Ambassadeurs and moved to several other locations over the next few years. Amid the dancing, clowns, and magic shows aimed at youngsters, various well-known musicians performed jazz. Soon the children began performing jazz themselves. The *Boîte à Joujoux* began featuring Baby Jazz, a "musical group of which the oldest is perhaps not twelve years old," one reviewer noted. The band was "very ingeniously trained . . . , [and] performs the most varied and the gayest rhythms of jazz with accordions, banjos, violins, and drums."[25] At one point, there were some fifty children in the orchestra.[26]

Although the music halls rapidly became one of the most popular Parisian entertainments in the 1920s, critical voices charged that their style damaged the French entertainment tradition by emphasizing foreign sounds, particularly the jazz that was now becoming a regular offering. Theater critic Gustave Fréjaville, for example, remarked in his book *Au music hall* (1923) that these places "during the war underwent a remarkable development. Tumultuous and full of light with blinding colors, a profusion of decorative effects, little or no text." For him, the shows had become a place where "tumult replaced harmony; frenzy replaced spirit; the Parisian muses have retreated before the invasion of black music and barbaric dances." Fréjaville called music halls a "noisy cosmopolitan camp, disorganized, where one can hear all the languages of the known universe." And although jazz was not the only cause of such a decline in these productions, for Fréjaville it was a big part of the problem. "One gets drunk on the jazz band," he declared, cataloging the music hall's offenses, "the raised legs, the big laughs, the great stupidity," the loudness, and the rhythm of it all.[27] "American music, the jazz band, exotic dances . . . the Russian and Swedish ballets, the audacious decorations," he lamented, "all of this has fallen pell-mell into the melting pot to melt into a loud, sparkling, motley sound: this is the music hall of today."[28]

The jazz in the music hall that Fréjaville attacked was certainly an imported music. But in spite of Fréjaville's characterization of it as "loud" and "exotic," it was frequently different than the music to which Parisians danced and listened in the nightclubs of Montmartre and Montparnasse. Rather than the spontaneous, improvised kind of jazz associated with black musicians, the music halls usually featured a more orchestral, symphonic jazz associated with white musicians. In 1920s Paris, two of the most famous names for this sort of music were Briton Jack Hylton and American Paul Whiteman, who played in music halls around Europe to enthusiastic audiences and much critical praise. At the height of their popularity in the mid-1920s, they headlined the evening in various Parisian theaters. The success of bands like Hylton's and Whiteman's began to alter the definition of jazz music in Paris that, since its beginnings in Paris, had been so closely associated with black players. Some depictions of Whiteman's and Hylton's music still emphasized the African American origins of jazz, and so did Whiteman and Hylton themselves. Yet many observers described their sound as being substantially different when compared to what they associated with black jazz musicians. In offering this so-called white jazz, music halls began to change audiences' perceptions about the music.

By the mid-1920s, both Americans and Europeans already knew Whiteman as the King of Jazz, although in France the title was translated as *Féérie du Jazz*—the jazz spectacular or fantasy.[29] He was born into a musical family in Denver, but after performing in the Denver and San Francisco symphonies, Whiteman changed course to try his hand at the more popular music that he loved, and by which he could more easily earn a living. Fired from his first such job for not being able "to jazz," as he told the story, Whiteman stood in the doorways of San Francisco nightclubs trying to decipher the musical code of the jazz bands he heard. When he realized that they were "faking"—by which he meant improvising individual solos around the melody (one of the very qualities that made jazz distinctive to many other musicians)—Whiteman decided to make a crucial change when he played the music. "Up to that time," he claimed in his autobiography, *Jazz* (1926), "there had never been a jazz orchestration. I made the first and started into the jazz orchestra business."[30] Whiteman combined the light, syncopated dance melodies of the jazz he heard with his orchestral training to produce jazz scores that a band could play without having to "fake" it.

Whiteman's success with this formula earned him record-breaking amounts of money in New York venues as well as nationwide popularity in the United States on radio and through phonograph records. He commissioned and debuted Gershwin's jazz symphony *Rhapsody in Blue* in his famous 1924 Aeolian Hall concert in New York. Whiteman also became known for "jazzing" classical works by performing pieces from the classical repertoire in a jazz style. For all of these accomplishments, Whiteman's musical legacy is controversial within jazz history because much of his work does not neatly fit within traditional definitions of jazz. Instead, his music lay at the intersection of several early-twentieth-century styles including jazz, pop, and orchestral music. But his role in helping to popularize jazz—or at least jazzy music that people called jazz—in Europe is clearer.[31]

Whiteman traveled to Britain in 1923 and received widespread acclaim from audiences, who filled his shows for several months. By then, he was already becoming quite popular in France through record sales, although he did not visit there until 1926. When he finally did play in Paris for the first time, audiences raved over his simultaneously running shows at Le Théâtre des Champs-Elysées and Les Ambassadeurs, the latter with the black American singer Florence Mills.[32] The program was "entirely unconventional," according to the Paris-based U.S. journalist Irving Schwerké, consisting of "pieces composed or arranged for jazz orchestra, not to forget jazz pieces for two pianos, two wind instruments blown by one man, for bicycle pump, etc.," along with *Rhapsody in Blue*. Despite using certain kinds of musical tricks, like a bicycle pump, Whiteman's work was perceived to be far less shocking to the ears of many listeners than other jazz of the day. "It is to be hoped that all French and other misguided jazz players," wrote Schwerké, "will go to hear Mr. Whiteman, and learn that jazz is not a riot of noise but something much more insinuating and subtle."[33] Many French critics and listeners agreed. The well-known composer André Messager startled many in the Parisian music world when he proclaimed, "*J'adore le jazz.*" But he specified bands like Whiteman's, which he called "a real jazz," rather than the music of the Montmartre clubs performed by black musicians.[34] Music hall producer Gabriel Astruc, in spite of his stated fascination with la musique nègre, agreed with Messager on the greatness of Whiteman's "real jazz, not that which the French confuse with the disorderly and noisy sounds of the musicians in the *dancings.*"[35]

Chief among Whiteman's European imitators in those years was the British dance bandleader Jack Hylton, whose act some advertisements and commentators referred to as a *"spectacle à la manière américaine"* or *"fantaisiste américain,"* indicating the persistent connection between jazz and the United States in the public's mind.[36] Already well-known to Parisians through phonograph records, Jack Hylton and His Boys fit into the established style of music hall entertainment by employing theatrical antics. For example, his musicians passed their instruments around to one another. "Everyone plays everything—and dances, and sings, equally," reported one account. Hylton himself conducted with great verve, "his hands explaining his music . . . his body elongates and shrinks. . . . He jumps, goes, twirls, comes back, boxes a little, then in an instant, seems to hold a sword, fakes, jabs, while the instruments appear to change themselves rising or falling and one doesn't know how."[37] Performing a variety of tunes including "marching songs, light popular music, [and] English romances," among others, Hylton visited big music halls and other concert venues in Paris and throughout France. His performance at the Paris Opéra in 1930 revealed to one reviewer the power of this music over the young people in attendance who otherwise might not have come to that location. The audience that night demanded a second encore.[38]

Wherever he performed, though, Hylton's playfulness did not disguise the differences between his music and that of black performers. "Jack Hylton plays nothing that he has not previously submitted to a harmonic grooming, eliminating all the accidents, all the roughness that alone would be able to retain some of the flavor," one reviewer remarked.[39] Another described Hylton's music as expressing "tumult but rhythm, thunder but precision."[40] Of a Marseilles show, one newspaper account noted the use of violins, the weak drums, and the similarities between some of his music and a Viennese waltz.[41] For another listener, Hylton's approach to jazz resembled more traditional European forms of music in spite of his clowning on stage. "*Le jazz* is transformed into a large classical orchestra," he observed of a Hylton show. "Jack has only one idea: to enter the Académie des Beaux-Arts."[42]

Many white bands with this lighter sound appeared in Paris, especially in the mid- and late 1920s. The Americans Billy Arnold, Ted Lewis, and Fred Waring and His Pennsylvanians, to name a few, played on music hall stages as part of a cohort of white jazz musicians who went to France during these peak years of the music's early success. Following much the same format as Whiteman and Hylton, and often compared to these bigger stars by the critics, such bands continued to popularize upbeat orchestral music called jazz on the French entertainment scene. Lewis, one reviewer noted, "is at once a tragic actor, clown, and dancer. His orchestra is made up of nine musicians, two singers, and one female dancer."[43] Lewis's style was more showy than musical, many commented, and as such his act fit neatly within the music hall tradition.[44] Waring's Pennsylvanians appeared to lack "the noisy and harsh explosions" of others.[45] "One must admit," stated a critic, "that these white bands have turned the daring revolutionaries [of jazz] into something classic and that their orchestras can take their place beside the large reputable orchestras."[46]

Through such bands, the image of jazz began to change.[47] The kind of songs performed in the music halls by people like Whiteman and Hylton made jazz available to listeners who might not go to Montmartre or did not like the music as black musicians played it. This sort of jazz seemed more balanced and less noisy to many listeners. As the Belgian critic and fan of black jazz Robert Goffin put it, men like Hylton and Whiteman made jazz palatable by softening its sound: "Paul Whiteman was the first to find a compromise between real [black] jazz and the prejudices of the bourgeois public, which could not swallow certain of the novelties of syncopated music."[48] These were certainly not the kinds of comments elicited by black jazz performers whose music was called wild, spontaneous, and outside the European musical tradition. In fact, some writers argued that Hylton's and Whiteman's style of playing was not only a corruption of the black style but the result of its having been Americanized. White players, they charged, had taken the true spirit out of jazz and homogenized it. Black jazz in the early 1920s, as one commentator described it, was "charming, emotional, and sympathetic." It came naturally to the black musicians, who he called "big children." But in the United States, jazz had "already changed because of contact with a civilization foreign to [the black] race." White jazz musicians were taking the music further from its original source and making it into something that reflected U.S. culture—"mechanical and industrial." "M. Hylton and his troupe," one writer charged, "are conventional, and one would say . . . that their genre has been standardized."[49] Such observations served to re-emphasize the true blackness of jazz, in the minds of many, against the white imitators.

The "wilder" sort of black American jazz was not excluded from music halls, of course, and it was readily associated with one of the most important performers of the 1920s and 1930s, Josephine Baker. Baker's success and the reasons behind it have been discussed at length by many scholars. Certainly many people in Paris, particularly artists and intellectuals, were ready to encounter her highly stylized image after having come into contact with African art and culture in the years before her 1925 debut. Much of what they responded to was her supposed savagery represented, for example, by the Charleston and more famously the *danse sauvage*, which her French producer Jacques-Charles had created to fit French conceptions of the sensualized jungle savage.[50] Baker performed these dances in time with the syncopated music that accompanied her, most notably the clarinet of Sidney Bechet and the other players in the jazz band that was part of her first Parisian show, *La Revue Nègre*. Indeed, the dance and music were so closely intertwined that they inspired the dance critic André Levinson to remark that

> she seems to dictate to the spellbound drummer, to the saxophonist who leans lovingly towards her with the pulsating language of the blues, in which the insistent ear-splitting hammering is punctuated by the most unexpected syncopations. In mid-air, syllable for syllable, the jazz players catch hold of the fantastic monologue of this crazed body. The music is created by the dance.[51]

But there were limits to Baker's relationship to jazz as a musical form because Baker and jazz fit the music hall tradition in different ways. Jazz made sense in the music halls because of the surrounding context of exotic music, and so did Baker at first. Yet Baker quickly became associated with another part of the music hall tradition: she joined a long history of female dancers like Deslys and, in the 1920s, Mistinguett. As a performer, Baker followed in the footsteps of the French women who preceded her as much as in those of other black entertainers. Furthermore, Baker may not have been as exotic as she sometimes seemed. Michel Leiris, for one, maintained that had Baker been dark-skinned, she might not have been as easily accepted.[52] Her race was significant, but variations in the visible marking of color could still play a critical role in determining whether a performance was more broadly acceptable.

With her husband/manager at the time, Pepito Abatino, Baker also made a conscious decision to change her persona from the banana-clad, shimmying, grinning, American girl who crossed her eyes to get laughs in 1925, to a more sophisticated, glamorous, Parisian music hall star. Baker left Paris in 1928 for a year-long European tour, during which she and Abatino recast her image. By the time of Baker's return to Paris in the 1930–1931 show *Paris Qui Remue* at Le Casino de Paris, Baker was beginning to emerge as a different kind of star. "The *danse sauvage* is finished,"

Baker proclaimed. "You have to grow and change all the time."[53] Baker began to appear in silky evening gowns and feathered bathing suits like those that the other female music hall stars were wearing, including Mistinguett, who Baker replaced at Le Casino de Paris in the fall of 1930. She spoke to the audiences and the press in French, and started to consider herself French as well: "I don't want to live without Paris. It's my country. The Charleston, the bananas, finished. Understand? I have to be worthy of Paris. I want to become an artist."[54]

Race was still a factor in Baker's life, and the revue at the Casino did not allow her to shed the exoticism that had helped to make her popular. The show had a colonial theme in honor of the 1931 Colonial Exhibition, and Baker provided what the producers believed to be a necessary element of blackness to the performance. She was even asked to be the grand marshal of the exhibition's parade until someone remembered that she was not from the colonies. But being black was becoming less important to her performance, as was her connection with black American music. The recordings she made in 1930 for Columbia were "closer to music hall songs than to jazz," according to Baker's biographer Phyllis Rose, even though Baker was backed up by a band named Jacob's Jazz. Baker was quickly leaving the connections with exoticism behind and assimilating into Parisian society, and in 1937, she became a French citizen. "A French music hall star had been born," Rose argues of this transformation, "but an American jazz performer seemed to have died."[55]

Still, black performance was a crucial component of the 1920s music hall repertoire, and black jazz remained part of the show, even while Whiteman and others were popular. In 1929, the revue *Blackbirds*, organized by the white producer Lew Leslie and starring an all-black troupe, arrived at Le Moulin Rouge just as it had been staged in New York—a fact that the press commented on frequently. Portions of earlier *Blackbirds* revues had apparently been performed in Paris, but never a show in its entirety. "In France we have never seen a real black revue," one reporter claimed. Baker's *La Revue Nègre* "was conceived and directed by the French in the French style."[56] *Blackbirds*, however, promised to be a more authentic representation of black life in the United States. Accompanied by a jazz band called the Plantation Orchestra, whose records were already known in France, the show prominently featured dancing.[57] Playing on traditional stereotypes, it also depicted scenes of plantations and life in Harlem. Yet the blackness of the performers was muted, according to one reviewer, who called the players "mulattoes and mullatresses . . . [who] were evidently chosen in order to seduce a public that likes them because of their light skin."[58] The show, said another, was "half-black, half-white," as symbolized by its two stars, Aida Ward and Adelaide Hall.[59] According to one observer, Ward sang with "grace and charm," and was "perfectly civilized," while Hall "on the contrary remained perfectly primitive," backed by the sounds of the jazz band.[60] In such a show, la musique nègre was present, but it was tempered and modified.[61]

As musicologist Henry Prunières noted in *La Revue musicale* of music hall jazz, "This is not savage jazz . . . , this is classic, civilized jazz, white jazz. . . . Perhaps it is too much like European music."[62] Whether or not that was the case, jazz in the music hall was certainly better adapted to that venue where performances were, by definition, more carefully scripted than in a cabaret in order to accommodate the logistics of large sets and special lighting. And rarely did a jazz band fill an entire music hall program, which placed jazz alongside other foreign, though still familiar, kinds of performance. Although black revues like *Blackbirds* or *La Revue Nègre* excited Parisian audiences and allowed them to revel in the exotic, they were not the usual sort of 1920s music hall fare. Rather, they were specialty programs, whereas white performers appeared to be more typical, according to the listings of music hall performers in programs and the journalistic accounts of the time. By the 1930s, French music hall orchestras were performing the more orchestral sort of jazz as a regular part of music hall shows as well. The orchestra for the 1931 revue *Paris Qui Brille* starring Mistinguett was the "melodic jazz of Edmond Mahieux," a French bandleader.[63] Of the 1931 Folies-Bergère show *L'Usine à Folies*, one reviewer wrote that this was "the most stunning jazz of the present moment, but it is jazz for a French taste directed by a talented [French] composer."[64]

As a result of this transformation, music halls widened the definition of what could be considered jazz and stripped it of some of its most pronounced racial qualities. In the process, they helped to reshape Parisian perceptions about this music. Not only did the music halls assist in changing the ways in which people thought about jazz by offering a different sort of sound, they also brought it to larger audiences. Music halls were spread around the city and took jazz out of the traditional entertainment districts. Some of the most important music halls were still to be found in lower Montmartre, such as Le Moulin Rouge and Le Casino de Paris on rue de Clichy and La Cigale on Boulevard de Rochechouart. Elsewhere, though, L'Empire was located on the Boulevard Wagram on the western boundary of the fashionable eighth arrondissement. Le Théâtre des Champs-Elysées that introduced Paris to Baker in 1925 was not far away on the Avenue Montaigne. L'ABC, which opened in 1934, was located on the Boulevard Poissonnière in the second arrondissement, L'Alhambra on the rue de Malte in the eleventh, and L'Olympia on the Boulevard des Capucines in the ninth, not far from the Opéra. In such different neighborhoods, jazz might not be as audacious as it was in places like Montmartre and Montparnasse, which were known for their rowdiness and play.

JAZZ AND THE AVANT-GARDE

Music halls were only one path by which jazz became a more familiar part of French entertainment in the 1920s. Avant-garde musicians who incorporated it into their creations were another. By the early twentieth century, many composers had already been seeking new sources of inspiration in folk melodies, foreign tunes, and other types of music that were not part of the standard repertoire in order to reinvigorate the European tradition for the new century. Some had already begun to use African American songs. As mentioned earlier, Debussy wrote cakewalks in the first few years of the 1900s, and Stravinsky had used black American rhythms in his work "Ragtime" (1919). The introduction of jazz to avant-garde music seemed the natural outgrowth of a larger avant-garde project in the 1920s to break down the old barriers between so-called art and popular music. Music historian Glenn Watkins has identified this tendency for appropriation and rearranging music from various traditions—a process that he calls "collage"—not only as part of the late-nineteenth- and twentieth-century search for ways to find transcendent sources of musical expression but also as a form used by European composers "who were interested in resuscitating their art in a radical new way."[65] For such individuals, the unique rhythms and harmonies of jazz promised to add just such a necessary vitality to older musical forms.[66]

One of the most significant connections between black American music and French composers began after World War I when Darius Milhaud and other members of the group of young musicians known as Les Six incorporated jazz rhythms, melodies, and instrumentation into their works. Les Six emerged out of a group of young admirers of Satie, the musical maverick who, in 1917, had composed the ragtime-inspired ballet *Parade* with a story by Cocteau. Attracted to the piece's musical simplicity and clear revolt against romanticism in French art music, composers like Milhaud, Francis Poulenc, Georges Auric, and others began meeting together to share their common musical project.[67] The entertainment trade newspaper *Comœdia* dubbed the group Les "Six" Français to distinguish them from the musicians known as the Russian Five. Several of these composers visited the popular entertainment venues of Paris—such as the music hall, cinema, and circus—to seek new inspiration for their music. In such places, they reveled in the playfulness, energy, and richness of what they saw and heard. Tired of the influence of German music and French Impressionism, and full of the desire to "fuse 'art' with everyday life," as musicologist Nancy Perloff puts it, these composers brought Parisian popular culture into the concert hall.[68] In the mixture of sounds, including jazz, that they encountered on their visits to music halls and cabarets, avant-garde musicians like Les Six found a means of renovating French music.

Of Les Six, Milhaud was the most outspoken about jazz and the one most clearly influenced by it. Auric had written a fox-trot in 1919 entitled *Adieu, New York!* that marked the end of his experimentation with black American music, but Milhaud's interest in jazz lasted several years into the 1920s.[69] Milhaud had recognized the power of the music early on when he heard Billy Arnold's (white) jazz band in London at the Hammersmith Palais de Dance in 1920, and found himself entranced by "the vital pulse of the rhythmic life of the music." He set about trying to incorporate the new sounds into some of his work right away.[70] Two years later on a trip to New York, Milhaud heard many kinds of African American music, including spirituals, when he visited Harlem. "I could not tear myself away [from the music]," he reported. "From then on, I frequented other negro theaters and dance-halls." When he returned to France, he listened over and over to the jazz records he had brought back with him.[71] Milhaud was not a novice at integrating non-European music into his own compositions. By the time he discovered jazz, he had already used the sounds of the South American folk songs and tangos that he heard while in Brazil during the war; the result was his ballet *Le Bœuf sur le Toit*, with a story by Cocteau.[72] Now in the early 1920s, jazz inspired him in new ways.

Much of Milhaud's appreciation for jazz was based on its musical innovations, and most of his comments focused on syncopation, percussion, new instruments, and new performance techniques. But like other observers of his day, Milhaud referred to blackness as one of the central characteristics inherent in the music itself: "Primitive African qualities have kept their place deep in the nature of the American negro."[73] Drawn from a rich tradition of black music that included spirituals and folk music, jazz played by black musicians was freer, more spontaneous and improvisational, and more dramatic for him than jazz played by whites. He certainly admired and respected the white bands of the day, like Whiteman's and Arnold's, which he called "serious jazz" where "nothing is left to chance, everything is balance and proportion, revealing the touch of the true musician, perfect master of all the possibilities of every instrument."[74] But it was black music that truly moved him. In his 1923 jazz-influenced composition *La Création du Monde* (The creation of the world), for example, Milhaud reported that he employed an orchestra similar to that in the black American musical *Liza*.[75]

Although many French bands in the 1920s seemed merely to be copying what the Americans were doing, Les Six wanted to unite jazz techniques with their own French compositions. In doing so, Milhaud hoped to enrich the French repertoire. "Instrumental chamber-music and concert sonatas still remain to be written for the jazz band," he remarked in order to encourage musicians, "especially for those instruments which jazz ordinarily brings together."[76] More specifically, efforts to incorporate jazz into the classical tradition could, he believed, help to revitalize French music at a moment when many composers were already seeking new directions. Part of Les Six's musical mission was to return to what they saw as a more authentically French style of music by escaping from the influence of Debussy's musical romanticism and the Wagnerism of the late nineteenth century. "What we want to do," Milhaud said in an interview, "is to recover the real French tradition which was lost in the nebulosity of impressionism, the tradition of Rameau, of Berlioz, of Chabrier."[77] In his attempt to return to a simpler and more classical style of French music, Milhaud did not recommend looking to the earlier classical composers but rather to the popular music from the music halls, circuses, and cabarets. In the process, American jazz (ironically, since it was an imported form) became a way of articulating a seemingly lost vitality within the French musical tradition that he hoped to reconstruct with a more muscular sound.[78]

Les Six's connection with jazz did not only involve composing it, performing it, and writing about it. Along with their literary companion Jean Cocteau, they helped to establish a nightspot called Le Bœuf sur le Toit (The Ox on the Roof), after the name of Milhaud's tango-inspired ballet, that became a crucial gathering place for the artistic, literary, and musical elite in Paris during the 1920s. Le Bœuf sur le Toit began as a small bar called Le Gaya on the rue Duphot (first arrondissement, near the Madeleine), which was already a well-known gathering place in the early 1920s.[79] Like many Parisian bars and cafés, it was tiny and crowded. But unlike most nightspots in 1921, Le Gaya was about to be "discovered." Milhaud heard about the place through his old friend Jean Wiéner, who played piano there, and Les Six moved their Saturday night meetings from Milhaud's apartment to Le Gaya's cramped quarters. Soon, much of the Paris that prided itself on being modern followed the group. Realizing the potential profit to be made from the popularity that his famous clientele was attracting, Le Gaya's owner made two important decisions. First, he moved the bar a few blocks to 28 rue Boissy d'Anglas off the Place de la Concorde (eighth arrondissement). Second, drawing on the avant-garde's reputation, he changed the name to Le Bœuf sur le Toit.

Once the new place opened on 15 December 1921, Le Bœuf sur le Toit became a true center for artistic culture of all types and a socially fashionable destination. Celebrities gathered there: not only Les Six but Picasso, Dadaism's founder Tristan Tzara, the Surrealist Louis Aragon, Russian dancer Serge Diaghilev, and other artists, writers, and musicians, along with various members of Europe's royalty.[80] Others came to watch the famous and soak up the trendy milieu they created. "Society mingled with painters and actors, men of affairs with writers," remarked author and chronicler Maurice Sachs, but the crowd was not always an elite one. "It was not unusual to meet there workingmen in sandals come down from Montparnasse," he recalled, and one could come dressed as one was.[81] For drinks, food, and the atmosphere of one of Parisian society's most important gathering places, Sachs rememberd, "it was impossible to finish a day without going there."[82]

Music completed the setting. Wiéner had played jazz piano at Le Gaya along with the black American saxophonist and banjoist Vance Lowry. They continued together at Le Bœuf sur le Toit, joined by the Belgian pianist Clément Doucet, who sometimes read detective novels while performing. Doucet had already been playing at Le Coliséum with a black drummer in 1919 and was familiar with jazz himself.[83] Often Cocteau, who as he put it, "found the jazz more intoxicating than alcohol, which does not agree with me," joined in at Le Bœuf on drums.[84] On a visit there, one could hear many kinds of music. As Milhaud recalled, Wiéner and Lowry "would pass from fashionable rag-time and fox-trots to the most celebrated works of Bach," of which Wiéner had become especially fond.[85] But Wiéner sometimes combined classical sounds with "*musique négro-américaine*," as he called music in the jazz idiom.[86]

Wiéner drew eclectically from both jazz and European art music as sources for inspiration. In his *Concerto franco-américain*, he blended the sounds of "the great classical form with black American composition."[87] The result was a jazz that, according to many accounts, was easier for Parisian audiences to understand. The sound of Wiéner and Doucet's jazz was quite different from that of the black musicians, most descriptions revealed, even though they performed with a black saxophonist and recognized their debt to black musicians. As one critic portrayed Wiéner and Doucet's performances, "They have lightened and ennobled the spirit of American music so well that they have profoundly modified it, perhaps without thinking."[88] Anthropologist and jazz fan Georges Henri Rivière remembered the two pianists playing in different styles, neither of which could be used to describe black jazz players: Doucet's performance was "Wagnerian," he said, while Wiéner's was "a baroque sort of music, perfected, and more logical, more mathematical."[89] Through their performances, these musicians were changing people's perceptions of jazz, according to many observers. "Jean Wiéner and Clément Doucet have acclimated the *blues* to Paris," wrote one critic. "They have naturalized it to French by imposing a very particular allure."[90] Milhaud remarked that Wiéner had incorporated the sounds of jazz in works like *Sonatine syncopée* and *Suite* for piano and violin in which he "uses the elements of *rag* and introduces them into pure music."[91] For Milhaud, Wiéner's *Concerto franco-américain* "is a skillful mixture of jazz syncopation and the quasi-military blaring of our polkas."[92] One French reviewer declared that it was "a long way from the primitive excesses to the codifications of Wiéner and Doucet," with their lighter, more balanced sound.[93] Leiris recalled his fondness for Wiéner and Doucet, who as he put it, had "invented a style of Parisian jazz which was pretty and original."[94] Such descriptions hardly sound like the jazz being played in Montmartre and Montparnasse.

Outside Le Bœuf, Wiéner played a crucial role in popularizing jazz music, perhaps more so than any other member of the avant-garde. First, he and Doucet had a successful recording and concert career that brought them much notoriety as they toured around the world. But Wiéner's efforts went further. Excited by the various musical developments of the 1920s, he introduced audiences to groundbreaking music, including jazz, through a series of concerts beginning in December 1921. The first of his "Concerts Wiéner" presented new musical sounds to a crowd largely populated by musicians and composers.[95] Held at La Salle des Agriculteurs, the show featured Billy Arnold's jazz band as its opening act—"a sum of considerable audible richness," one reviewer observed.[96] They played a combination of jazz, various U.S. folk songs, and as one reporter noted, "a curious Chinese rhapsody."[97] Second on the bill was a demonstration of technology performing the sounds of musical modernism in a rendition of Stravinsky's *Le Sacre du Printemps* by a player piano. Reactions among the audience were mixed, as Wiéner recounted in his autobiography. The composer Albert Roussel got up shortly after the jazz began and left the hall, "slamming the door." Maurice Ravel was more generous, however, telling Wiéner after the concert, "It was marvelous."[98] Later "Concerts Wiéner" also combined jazz, blues, and ragtime music with works by Arnold Schoenberg, Stravinsky, and Satie, thus connecting a wide range of challenges to traditional art music both from the avant-garde and popular culture.[99]

Much of the avant-garde eventually lost interest in jazz because, by the mid-1920s, this music was becoming too well-known. After a few successful years, Le Bœuf sur le Toit moved to the rue de Penthièvre (eighth arrondissement), but the famous people did not go with it, and only the tourists remained to remember the legacy. Jazz "had now become official, and won universal recognition," Milhaud explained in his autobiography. "White men, snobs in search of exotic colour, and sightseers curious to hear negro music, had penetrated to even the most secluded corners [of Harlem]. That is why I gave up going."[100] As Milhaud's comments illustrate, jazz had lost its status as an outsider music in avant-garde circles. The jazz that was once an escape from the traditions of European music had now become too much a part of that tradition to offer any challenge to mainstream culture. Milhaud and others had relied on the newness and modernity of jazz for their project, and thus rejected jazz when it ceased to be so. Ironically, of course, the avant-garde had played an important role in the very transformation of jazz that they ultimately held in contempt. They had helped to popularize the music, making it into something more familiar to the French audiences and composers who appreciated avant-garde music. On a more basic level, though, their interest had not really been in jazz but instead with revitalizing French music. Like the many other kinds of "exotic" music on which they drew, jazz could only go so far within the framework of art music once its resources were exhausted without transforming European music into something very different.

By the end of the 1920s, jazz bands were still primarily American. But there were growing numbers of French bands who, drawing especially on the music hall style of jazz, began to play jazz too. Like music halls and the avant-garde, French musicians would have to confront the ambiguities of jazz's racial content and decide whether to remove or embrace it. As we will see, some continued the process of moving away from jazz's black roots by offering a Latin style of jazz. Others heard in black jazz the echoes of an older French tradition.

6

MAKING

JAZZ FRENCH

Parisian Musicians and Jazz Fans

Despite the fact that jazz was beginning to reach more and more listeners through music halls, radios, and records during the 1920s, by the end of that decade, large numbers of people from outside France still comprised much of the audience for jazz in Paris. Therefore, when many of the tourists and expatriates—especially the Americans—began leaving Paris in the early 1930s, the jazz scene appeared to be dying. And the dwindling vitality of the music became more pronounced when record shipments from the United States slowed because of the depression. At first, few French bands appeared to offer much hope to jazz fans as the music's American practitioners began to disappear and its popularity seemed to be waning. Those who played noisy music in the early days of jazz had not gained the reputations of bands from the United States. In any case, most audiences in Paris had always seemed to pay more attention to the Americans than to these early French performers because they believed that the French simply could not play jazz as well.

Yet the "death of jazz," as some observers described this decline in jazz's presence in Paris, was somewhat misleading. Rather than dying, the jazz community in Paris was evolving. Starting in the late 1920s and early 1930s, a younger generation of French musicians who had been absorbing the lessons of imported American tunes during the previous decade now began to enjoy greater success with jazz music and French audiences. After performing for a time with the popular bands of the era like Hylton's, French jazz musicians formed their own, increasingly well-known groups. By the end of the 1930s, France's legendary jazz band, the Quintet of the Hot Club of France, had come from this cluster of new French performers. Indeed, the reputations of the Quintet and its renowned soloists Django Reinhardt and Stéphane Grappelli persist even today. Other

French musicians like Ray Ventura and Grégor also won fame and fortune in the 1930s, and Ventura continued to play for many years afterward.

These new musicians, along with their fans, worked hard to create a broader audience for jazz in France through their performances. But perhaps the most significant fact about them was their claim that they were not simply jazz musicians: they were French jazz musicians. When performed by Ventura, Grégor, or the Quintet, jazz no longer seemed to threaten French music by Americanizing or Africanizing it, as many critics had charged in the 1920s when jazz was so frequently labeled as foreign. These French players were instead absorbing jazz into the tradition of French entertainment. They did not alter the music itself—that is, they did not necessarily try to invent a "French jazz" with different or unique musical qualities. Rather, they began to change what this music meant to French listeners. Through their efforts, they demonstrated that jazz had ceased to be simply an American import and was now becoming a homegrown French art.

THE DEATH OF JAZZ?

By the end of the 1920s, many people in Paris were becoming tired of jazz music, even when played by Americans, and critics began predicting its death for a variety of reasons. Some observers believed that the public was simply saturated with jazz and was looking for something fresh. Several writers noted the revival of gypsy orchestras and waltzes as more traditional alternatives. According to one author, himself no lover of jazz, the change was not too surprising since jazz would come and go like all musical fads. "Gypsies are a little less black . . . ," he remarked sarcastically, "but just like the jazzmen they style their hair with salad oil."[1] "The cycle is complete," remarked another on the return to gypsy and waltz music.[2] Chanson composer Esther Lekain predicted a "triumphal return" for the chanson even after "its finesse and its candor [had been] humiliated by the arrogant jazz band."[3] Others argued that jazz, having reached its peak, was simply not making any new contributions to music. André Messager, the composer who had previously startled colleagues by announcing his adoration of jazz, soon noted, "It seems to me that if 'jazz' is not yet old-fashioned, it is not progressing."[4] Jazz, argued another composer in the mid-1930s, "from the point of view of orchestral arrangements has not made much progress for twenty years!"[5]

Questions also arose about just how influential jazz had really been even at the height of its popularity. Some claimed that although its contribution was significant, perhaps musicians had overstated the value of this new sound in the rush to embrace it. When composers brought jazz effects to other kinds of music, the product was questionable, in the mind of one observer: "We have had many occasions to hear several famous works distorted from their original sense and transposed into a jazz style. The result has always proved to be mediocre."[6] There was too much "deep melancholy" and "despairing tenderness," claimed another critic, for jazz to become fully a part of French musical life. Older kinds of music were coming back, he concluded, because "the Frenchman is troubled" by jazz music.[7] Once the newness had faded, jazz sometimes seemed to have been little more than a fad to many. By 1929, one author could remark that "at the present time, nothing shocks the public less than a new jazz."[8] "Jazz was the amusement for a moment," said one composer looking back on the 1920s. "Today when its vogue seems to be exhausted, one realizes that at bottom it brought nothing to music."[9]

One measure of the death of jazz appeared to be an imbalance between the supply of the music and the demand for it. In a 1931 interview with the newspaper *Candide*, the black American singers Layton and Johnstone, who were popular in France throughout the 1920s, described a "crisis of jazz and American songs." "In America, there was a crisis of overproduction in songs just as in cars and other areas," they noted. "Above all in talking films, the number of songs multiplied infinitely; there too the ability of the public to digest is limited." The result was a surfeit of mediocre music because "songs are a popular art, made for a rather mediocre public."[10]

More significantly, the economic problems of the late 1920s and then the depression years further reduced the presence of jazz in France. Already in 1927, some black musicians had difficulty finding work in increasingly troubled economic times, and many clubs at least appeared to be replacing black jazz musicians with whites. As Joe Alex, Josephine Baker's old partner from *La Revue Nègre*, put it, "Nightclub owners have suppressed one of every two jazz bands and it's black jazz that, for financial reasons, has given way to white jazz."[11] "Stopped in their conquests and their excesses by the [economic] crisis and the unemployment," wrote conservative critic Henry Malherbe a few years later, "the virtuosos of color have returned in numbers to their hectic native cities."[12] Although nightlife certainly continued during the 1930s, audiences were becoming harder to find, especially when French musicians tried to play jazz since they were still generally thought to be bad at it. As one American observer remarked in 1933, "European orchestras cannot play good dance music—that is, the jazzy peppy kind."[13] Even the records on which French listeners often relied for the latest songs from the United States were harder to buy. The U.S. record industry was suffering both from the overproduction that Layton and Johnstone had described and depression economics. The result was a temporary reduction in the number of records pressed and sold. The "race record" market—records by black musicians for black audiences— quickly dried up in the United States except for certain bands like Duke Ellington, Fletcher Henderson, and King Oliver, whose recordings survived a bit longer thanks to the demand among college students.[14] Two of the major British record companies that provided many recordings to the continent, the Gramophone Company–His Master's Voice (HMV) and Columbia, together declined 90 percent in profits in 1930–1931, forcing them to merge in order to stay in business.[15]

However, if jazz seemed to be dying, according to many critics and observers in the late 1920s and early 1930s, not everyone in Paris believed it. There was, in fact, much evidence to prove that jazz was far from obsolete, particularly in the dance clubs that still attracted large numbers of wealthy visitors who were not as seriously effected by the depression. "What dancing and merrymaking!" exclaimed the magazine *Femina* in 1934. "One dances at Ciro's, one dances at the Ritz, one dances everywhere . . . [and] the tediousness of depressions seems far away."[16] "Jazz" continued to be one of the generic terms for dance music in these years, and jazz bands could still find work in the dancings that survived.

Nor did the wave of articles in the press about the purported exhaustion of the new music worry many of the people who had become jazz fans during the 1920s. Instead, the partisans of jazz frequently replied to such statements with their own analyses of the situation. A *Billboard* magazine article from the United States described what it characterized as the "bankruptcy of American jazz-bands in the cabarets and other public establishments in Paris," but one of jazz's French supporters responded to that statement by saying that the situation was actually quite the opposite: although French bands struggled to find work, American bands had plenty of jobs, thus suggesting that demand for the music was still high enough to support many working jazz players from abroad.[17]

Others from the more traditional ranks of the French musical community who were also jazz aficionados also doubted the truthfulness of the claims of those predicting the music's demise. If there was a problem, for

Henry Prunières, editor of *La Revue musicale*, it was not with the music but with the way people were treating it. "There is currently a conspiracy against jazz," he charged of European music publishers, who "make much more from the pieces they record themselves than from what they import." Prunières maintained that the result was a decline in the supply of "good jazz" records rather than a decline in demand.[18] Music critic Émile Vuillermoz argued that "every morning we hear that jazz is dead. This is not correct and is, besides, not desirable." All that was disappearing, he concluded, were "the fox-trot and stereotypical tangos, the interchangeable and monotonous pieces that lack creativity."[19] And according to some observers, only the popular and showy kind of jazz was on the downturn. "The amateurs who announce the disappearance of the genre are victims of a misunderstanding," wrote music critic André Hoerée. "They are speaking of Jack Hylton or Paul Whiteman. In this respect, they are not wrong."[20]

JAZZ À LA FRANÇAISE

Even though certain kinds of jazz performances seemed to be falling from favor, a new group of French musicians was starting to take their place. By 1927, American bandleader Paul Specht had begun to notice "real European musicians of the younger class becoming more efficient in playing modern dance music of the rhythmic, syncopated style than American musicians."[21] And in the late 1920s, newly prominent names on the Paris jazz scene seemed to confirm Specht's observation. A cohort of French jazz musicians was now gaining more attention—men like André Ekyan, Stéphane Mougin, and Alix Combelle, among many others. They were young, usually in their early twenties, and had frequently, but not always, been trained at conservatories. At some point along the way, they had encountered jazz, either at a concert, on a phonograph record, or in a nightclub, and chose to devote their careers to this music.[22] They often toured around France and Europe after joining one of the many successful dance bands, making names for themselves among the most fervent aficionados of jazz, particularly when they performed solos that allowed them to showcase their individual talents. Many of these players went on to make records, lead bands, and open clubs of their own.[23] But these French players were different from the other musicians who had preceded them because of their prolonged exposure to American music. Whereas French bands in the early 1920s were composed of musicians quickly trying to learn a new style in order to remain competitive with the imported groups, these newer players had spent their adolescence in the years when jazz was thriving. They had thoroughly imbibed its rhythms in the dance halls and from records.

The first widely famous French jazz bandleader of the era was Grégor, an assimilated Armenian immigrant (whose given name was Krikor Kelekian) with a flair for dancing and theatrics, including wearing a monocle and riding around in a white limousine.[24] After playing with some earlier orchestras, Grégor brought together the best French musicians of the day in what he claimed (not necessarily accurately) was the first all-French jazz band, debuting it at the Cirque de Paris in 1927. Indeed, Grégor's skill as a bandleader lay in identifying and hiring the talented young musicians emerging in Paris, and playing in his band became a way for many French jazz musicians to meet.[25] "Grégor et ses grégoriens" performed in the orchestral jazz style of Whiteman and Hylton, and Grégor himself was an important part of the act as "mime, dancer, singer, always moving, dragging out notes from the trumpets, crying with the violin." Such behavior placed him clearly within the tradition of a bandleader like Hylton, who was also famous for his onstage antics.[26] Léo Vauchant concluded that in spite of Grégor's own lack of musical ability, he "could tell a good player from a bad one and his band were all pros."[27] Grégor's band performed in Europe and toured in South America, playing in a variety of styles including, according to one description, "Spanish, Hungarian, German, Cuban, Russian, and finally French."[28]

Although the band employed these different ways of playing, Grégor put forward his music as self-consciously French, assigning a new and distinctly national meaning to what was by then the familiar sound of jazz. "For two years," Grégor said in a 1930 interview, "we have freed ourselves from our dependence on the Americans: before we had to copy the fantasies of the boys in Charleston pants who had the public's favor all for themselves while French bands were viewed with suspicion." He asserted that his band performed a "Latin style of jazz"—rather than "American" or "nègre"—with a sound that was "more colorful, more nuanced" than that of other jazz bands, although what that actually constituted in musical terms was far from clear.[29] Music hall historian Jacques Hélian put it even more strongly when he argued that Grégor "declared open war on the Anglo-American productions that invaded France more and more."[30] Grégor et ses grégorians "hide nothing" of their Frenchness, one writer put it at the time. "They proclaim it on their huge posters."[31] When Grégor et ses grégoriens opened at the Empire music hall, according to jazz critic Hugues Panassié, the blue, white, and red music stands formed a French tricolor.[32] This nationalist twist was not always successful, however. Panassié also remembered that because the show was billed as a "French jazz band," not too many people showed up since audiences still thought that French musicians were incapable of playing jazz as well as the Americans.[33] More generally, the reception of Grégor's ensemble was mixed. Léo Vauchant, who played with Grégor at times, said that "Grégor was not really a musician. He was a good dancer."[34] A critic in the entertainment newspaper *Comœdia* remarked that "the jazz of Grégor is a very mediocre imitation of Jack Hylton's."[35] But many still recognized the significance of Grégor's band as one of the first to be proudly composed of French musicians.

Grégor was not only important as someone who brought young French jazz musicians together. He was also the founder of France's first magazine devoted to jazz. *La Revue du jazz* only lasted for eight months from its beginning in July 1929 and never found a readership outside the ranks of music professionals. But it was the first printed forum in France exclusively devoted to jazz. It thus constituted a founding institution in the French jazz community, even as it served as an advertisement for Grégor's own band. Within these pages, Grégor and other contributors proclaimed the value of French musicians, published descriptions of records and bands, and addressed professional issues for musicians, such as how to perform various styles of music. Articles by critics also began to establish standards for jazz by setting it apart from other musical forms both in terms of its actual performance and in the theory behind the music. The magazine enabled the jazz musicians who read and wrote for it to identify themselves as part of a distinct subset of the French music scene with their own particular interests. By sharing news and views about jazz, they created a community in print that they hoped would grow as more people discovered the magazine and the music.[36] In the journal's first issue, Grégor announced the need for such a publication: "In France we have been lacking a professional periodical that brings together publishers, bandleaders, and dance musicians. The Americans have 'Metronome,' the English 'Melody Maker,' the Germans 'Der Artist,' now we have, 'La Revue du Jazz.' "[37] Although *La Revue du jazz* did not last long, its impact was great. Later publications self-consciously continued to promote French musicians just as Grégor had done. The jazz press that emerged out of these early efforts soon became one of the most crucial aspects of the jazz community in helping to assign a national meaning to the music.

If Grégor was not enough proof that jazz in Paris was far from dead in the late 1920s, the success of the bandleader Ray Ventura made such a conclusion clear in the minds of many French audiences and critics. Ventura began performing in 1924 with a group of high school friends calling themselves the Collegiate Five, but the group's big break came in 1926 when they were hired to play during Easter vacation in the resort town of Deauville.[38] After a few more years of school and various musical jobs, often while his band members pursued other professions such as banking or retail trades, Ventura hit on the idea of "jazzing" songs from the French repertoire.[39] Whereas Grégor performed music that he described vaguely as being in a French or Latin style, Ventura actually performed traditional French chansons with which audiences were already familiar, such as "Sur le pont d'Avignon," "Malborough s'en va-t-en guerre," and "Frère Jacques."[40] In doing so, he did not remake jazz but rather united this modern music with a repertoire drawn from the French past in the minds of listeners. Like Grégor, Ventura was not changing jazz's musical form but its associations.

The critical response to Ventura was frequently positive. In 1930, the musical trade magazine *Jazz-Tango* described Ventura's band as "finally a French jazz under a Frenchman's direction."[41] A 1931 headline in *Candide* read, "A French Jazz: Ray Ventura," and a Marseille newspaper raved, "Finally a French jazz! with French words by French composers."[42] "Ray Ventura et ses Collégians," as his band became known, undermined the critics who had charged jazz with being a foreign sound or a music that would continue to erode the artistic traditions of France. Instead, wrote one reviewer, Ventura's music "is truly a promenade that we take through the French countryside."[43] In a 1932 public lecture, French author Gérard Bauer outlined the history of jazz. Ventura and his band performed their jazz-styled French folk songs near the end of the talk. "We must renew jazz," Bauer claimed, and Ventura's jazz was the key. "Listen to them," declared Bauer, "You will see that it is not unnatural to portray your [France's] youth in the current style."[44] Of Ventura's performance at this appearance, the entertainment trade newspaper *Comœdia* noted that he played "popular French tunes," and that "tunes from our operettas given over to the spirited and hilarious caprices of this jazz take on a new youth, a drunken spring."[45] Another account depicted the songs Ventura played as "the prettiest of our tunes, that is to say the old songs of France that are in all of our memories: Les Cloches de Nantes, Malbrough [sic], Au Clair de la Lune, etc."[46] Ventura himself seconded the idea that his work was just a new interpretation of music from deeper French traditions. Arguing that most jazz bands had long since departed from their black American roots, he maintained that "all the large jazz orchestras simply play popular music of their countries." Therefore, he concluded, "there is no reason why one cannot . . . play light French music with these same orchestral principles."[47] Ventura performed his music in the United States in 1929, where his concerts were broadcast on the radio in New York, and he wrote film scores, including one for the adaptation of Maurice Dekobra's novel *Minuit Place Pigalle* (1934), which was set among the cabarets of Montmartre.

Alongside Ventura, a number of other young musicians were also at the heart of the growing jazz community in Paris. Clarinet and trumpet player Philippe Brun began his musical career at the age of sixteen heading a small café orchestra, but he did not discover jazz until a job in Biarritz with an American band. From that time on, he learned more and more about popular music from the United States. Listening to records and other musicians, Brun became one of the best jazz players in Paris and performed with Grégor et ses grégoriens until he was stolen away by Hylton's band, much to Grégor's bitter disappointment.[48] The respected music critic Henry Prunières wrote warmly of Brun: "I did not imagine that a Frenchman could assimilate at this point the spirit and, if I may say, the poetry of jazz."[49] André Ekyan also learned his technique from listening to American records. Although trained as a dentist, Ekyan bought a saxophone and started performing in the clubs of Montparnasse and Montmartre. According to one writer, "All he lacked was what the rest of the important French musicians and composers lacked, formidable publicity."[50] Later in the 1930s, Ekyan led the orchestra at Le Bœuf sur le Toit, the early 1920s home of the avant-garde, before founding his own nightclub. Stéphane Mougin had won a prize in piano at the conservatory where he studied classical music, but he left it behind for jazz. Not only an influential player, Mougin also became one of the most important vocal advocates for the economic cause of French musicians and helped to rally them together on behalf of their common interests. Bands like the Pathé-Nathan Orchestra and Roger Berson's band further contributed to what one author called "the blossoming of such national orchestras" thanks to growing numbers of live performances and the release of recordings by French bands.[51] And many other musicians had similar stories.

As jazz musicians like these gained greater prominence during the 1930s, many French performers began to incorporate jazz into other kinds of popular music as well.[52] The composing team of Mirelle and Jean Nohain, for example, blended jazz techniques into their chansons to produce what two music hall historians called "an original synthesis between French tradition and American music."[53] Chansonnier Georges Tabet, of the team Pills et Tabet, was an enthusiastic jazz fan who performed with many French and American jazz musicians throughout the 1920s and 1930s.[54] Even more successful at combining French chansons with the spirit of jazz, if not its improvisation or blues basis, was Charles Trénet.[55] The handsome Trénet, nicknamed "the singing fool," wrote jazz-influenced chansons filled with rhythm and humor, and played with some of the rising stars of French jazz.[56] Trénet had been directly influenced by jazz records in his youth while living in Germany with his mother. Back in Paris by the early 1930s, he came to know most of the Parisian musical and artistic avant-garde through his visits to places like La Coupole and Le Bœuf sur le Toit, with their jazz-infused atmospheres.[57] Also in the early 1930s, Trénet began writing songs and singing with Johnny Hess in the duo Charles et Johnny at various music halls around Paris. Hess had been playing at the College Inn, a club that many U.S. and French jazz musicians visited, and the influence of the music came through in the melodies he wrote.[58] When Trénet went into the military, Hess pursued a solo career and sang such jazzy hits as "Je Suis Swing" (1938) in the midst of the popularity of American swing music in the later 1930s.[59] "Swing is not a melody/Swing is not a malady," the lyrics went. "But as soon as it pleases you/It grabs you and won't let go."[60] "For me," Hess said in an interview later in life, "music was—and is always—that of Duke Ellington, Eddy South, Arthur Brigg [*sic*] and Earl Hines, and the word 'swing' was synonymous with music."[61]

As the French jazz community grew and strengthened in the late 1920s and early 1930s, a new periodical replaced Grégor's ill-fated *La Revue du jazz*. Begun in October 1930, *Jazz-Tango* (for a while called *Jazz-Tango-Dancing*) became the primary publication for French dance bands, providing them with a constant source of news and reviews along with a forum in which to discuss professional issues.[62] Drawing on the writing talents of musicians and young jazz critics, the magazine was quickly filled with profiles of French players, reviews of shows and records, articles on the techniques of jazz performance, and philosophical statements about jazz and its musical merits. *Jazz-Tango* informed its readers about jazz within France and around the world, offered advertisements for musical instruments and bands seeking work, provided reissues of older records and a service for finding rare discs, and reviewed (the few) books on jazz. As the title suggested, the editors did not perceive jazz to be entirely different from other kinds of dance music, like the popular tango. Since bands were often expected to play all sorts of dance tunes at a performance, especially at a dancing, everyone could benefit from the periodical's broader coverage. But the magazine had another agenda too. In its first issue, the editors announced their specific intentions to promote French musicians to the public, introduce young French musicians and composers to jazz, and keep readers current on musical developments in France. Like Grégor's earlier publication, the names in *Jazz-Tango*'s pages also gave readers a way to begin identifying the important French jazz musicians as part of a distinct community.

Like *La Revue du jazz*, *Jazz-Tango* disseminated information about jazz, excited a passion for the music, and offered readers a means of claiming an identity as French jazz fans. But beyond these concerns, the editors hoped to use the pages of *Jazz-Tango* to unite French dance musicians into a self-conscious labor lobby—to be "the organ of the defense of Dance Musicians," as they put it.[63] The years during which this magazine lasted (1930–1936) were not easy ones for France and its musicians as the effects of the depression created unemployment as well as economic uncertainty. Musicians in particular were faced with both the problems of declining numbers in the audience who could afford an evening's entertainment and the competition from foreign bands; the latter was always a problem, but now more than ever. For its readers, *Jazz-Tango* soon became a forum in which to offer suggestions about how to deal with the tough times in the music business and come together on economic issues. And it gave performers a place to rally as French people with a particular national interest, as we will see in the next chapter.

The late 1920s and early 1930s were the years when a new, self-consciously French jazz community emerged in Paris. Musicians fashioned for themselves an identity not simply as jazz players but as French jazz players—no longer the contradiction that such a notion had seemed in the early 1920s when jazz was thought to be unquestionably foreign. These musicians demonstrated the continuing ability of French artists in the interwar era to absorb elements of other cultures and make those expressions their own. They wanted audiences to realize that French musicians could play just as well as the foreign bands that had been so popular in Paris since the end of the Great War. They removed many (if not all) of the associations of jazz with the United States and Africa, replacing them with connections to France. Players like Ventura rooted the interpretations of jazz in the French tradition by performing chansons that were part of an older French musical repertoire. Many others reinvented the chanson format by bringing jazzy musical elements to it. Doing so gave something of a nostalgic twist to a music that so many critics had charged with being a modernist assault on French culture. But such nostalgia was not for a purely traditional France. Rather, these performances suggested that what was perceived to be an authentically French music need not die with the modern age of jazz, nor did it necessarily emerge only from the French soil itself. Instead, it could be recovered and repackaged to younger audiences in the style of the day. The past and present could be combined to express the best elements of both.

Bringing jazz into the French repertoire ran counter to much of the cultural and economic isolationism of the 1930s. Many in France perceived foreign influences to be an even greater threat than they had been in the 1920s. Now the need for jobs was more imperative, and new U.S. imports were still replacing French products on store shelves. Some people responded by attempting to cultivate a stronger sense of duty to France in order to offset the effects of the depression. The press, for example, urged shoppers to buy French goods to protect both the French economy and France's artisan culture. The women's magazine *Femina* linked a sense of fashion with civic responsibility when it asked readers not to "wear old dresses, [but to] buy new ones and buy French: buying French proves not just patriotism, but good taste."[64] In response to the Americanized bars and cafés of the 1920s that prominently featured jazz, some new establishments reminiscent of the late-nineteenth-century Montmartre cabarets like the Chat Noir opened their doors for business. "The dancing is dead," reported one newspaper, "and, on its ashes, appears a new genre of cabaret-restaurant, a *cabaret-chantant*, the 'French cabaret'."[65] In mass culture too, particularly the film industry, many critics and policy makers attempted to determine the national characteristics of French film as a way of combating the U.S. influence. Responding to intellectuals' calls for action, the government established a commission to study the film industry and attempted to negotiate an acceptable ratio of French to American films.[66] In other words, many people argued that cultural expressions of France, whether in dress, film, or musical entertainment, emanated exclusively from France's own soil.

Rather than a primarily negative reaction, however, such as tariffs, quotas, or restrictions designed to exclude foreign imports, the responses of French jazz musicians and fans were more frequently positive and creative. Amid the xenophobia of the interwar years, French jazz musicians illustrated a more open side of French culture. Although they sometimes did seek to keep foreign musicians out of Paris, French players introduced a new national interpretation of jazz to French ears as a way of coping with the challenges of the day, instead of attempting to eliminate jazz altogether.

As these musicians show, the emerging jazz community formed in part as a defense against foreign influences even while retaining ties to musicians elsewhere in Europe and the United States and looking outside France for musical inspiration. Indeed, many jazz figures central to this story were immigrants—Grégor, Django Reinhardt, Stéphane Grappelli—and thus outside many traditional views of what it meant to be French. By keeping international connections strong, Parisian musicians revealed something about the ambivalent relationship of French and foreign cultures in the interwar period. Unlike many integral nationalists in the 1930s, they largely rejected the fear of those listeners who believed that France was being swept away by an invading and degenerate music. At the same time, they did worry about the continuing influx of foreign musicians and often tried to remove certain foreign elements by emphasizing, for example, a Latin style of jazz or rooting jazz in the more familiar chanson tradition. Retreating from total xenophobia, they may not have completely embraced cosmopolitanism. But they did manage to blend French and foreign music to retain the best qualities of both. French jazz musicians saw their music operating in two different, but completely intertwined contexts: in France and around the world. Jazz spread internationally from its earlier days thanks to technology—like records, radio, and film—bands that toured, and a burgeoning jazz press that promoted the music in its own publications. Yet it was simultaneously being shaped into particular national expressions.

The cakewalk, a style of African American dance, became popular in the United States and France during the late nineteenth and early twentieth centuries. Many historians see it as a precursor of the dancing that accompanied jazz. Courtesy of Getty Images.

(*Below*) African American musicians performing in the nightclub La Boull Blanche, circa 1930. Courtesy of Getty Images.

A French banjoist and an American drummer playing together in a Parisian club, 1929. The banjo was a common instrument in early jazz music. Courtesy of Bettmann/CORBIS.

(*Below*) Patrons had to dress well to visit the famous Montmartre nightclub Zelli's in 1929. Courtesy of Bettmann/CORBIS.

To many Parisians, jazz fit in well with the flashy spectacle of the music halls of lower Montmartre, such as Le Moulin Rouge in 1929. (*Below*) Jack Hylton and His Boys in 1931. This orchestra of white musicians, and many others like it, performed in music halls throughout Paris during the 1920s and 1930s. Both images courtesy of Getty Images.

(*Above*) The Quintet of the Hot Club of France in 1934, featuring Stéphane Grappelli on violin (far left) and Django Reinhardt on guitar (center). Courtesy of Bettmann/CORBIS.

(*Right*) A poster for a 1934 concert by the Quintet of the Hot Club of France in L'Ecole Normale de Musique, where the Hot Club de France sponsored many concerts during the late 1930s. Courtesy of Christian Senn.

Administration de Concerts A. et M. DANDELOT, 83, Rue d'Amsterdam

SALLE DES CONCERTS DE L'ECOLE NORMALE DE MUSIQUE
78, Rue Cardinet *(Métro Malesherbes)*

Dimanche 2 Décembre 1934, *à 10 HEURES PRÉCISES DU MATIN*

LE HOT CLUB DE FRANCE

présentera un orchestre d'un genre nouveau de

JAZZ HOT

Jungo **REINHARDT**   Roger **CHAPUT**
Guitare   Guitare

Joseph **REINHARDT**   **VOLA**
Guitare   Contrebasse

Stephane **GRAPELLY**
Violon

avec le concours de

J. **CAHAN**   M. **MOUFLARD**
Pianiste   Trompette

BILLY TAYLOR
Batterie

et deux des meilleurs saxophonistes actuellement à Paris

PRIX DES PLACES (tous droits compris)

Fauteuil : 12 fr. — Étudiants : 10 fr. — Membres du Hot Club : 8 fr.

LOCATION : à l'ÉCOLE NORMALE DE MUSIQUE, 114, bis, Boulevard Malesherbes - chez DURAND, 4, Place de la Madeleine - chez MM. ESCHIG, SENART, ROUART-LEROLLE, à la BOITE A MUSIQUE, 133, Boulevard Raspail ;et à l'Administration de Concerts A. et M. DANDELOT, 83, Rue d'Amsterdam, (tél. ligne spéciale) Trinité 31, 34.

DISQUES SWING

25 c/m - **25**^{FRS}

COLEMAN HAWKINS & HIS
ALL STAR " JAM " BAND

COLEMAN HAWKINS and ALIX COMBELLE (saxophones ténor),
BENNY CARTER et ANDRE EKYAN (saxophones alto), STEPHANE
GRAPPELLY (piano), DJANGO REINHARDT (guitare), D'HELLEMMES
(contrebasse), TOMMY BENFORD (batterie).

SW **1** HONEYSUCKLE ROSE
CRAZY RHYTHM

Pour la première fois dans l'histoire du jazz, un disque, au lieu de grouper
des vedettes jouant d'instruments différents, réunit quatre des plus grands
saxophonistes du monde, deux noirs et deux Français. Cette formule nouvelle
donne des exécutions entièrement différentes de tout ce qu'on a entendu
jusqu'à présent. Dans *Crazy rhythm*, Ekyan, Combelle, Benny Carter et
Hawkins dans l'ordre, improvisent chacun un solo, de telle sorte que l'auditeur pourra comparer le style de ces merveilleux musiciens. *Honeysuckle
rose* met en valeur la richesse et la plénitude sonore du quatuor dans les
ensembles arrangés par Benny Carter, et donne l'occasion d'entendre une
des plus géniales improvisations d'Hawkins.

QUINTETTE DU HOT
CLUB DE FRANCE

DJANGO REINHARDT (guitare - solo), STEPHANE GRAPPELLY
(violon), MARCEL BIANCHI et PIERRE FERRET (guitares), LOUIS
VOLA (contrebasse).

SW **2** CHICAGO
CHARLESTON

La réputation du Quintette du Hot Club de France n'est plus à faire.
C'est le seul orchestre « hot » européen qui ait forcé l'admiration du pays
du jazz, l'Amérique. Il n'est pas téméraire d'avancer que *Chicago* et
Charleston sont deux des plus beaux enregistrements de ce groupement,
tellement les improvisations de Grappelly au violon et de Django Reinhardt
à la guitare débordent des idées les plus riches et originales.

The first Swing Records catalog, 1937.
The label, founded by Charles Delaunay
and Hugues Panassié, placed recordings
by U.S. and French performers on
equal terms and often had them playing
together on the same record.
Courtesy of the Institute for Jazz Studies,
Rutgers University, New Jersey.

DICKY WELLS & HIS ORCHESTRA

DICKY WELLS (trombone), BILL DILLARD et SHAD COLLINS (trompettes), HOWARD JOHNSON (saxophones alto), SAM ALLEN (piano), ROGER CHAPUT (guitare), BILL BEASON (batterie).

SW **3** HOT CLUB BLUES
I'VE FOUND A NEW BABY

        Dicky Wells et les musiciens qui jouent avec lui dans ce disque, à l'exception de Chaput, sont les principaux solistes de l'orchestre Teddy Hill, qui a cet été à Paris accompagné au Moulin-Rouge la revue du Cotton Club. — *Hot Club Blues* est un de ces « blues » si caractéristiques de l'âme noire, chacun des musiciens exprimant sa nostalgie dans un solo déchirant.

ANDRÉ EKYAN

(solos de saxophone alto, accompagnés à la guitare par **DJANGO REINHARDT**).

SW **4** TIGER RAG
PENNIES FROM HEAVEN

        André Ekyan est considéré à juste titre comme le meilleur saxophoniste alto de jazz français. Ce disque met admirablement en valeur son extraordinaire technique, sa sonorité ravissante et son aisance dans l'improvisation qui le rendent comparable aux plus grands spécialistes américains. L'accompagnement du célèbre guitariste Django Reinhardt est d'un swing et d'une plénitude inouïs.

TEDDY WEATHERFORD

(solos de piano)

SW **5** TEA FOR TWO
WEATHER BEATEN BLUES

        Teddy Weatherford est considéré comme le plus grand des pianistes de jazz avec Fats Waller et Earl Hines. Sa puissance et son « swing » sont insurpassables. Sa version du fameux *Tea for two* est extrêmement originale et son *Weather Beaten Blues* donne une idée de la forme à la fois la plus primitive et la plus pure du jazz, enrichie par l'apport créateur personnel d'un grand artiste.

(Textes de Hugues PANASSIE)

Hugues Panassié (lower left) listening
worshipfully to an African American
band during his 1938 visit to New York.
Courtesy of Charles Peterson/Timepix.

7

NEW

BANDS

AND

NEW

TENSIONS

Jazz and the Labor Problem

French bands like Ventura's, Grégor's, and others confronted the cultural dispute over jazz's foreign origins by replacing a supposedly black American jazz with what they believed to be a French or Latin style. Meanwhile, other musicians grappled with a different issue: the threat that jazz posed to French musicians' jobs. To many French performers throughout the interwar era, the problem of jazz as a foreign music had more to do with the players who came from abroad and took their jobs than it did with jazz's challenges to French civilization. Ventura and Grégor were quite popular, but theirs was a success that not every French musician achieved. Even amid the 1920s dance craze, some players protested against what they saw as a potent threat to their wallets. By the late 1920s, and especially the depression era of the 1930s, the process of transforming jazz into something French became a necessity in order for many French musicians to reassert their economic interests.

LABOR TENSIONS IN THE 1920s

Ever since jazz's arrival, it had caused a certain amount of economic resentment among French musicians. Eager theater owners, who wanted to draw in larger audiences in order to pay the hefty entertainment taxes, turned to U.S. musicians to fill seats. Furthermore, because Americans did not always belong to French musicians' unions, club and theater owners could bypass any problems that might ensue from such an affiliation. Precisely because of these two facts of the postwar political economy, jazz had always threatened to take jobs away from French musicians. The persistent belief among many Parisian audiences throughout the 1920s that the French simply were unable to play jazz not only increased the demand for American players but also heightened the sensitivity of French musicians to the presence of foreigners in their jobs. "In most of the nightclubs, French musicians are totally banned," complained the head of the Parisian musicians' union, the Chambre Syndicale des Artistes Musiciens de Paris, undoubtedly with more than a bit of hyperbole. "The owners maintain that their clientele will only accept foreign orchestras. This may be true, but perhaps the clientele does not consider the disastrous consequences of its taste for exoticism." Those consequences, he and many others argued, were unemployed French musicians.[1]

From the start, however, French musicians were not satisfied with what they believed to be this aesthetic misjudgment on the part of audiences and its impact on their pocketbooks. In 1924, the Chambre Syndicale struck over the issue of wages and the rights of musicians to take up a collection from audience members as a way to supplement their regular pay. According to a report in the files of the Paris police, one source of the dispute was the fact that "foreign artists, for the most part *les noirs*, receive 120 francs to 150 francs per night and sometimes more, but the French musicians . . . only receive 25 francs."[2] Also in 1924, protests by French musicians moved Paris police to take away all the working papers of between twenty and thirty American jazz players, except for their passports, and to issue a deadline for their leaving the country. As the *New York Times* reported, "Once or twice before there has been a protest from French musicians against the presence in Paris of foreign players," but such earlier problems were resolved because in the midst of a dance craze there was enough work for everyone. "French directors of the dancing clubs admit tonight," continued the article, "that without the American jazz musicians they will not be able to do so much business" since audiences greatly preferred the Americans to any French musicians labeling themselves a jazz band.[3] By 1929, composers called on radio stations to play only French music since, as one press account of their demands put it, "in the dancings, as in our broadcast studios, one hardly hears anything but Anglo-Saxon music!"[4]

Protesters often cited a Parisian municipal law stating that no more than 10 percent of musicians on stage could be foreigners. Outside Paris, the 10 percent law did not apply, though, and in some of the resort towns the problem of foreign musicians could be worse. One 1929 article told the story of U.S. and British students who came to France to study the language or vacation for the summer. They paid their way, according to the report, by playing jazz in tourist havens like Deauville, thereby taking away jobs from French musicians.[5] In 1926, the head of the musicians' union wrote to the minister of the interior to explain why musicians were on strike in Nice and ask for his intervention. Foreign bands were taking the jobs at southern casinos, he contended, thereby supplanting Parisian musicians who usually went there for the season. "The intense unemployment in our corporation threatens to get worse every day," he remarked. The union's members demanded to know "whether they would be condemned to death by hunger while foreigners received jobs even better than those they asked for."[6]

The sources of friction among jazz musicians went beyond nightclub performances, but the problem of foreign musicians was also bigger than jazz. The Opéra group of the Syndicate of Lyrical Artists, for example, had protested in 1920 that the number of foreign singers on the stages of state-funded theaters was exceeding the designated maximum.[7] Meanwhile, French composers sought to cap foreign music by arguing that because of "the dropping royalties collected for French song writers and composers . . . programs be limited to five per cent [sic] of foreign music, not including the works of foreign composers who may have resided in France for the past ten years."[8]

Musicians in France were not alone in their concerns. Other countries in Europe also experienced a growing interest in American music after the war, with a resulting influx of players from the United States who posed a challenge to their musicians too. The response in several European countries was to erect barriers to the immigration of American musicians because of fears about foreigners taking away the jobs of native performers.[9] When Whiteman arrived in England for the first time in 1923, for instance, a representative of the Labour Ministry met him and his band only to inform them that they could not perform because they did not have working papers. Whiteman was only allowed to play when the nightclub that had brought him across the Atlantic agreed to hire an equal number of British musicians for the show and pay them the same wages as the Americans.[10] Similarly, in 1924, angry German musicians persuaded the police to try and find reasons for deporting U.S. and English bands playing jazz because the German public demanded the foreign artists over native ones.[11]

Other such cases revealed the widespread desire of each nation to keep their own entertainers employed. "Free trade in jazz is the battle cry," remarked a *New York Times* article in 1926 of the larger, European-wide problem, "with a wall against syncopating immigrants as the alternative."[12]

LABOR TENSIONS IN THE 1930s

Although foreign players were always a source of tension between U.S. and French musicians, protests against them gained renewed significance and intensity by the 1930s as France slid into a depression. Proceeding more slowly than elsewhere in Europe, the depression did not have the same dramatic impact in France as in other countries. But the years of economic downturn clearly heightened the tensions that ran throughout the economy, such as a nationwide conflict over immigrant labor that had been partially masked by a preceding period of stability and prosperity. In the industrial sector of the economy during the 1930s, many French workers came to resent the foreign laborers who had helped to rebuild the country after the Great War. Calls for limiting and regulating immigrant labor poured into government offices from workers and labor leaders hoping to stem what seemed to be a tide of job loss for the French.[13] Even middle-class professionals like doctors and lawyers worked to guard their talents from foreign competition.[14]

French musicians believed that they could make a particularly strong case against foreign labor. The government had regulated industrial workers and directed them toward the economic activities that needed the most help during the 1920s.[15] By contrast, musicians argued that their trade had been far less regulated at the beginning of the interwar period and that the few limitations that existed on foreign performers had been poorly enforced. "The protective legislation has nothing to offer French musicians," the Paris musicians' union asserted, and it continually worked for greater regulation of foreign labor throughout the interwar years.[16] French musicians frequently earned less than their foreign counterparts, and the higher wages for American bands did not necessarily raise the standard pay scale for all musicians.

Important, too, was the vulnerability of entertainment in Paris to the condition of the international economy since it largely relied on audience members from around the world with the resources to travel. During the course of the 1930s, the French tourist trade that had sustained much of the entertainment business shrank, having been damaged by the falling value of the franc. Between 1929 and 1933, income from tourism fell from 9.6 billion to 4.3 billion francs and remained below 3 billion for the rest of the era.[17] The 1931 Colonial Exposition provided work for many musicians to entertain the tourists in Paris, but it was only a temporary respite. When the event was finished, many musicians returned to being unemployed.[18] And even though many American musicians had gone home with the advent of tougher economic times, some chose to remain in France and others continued to visit from abroad. The result for French musicians was a persistent competition for a shrinking number of jobs—and a growing frustration.

The journal of the Parisian musicians' union, *L'Artiste musicien de Paris*, recorded the ways in which many musicians viewed their profession during these years of crisis, and it offers insights into how they responded throughout the era. Indeed, the main problem for Parisian musicians was, according to *L'Artiste musicien*, the presence of outsiders taking their jobs, both from abroad and elsewhere within France. Throughout the 1920s and 1930s, the journal regularly ran an announcement warning musicians from the provinces to stay away from Paris when looking for work so as not to aggravate unemployment in the capital. To limit the number of non-French musicians at work, the musicians' union itself had stopped admitting foreign members by the early 1930s. It also urged its members to report any instances of foreigners performing in violation of labor regulations to the secretary general and to give "their names, addresses, the instruments they play, and to add if they are singing in foreign languages."[19] The union forbade its members to perform in any venue that habitually employed too many foreigners.[20] In addition, it reminded members of the limitations on foreign musicians: 10 percent of an orchestra, later 5 percent or a minimum of five French performers for small bands.[21] Some jazz clubs got around the laws by hiring French musicians who sat in the audience or next to the bandstand while the Americans actually performed, although this was an old trick that had been used in the early 1920s too. *L'Artiste musicien* frequently informed readers of the number of unemployed during this period, however the accuracy of such statistics is impossible to assess. Reports ranged in February 1932 from five hundred to two thousand unemployed depending on the source; the secretary general of the union himself suggested about one thousand.[22] By 1935, another account noted that 25 percent of the five thousand unionized musicians were unemployed.[23]

Musicians had openly protested foreign players at work in Paris in the

1920s, and by 1931 they were doing so again. Reprinting favorable articles from other Parisian daily newspapers, *L'Artiste musicien* offered its readers sympathetic accounts of unemployed musicians who challenged establishments that employed non-French performers. "A group of two hundred unemployed French musicians met Friday evening in a café on the Boulevard des Italiens to protest against an establishment that only hired orchestras composed of foreigners," began one article. The "firm but calm" demonstration extracted a promise from the café owner to hire more French artists in the future.[24] In other cases, according to *L'Artiste musicien*, the foreign bands fled at the sight of the arriving French protesters. The always favorable reports of such action typically described the protesters as peaceful and orderly. Nevertheless, audiences were sometimes shocked by these protests as well as the arrival of the police who were called in to intervene.[25]

If work at home seemed scarce, it was also hard to find outside of France. "We are not driven by a narrowly nationalist spirit," according to one account of a speech given at a protest in Paris. "But there are thousands of unemployed French musicians and the doors of other countries are closed."[26] The head of the musicians' union defended the protests occurring in Paris in part as a reaction to the closing of other countries to French musicians.[27] Indeed, the French did experience problems similar to those of American musicians in getting into other countries—not surprising given the common desire to protect the entertainment industry along national lines, but certainly ironic given their advocacy for the same kind of regulation at home. In 1931, *L'Artiste musicien* reported, for example, that five French musicians planning to participate in a chamber music concert were not allowed to disembark at Newcastle because of the British government's labor regulations.[28]

Although all kinds of musicians suffered from these problems—as *L'Artiste musicien* indicated, since it rarely mentioned jazz specifically—jobs for jazz bands presented a visible battleground for the struggle between employed foreigners and unemployed French people because jazz musicians were especially aware of the number of foreigners in their midst. According to jazz musician Maurice Bedouc-Ennouchy, in 1931 those "who had until now not wanted to see the danger of the mass introduction of foreign musicians are beginning to react passionately."[29] Two surveys that he conducted of Parisian nightclubs and music halls provided startling statistics to the readers of *Jazz-Tango*. In November 1931, the 46 foreign orchestras he examined employed only 41 French musicians compared to 236 foreigners. The figures had gotten worse by December 1931, with only 21 French musicians compared to 246 foreign ones working in 47 foreign orchestras. The number of foreign musicians remained relatively stable, in other words, while the number of French musicians was dropping precipitously. Furthermore, Bedouc-Ennouchy noted, French orchestras were much more generous in employing foreigners than the foreign bands were in hiring the French.[30] Verification of such statistics is impossible since Bedouc-Ennouchy did not indicate which bands or performance venues he surveyed, and one cannot be sure that his efforts were exhaustive. Nevertheless, the accuracy of his numbers is not necessarily as important as the perception of a crisis that they both reflected and helped to perpetuate. Bedouc-Ennouchy also charged that the laws regulating foreign labor and requiring a work permit were not being followed. For example, when a labor inspector challenged a pianist at a club on the rue Pigalle, Bedouc-Ennouchy wrote sarcastically, the pianist "told him that his papers were in order, [but] that he had forgotten his papers . . . , [and] the inspector goes away with a clear conscience, probably makes an optimistic report to his boss, and waits for the end of the year to receive his bonus."[31] There were instances when the authorities took action, however. A *Jazz-Tango* correspondent in Marseilles reported in February 1931 about a crackdown by local authorities on musicians working under tourist permits. The foreigners were forced to pay a special tax and have their permits renewed on a regular basis.[32]

The most common response of French musicians to the threat of foreign labor was a call for regulation. Many advocated limits, or sometimes outright bans, on foreign bands. Musician Louis Dor offered the suggestion that "in the current state of crisis that one finds oneself in, one of the first steps to take is to dismiss bad foreign musicians."[33] In response to a running column in *Jazz-Tango* that asked musicians from all nations, "Should we ask our respective governments to close the border to our foreign colleagues?" pianist Stéphane Mougin replied, "Without a doubt, we must stop foreign musicians who flood into France in order to protect ourselves immediately." Only governments had the power, Mougin argued, to confront problems with the international distribution of labor, "which refers not only to one country, but to a community of countries."[34] Not everyone believed that erecting barriers to musicians would solve the problem. One Belgian musician writing in *Jazz-Tango* argued that such obstacles to the freedom of movement would "aggravate the situation." "I repeat," he implored, "it is urgent to find a solution that is equitable for everyone."[35]

But his was a lonely voice since some kind of limit made sense to most others, and musicians' unions continued to lobby for just such a change.

On further reflection, many musicians realized that the presence of foreigners was only part of the problem. Much of the need for change lay in audiences' demands and their perceptions about what made a good jazz band. Mougin identified the popular preference for black Americans, simply because of their race, as a major obstacle for French musicians. He denounced this "Négromanie" in a few *Jazz-Tango* articles because "by a curious destiny, skin color assured a musician, even a bad one, greater respect than if he were born white."[36] The issue of quality, Mougin made sure to point out, was at the center of his argument. He was not attacking black musicians for being black but rather *bad* black musicians who got jobs because French audiences thought their music would automatically be better than any white musician's, including a French one.[37] Yet the suggestion that there was such a thing as a bad black musician was significant. Throughout the 1920s, African American musicians were revered in many jazz circles because being black was what supposedly enabled them to play jazz well, in part because of rhythmic abilities believed to be derived from African ancestors. Some observers had already begun to move away from a direct connection between music and race. As we have seen, Ventura observed that most jazz had, in practice, become detached from its African American roots, and he hinted at a separation between race and musical style. Music halls had also frequently lessened the racial aspect of jazz by presenting white jazz bands. But Mougin's remarks constituted one of the first sustained and thoughtful arguments to separate the discussion of jazz music from the race of the performer, and these comments were especially important having come from someone as well-known among French players as Mougin. Once the separation of jazz music and race was made in the audience's mind, Mougin maintained, French musicians could more easily find work because audiences would more readily listen to French musicians.

Although foreign musicians appeared to be the most significant problem that French jazzmen faced, other factors made unemployment worse as the depression deepened. The high taxes on entertainment that had persisted since the days of the Great War now seemed to be shrinking audiences further and taking money out of musicians' pockets. *L'Artiste musicien* reported ongoing lobbying efforts to have those taxes changed, though with little effect. Even more crucial were musicians' outcries against mechanical music, the label used to describe the expanding technology of record players, radio, and beginning the late 1920s, sound film. The Chambre Syndicale des Artistes Musiciens de Paris forbade its members from playing in any venue where a radio was regularly used.[38] In 1930, another union, the Syndicat des Musiciens de la Région Parisienne, circulated a tract calling on audience members to refrain from patronizing any place that used phonographs because it went against "real and living music." Such devices were "a decay of the musical arts, [and] French culture," the union contended, and it instructed members to resist this form of Americanization.[39]

The French had relied on mechanical music, phonograph records in particular, to learn jazz and other kinds of dance music in the first place. But throughout the 1920s and especially by the early 1930s, many musicians held that as much as mechanical music had done to spread jazz, it was reducing the size of audiences that might come out in the evening to hear a French jazz band because it provided an alternative to live music. Records and radios were simple to use and increasingly available in France; the French listened to a million radios by 1932 and five million by 1939 as prices continued to fall.[40] As technology improved by the 1930s, moreover, radio stations became able to play records and eliminated the need for live bands, which might normally find work on the airwaves.[41] The problem became worse as record companies often supplied new releases to radio stations free of charge.[42] Sound film in particular ravaged the orchestra business and put thousands of Parisian musicians out of a job because bands were no longer needed to provide the accompaniment to silent films. Musicians in the United States faced this problem as well; within three years of the release of *The Jazz Singer* (1927), some 22,000 musicians were out of work.[43] "The financial benefit to theater directors," Mougin claimed that these businessmen had concluded, "was real, why not profit?" Sound film "threw hundreds of musicians, whose lot is becoming more uncertain, into the streets," Mougin asserted.[44] And as Mougin reminded his colleagues, any collective action taken by musicians would have to operate within these realities of the music business. Mechanical music, for him, was "nothing but the result of modern industrialization," but the union that should be protecting the interests of musicians was not succeeding because this industrialized popular musical production had divided musicians into two groups: those interested in preserving their art and those willing to please the public "according to the popular fashion."[45] "We are slaves to public tastes," he declared; musicians were limited by the demands of audiences regardless of whether they were unionized.[46]

For all the discussion of problems and crises—whether foreigners, taxes, or mechanical music—the central theme uniting the many proposed solutions to the issues of unemployment, especially in the journal *Jazz-Tango*, was overwhelmingly the promotion of French musicians as talented jazz players. Unable to stop the growth of mechanical music and ineffective in protesting against foreign musicians, French jazz players wanted to let audiences know that they could, in fact, play jazz and other kinds of dance music just as well as any band. Maurice Bedouc-Ennouchy wondered why in people's minds, "a Pole, an Italian, a Czech, even a Spaniard, plays an 'Argentine' tango better than a Frenchman?"[47] One observer praised the abilities of French bands by saying, "It is hard to find foreign musicians who can do what French musicians can: adapt to all necessities."[48] In this self-promotional effort, Mougin encouraged jazz musicians to rally to *Jazz-Tango* as the only journal concerned with promoting their interests and working to spread jazz music as something the French could play.[49]

Foreign musicians hold an ambiguous place in the history of jazz in France. They were the original sources of the music and remained the inspiration for many French players. People listened to records from the United States, frequently with great care, in order to glean as much from them as possible. When many of the most famous American musicians visited Paris, they were treated with great fanfare by a growing number of jazz aficionados. But at a moment of economic crisis, foreigners were often as much a threat to French musicians' material interests as they were a boon to their musical fascination.

Mougin and others did propose schemes to restrict and exclude American musicians, and their words did sometimes sound like those of the more xenophobic nationalists of the era who stirred up feelings against foreigners. But French jazz musicians who called for such restrictions limited themselves to speaking of foreign musicians in tough economic times. Cultural nationalists of the interwar era had identified jazz as a threat to France because of its foreignness, primitiveness, and modernity, seeking to remove it from French musical life altogether. By contrast, many French musicians appreciated jazz even though they preferred that the Americans who created it would remain at home. But they did not hope to exclude jazz from France altogether. Instead, they continued to welcome this music so that they could perform it themselves and reap the financial rewards of its popularity. Jazz itself did not constitute a grave economic threat to their interests. It actually offered the possibility of monetary reward given its popularity, but only if detached from its roots and performed by French musicians themselves. In the midst of the cultural nationalism of the 1930s, jazz musicians rejected excluding jazz as a threat to French culture and saw it as a way to save their jobs. Throughout this period in which *L'Artiste musicien* reported on the crises of French musicians, for example, it never stopped advertising the sale of jazz instruments or sheet music for American songs to its readers. Jazz as a musical form was certainly not dead, nor did it have to be foreign, these musicians were arguing. Rather, it needed to become French.

8

THE

DISCOVERY

OF HOT JAZZ

Most of the French bands of the late 1920s followed in the orchestral or symphonic tradition established by Whiteman and Hylton. Individual players within these bands were allowed to take wilder and more spontaneous solos, but as a whole, their sound was the lighter one designed to appeal to a broader audience's tastes. Their main difference from Whiteman and Hylton was their use of French musicians, and in Ventura's case, the performance of French chansons. But during the 1930s, many French musicians and a growing number of listeners also began to discover "hot" jazz, the spirited, improvisational music associated with Louis Armstrong and other black American, New Orleans–style players. The arrival of hot jazz divided the French jazz community into fans of symphonic jazz and fans of hot music. It also created additional tensions between musicians since hot aficionados were now actively promoting a new group of American players at the same time that many French musicians were hoping to restrict foreigners for economic reasons.

In spite of these conflicts, however, the story of France's discovery of hot jazz reveals another twist in the process by which jazz music became a part of the French musical and cultural repertoire. Those who loved it were especially impressed with its supposed blackness—a seeming retreat from the kind of adaptation that Ventura, Grégor, and others had brought about by modifying the racial connotations of jazz. Hot fans reemphasized the African American origins of jazz music at a time when white musicians were more clearly in vogue. Yet as many did with orchestral jazz, hot proponents also advocated its being played by French musicians, arguing that they could and must learn to perform in a black style in order to create what the critic and chief propagandist of hot music in France, Hugues Panassié, called "real jazz." Going even further, Panassié linked the sound of hot jazz with a tradition of French popular culture that he believed was dying in the modern age. For him, some of the racial qualities of hot jazz revived an image of an older, more traditional France. Hot jazz, it seemed to him and others, was not so foreign after all.

LE JAZZ HOT

By the time that hot music came to France, it had been flourishing in the United States for several years. Hot New Orleans musicians like Jelly Roll Morton and King Oliver had begun playing in the late 1910s and early 1920s. Oliver's band was where Armstrong had first honed his skills. The original hot style was a kind of group improvisation with no particular instrument taking the lead. Instead, each musician blended into the overall uproar. As the jazz historian Ted Gioia has described the hot sound:

> The most characteristic moment in these recordings of early jazz takes place when the lead instruments, usually cornet, clarinet, and trombone, engage in spontaneous counterpoint. The trombone takes over the low register, providing a deep, deliberate bass melody; the clarinet plays more complex figures, often consisting of arpeggios or other rapidly fingered patterns; the cornet moves mostly within the middle register, playing less elaborate melodies than the clarinet, but pushing the ensemble forward with propulsive, swinging lead lines.[1]

The musicians who perfected this brand of music began to spread it throughout the United States in the 1920s when they, like many African Americans during this period, left the South and moved northward in search of better economic opportunities. Some began to refine and emphasize their solo skills so that they would be memorable to audiences and club managers in the competitive atmosphere of the South Side Chicago nightclubs where they frequently played.[2] Soon, other schools of jazz emerged that were based in part on the New Orleans sound, like the "Chicago jazz" of the white players Bix Beiderbecke, Jimmy MacPartland, and others.[3] Musicians themselves used the term *hot* to describe this kind of spontaneous music as, for example, Armstrong would do in his famous Chicago recordings of the later 1920s, *The Hot Fives* and *The Hot Sevens*, or in the song title "Hotter Than That."

The basis of a hot performance was improvisation, in which musicians played around a composed melody while adding their own unique twists and turns—what bandleader Whiteman had derided as mere "faking." Whereas two "straight" performances of the same piece would bear a striking similarity to one another because musicians respected the written notes, two hot performances would be remarkably dissimilar since the musicians improvised on the melody differently each time. Drawing on this distinction stressed by American jazz musicians, many fans in France repeated the notion that there were two kinds of jazz performance: straight and hot. To play straight meant to play notes just as they were written in the musical text, faithful to the melody and harmony that the composer had intended. To play hot, though, according to an author in *Jazz-Tango*, meant "to interpret a melody according to its own idea, that is to invent a variation on this melody respecting the rhythmic base and harmony."[4]

Despite its growing popularity in the United States throughout the 1920s, hot jazz was not really well known in France as a distinct kind of jazz until the late 1920s. Writing in February 1931, Panassié noted that "it is not very long—around two years—that Louis Armstrong has been known by the French who are interested in jazz."[5] Music critic Henry Prunières, writing in 1932, said that until about a year earlier, jazz was still thought of in France as the dance music of the 1920s: "All this has been abruptly changed since the appearance of what we in Paris call 'le jazz hot.' In one stroke it became the rage here."[6] Previously, hot records had not been widely available in France. For instance, none of Armstrong's recordings were released on a French label until 1929.[7] Furthermore, U.S. music companies had usually designated hot records as "race records" in their catalogs because these recordings were targeted at African American audiences. But the category was largely unfamiliar to the French.[8]

As Armstrong and other hot performers became better known by the late 1920s, they inspired many French musicians to perform in the hot style. In 1929, Mougin wrote an analysis of hot music in Grégor's *La Revue du jazz* in which he attempted to define what this kind of playing actually meant. "Literally speaking," the pianist explained, "'hot' means '*chaud*.' But '*chaud*,' in the figurative sense, which means 'to play with heart, with fervor.' And nothing else."[9] Many believed that the fervor he described had been removed from jazz over the course of the 1920s in order to make it more popular. Now it was being rediscovered. The result was what one U.S. observer called "a lively European vogue" for hot records by 1932 that, he claimed, "are exported in tremendous quantities."[10]

Increasing numbers of hot records available in France and the promotional efforts of those who loved the music created a growing audience for hot music. That popularity soon made possible the arrival of some of the biggest names in American jazz at the time. In July 1933, Duke Ellington debuted in Paris at the Salle Pleyel, and his presence helped to bring the term *hot* into mainstream press accounts as more writers adopted this American label to depict Ellington's music. Ironically, Ellington's trip was sponsored by Hylton, one of the foremost exemplars of orchestral dance music, but some French reviewers were quick to note the difference between the two men. "One knows that the jazz aesthetic is comprised of two very distinct currents," wrote music critic Émile Vuillermoz in a common observation, "that of *straight* jazz practiced by Paul Whiteman, Jack Hylton, Ted Lewis, Ray Ventura, and other famous groups, and *hot*, defended by Louis Armstrong, Eddie Condon, Henry Allen, the Mound City Blue Blowers, McKinney's Coton [*sic*] Pickers, and Duke Ellington, who is one of the most representative champions of this technique."[11] Still, the reputation of hot music was not completely established by the time of Ellington's arrival. According to some accounts, before his visit Ellington was already famous in France thanks to recordings; he was "known to everyone," as one reviewer put it, "since his works are extremely widespread."[12] But Jacques Canetti, the organizer of the concert, remembered that the Gaumont Palace refused to book Ellington, and that only Canetti's persistent efforts to sell this "inexpensive black orchestra" allowed him to secure La Salle Pleyel for the show.[13]

Once Ellington got there, the audiences that came to hear him were a blend of youth and fashion, as one writer remarked: "Young girls with platinum wigs, adolescents with shiny, plastered hair. . . . Some wore only a sleeveless shirt and golf pants. Africans with ebony faces. Dancers from fashionable cabarets. Movie stars. Artists from the extreme edge of the avant-garde. And above all the socialites with a passion for Americanism drunk with negromania."[14] Indeed, the presumed blackness of Ellington's sound attracted many listeners. It was, for one reviewer, a "fantasy disciplined by primitive musicality, by the rhythmic instinct of this orchestra that offers an incomparable imagery of noises, images where the melancholy of the plantations alternates with the brutal poetry of the jungle."[15]

As this response to Ellington suggests, for some jazz had not come far from the timeless image of primitive Africa, particularly when played by a black band. But by now, the racial connotations of jazz were becoming more complicated. The reintroduction of so-called primitive sounds into Paris during the 1931 Colonial Exposition undoubtedly reinforced the link between jazz and Africa for some observers by putting African culture and performance on display. In an article about the musical exhibits, one writer mentioned how jazz had "brought us a strange rapprochement" with African culture that could be seen again at the exposition.[16] Yet the two were not always interchangeable. One photo essay on the exposition in *Paris Music Hall* magazine, for example, made an important distinction between jazz and the music of the colonies. On the left side of the page under the heading "What One Will Not See," the magazine printed pictures with the captions "The sound of a frenzied jazz of 'Coloured Girls' dancer with a belt of bananas"—making reference to Baker's famous dance—and "Happy Hawaiians charming us with the nostalgic sounds of their guitars." In other words, one would not see the exotic kinds of shows that had been associated with the broad category of jazz music during the 1920s. Instead, according to the magazine, one would see "splendid négresses attending tranquilly to their housework at the Colonial Exposition."[17] Based on these photos, the focus was on "authentic" colonial life rather than an aestheticized interpretation of *la vie nègre* that many still associated with jazz. Other observers also noted with great care the musical distinctions between the sounds of the colonies on display at the exposition and jazz. One article contrasted the two, asserting that la musique nègre (by which the author specifically meant music from the colonies) was "a music singularly more primitive" than jazz, one that was "close to nature—abrupt onomatopoeias of wind in the branches and murmuring of rivers on the rocks of the rapids." Jazz, on the other hand, contained none of these qualities. The "real musique nègre [has] no relationship with that which has recently been brought to Europe by Americans."[18] Even outside the Colonial Exposition, other intellectuals had already begun to notice just how un-African jazz was. Ethnomusicologist Stéphen Chauvet, for one, had already argued in his book *Musique nègre* (1929) against thinking of jazz as a truly authentic African music: "But there is nothing less specifically nègre, nothing that resembles real *musique nègre*, the *musique nègre* of Africa that is, less than jazz."[19]

In spite of these distinctions, jazz was among the musical presentations at the Colonial Exposition, but it functioned differently than colonial music. For example, at an exposition soirée on the evening of 8 July 1931, after a series of performances on colonial themes, the program announced "*On dansera*," featuring music and dancing from Martinique as well as two jazz orchestras, that of Master Jack—who had also performed at the Exposition des Arts Décoratifs in 1925 and at other social functions during the Colonial Exposition—and Maurice Maire.[20] Juxtaposing these two musiques nègres suggested their relationship, but jazz played a role much more fitting to high-society dance music than that of merely another exotic exhibit.

Even if jazz was not as clearly African as many had once thought, by 1933 Ellington's music—"primitive, vehement, truculent, hyperbolic," as one review put it—could still be distinguished by many listeners from that of Ventura's "Latin art," which this same critic described as having a "measure of gaiety controlled by spirit."[21] Such terms helped to strengthen the distinctions between black American jazz musicians and French performers by harkening back to the ways in which jazz had been identified in the early 1920s. Most important by this time, one kind of jazz musician was homegrown and the other imported—a significant fact at a moment when economic tough times implied to many that one should support the people of one's own country.

Ellington was not alone among the U.S. jazz stars to appear in Europe. In 1934, Armstrong made his Parisian debut, also at La Salle Pleyel, after having performed elsewhere in Europe. As Panassié recalled:

> Louis' entry onto the stage was something unforgettable: while the first measures of his orchestra resounded, he made his appearance running, like a rocket, brandishing his trumpet, offering a few words covered by the noise of the music. He stopped, laughing, in the middle of the stage."[22]

Milhaud, who had written favorably about some of Armstrong's work, walked around during the intermission repeating "very 1920, very 1920," according to Panassié, suggesting connections between this work and that of the early era of jazz when so many people fell in love with it.[23] Not everyone was impressed, of course. One reviewer even claimed that he was "very bored."[24] But many among the growing number of jazz aficionados had just the opposite reaction, and after the performances, Armstrong met with French musicians in the nightclubs of Montmartre. Musicians and fans encountered a string of hot musicians during the early 1930s, including Sam Wooding, Muggsy Spanier, Coleman Hawkins, Bill Coleman, Benny Carter, Eddie South, and many others, as these players traveled to France and found receptive audiences, especially in Paris.[25]

THE HOT CLUB DE FRANCE

If some Parisians were bored with Armstrong, Ellington, and other hot jazz players, at least one group of French listeners was extremely excited. In November 1932, *Jazz-Tango* announced the formation of a club of aficionados devoted to hot music above all other kinds of jazz.[26] The newly created Hot Club de France wanted to bring together the fans who appreciated the hot style of playing. It also hoped to educate the French public about the value of hot music: "The Hot Club wants . . . to diffuse *le hot*, and to finally obtain for it the recognition it deserves."[27] The group had originally been formed a few years earlier as the Jazz-Club Universitaire by two young students, Elwyn Dirats and Jac Auxenfans, who organized dances for their classmates; dance music and jazz had remained popular among young people, and students in particular, through events like the Association des Étudiants dances held in the Latin Quarter.[28] Dirats and Auxenfans sought out further help for their group and engaged the assistance of Hugues Panassié, a twenty-year-old jazz aficionado who had been writing articles and reviews of the press for *Jazz-Tango* since its early days. Panassié was quickly becoming known within jazz circles for his opinions on the music, and he seemed like a logical person to turn to in order to advance the cause of hot jazz. Panassié was skeptical at first, not only of Dirats's and Auxenfans's grandiose schemes for their organization but because of what seemed to him to be their ignorance of the music they wished to promote. With the encouragement of his friend and fellow enthusiast Jacques Bureau, Panassié went to the headquarters of the Jazz-Club Universitaire. Finding the efforts of the group to be serious after all, Panassié and Bureau joined it.

Soon other young fans became associated with the group. Pierre Nourry, who possessed the all-important ability for organization, eventually became the general secretary. Panassié assumed the position of president with the stipulation that the general secretary take on all of the organizational responsibilities. Jean-Louis Levy-Alvarez, whose father owned a popular record store that featured jazz, and Michel Prunières, whose father Henry Prunières edited the influential journal *La Revue musicale*, added their names to the growing roster. The club made Armstrong its honorary president. Dirats and Auxenfans had bold plans for the group, which they continually pronounced at most of the early gatherings. "These meetings," remarked artist Charles Delaunay, who would soon join the group, "gave way inevitably to the interminable discourses of Dirats and Auxenfans who never stopped discussing their administrative concept of the club and its developments: publicity, advertising, radio, records, concerts, films, conferences, nothing missing. They already predicted innumerable telephone lines, a secretarial staff, typists, accountants." But as Delaunay explained, the club finally "decided to put words into action."[29]

At Panassié's recommendation, they changed the group's name to the Hot Club de France and publicized it in *Jazz-Tango*. The immediate plan, reflecting the ideas of Dirats and Auxenfans, was to expand the group's numbers and spread the music as widely as possible. To do both, they hoped to embark on an active publicity campaign on behalf of hot music and the Hot Club. They wanted to establish regular radio broadcasts of hot jazz accompanied by explanations of the music, something that they soon achieved with the help of Bureau, who was already playing jazz records on the small Paris radio station Radio L.L. Right away, the Hot Club became the most significant influence on the coverage of jazz in *Jazz-Tango*, and eventually it published a special section of Hot Club news contained within the magazine. Belonging to the Hot Club—at a yearly cost of twenty-five francs, reduced to fifteen for the initial membership drive—one would receive a subscription to *Jazz-Tango*, announcements about upcoming concerts, and special admission prices to events. By writing letters to record companies, the Hot Club also sought to persuade them to release U.S. hot records in France so that more people could hear the music.

Despite their broad outreach, the number of people who wanted to join was quite small, in part, Panassié suggested, because the readership of *Jazz-Tango* was largely composed of professional musicians whereas the Hot Club really aimed to target amateurs and fans who liked listening to hot jazz. Furthermore, the circulation of the magazine was not large. After several months, the group had only succeeded in attracting around one hundred members from all over France, much to their disappointment. Panassié, Dirats, and Auxenfans then went to see the director of Poste Parisienne, one of the larger radio stations in the capital. After listening to the records by Armstrong and a few other musicians that Panassié and his friends had brought, the director informed them that he did not especially like the music and did not find it well suited to the radio.

The next promotional idea, which proved to be more successful, was a hot music concert. Levy-Alvarez's father owned La Boîte à Musique, a Montparnasse record store that was a favorite of many jazz fans in Paris, and he offered his basement to the Hot Club since they lacked sufficient funds to rent a concert hall. The basement could hold about eighty people and a piano, and the elder Levy-Alvarez publicized the gathering among his customers. Panassié engaged pianists Freddie Johnson and Garland Wilson to perform for free, along with singer Louis Cole and composer Spencer Williams, who also sang. While Nourry drove around the city to pick up the musicians and bring them to the makeshift stage on 1 February 1933, the audience gathered, growing larger and larger to the point of overflowing. Panassié played some Armstrong records for the swelling crowd until the musicians arrived. Panassié recalled that

> the air in that little room quickly became unbreathable. We literally suffocated in the overcrowded basement, but the public was so excited by the playing and the sight of the two pianists who took turns with one another for more than an hour that no one seemed to suffer too much. The people sweated great drops, it's true, but they showed such a delirious enthusiasm that we no longer knew if they were hot because of the music or the atmosphere of the room.[30]

With such a crowd, the Hot Club seemed to be off to a good start despite its small membership, but the next concert on 1 March 1933 was not such a success. Not only did the audience consist of a mere twenty people but the musicians themselves also forgot to come, so the audience had to make do with listening to some hot records instead. Such a poor showing demonstrated that the support for hot music was not yet as firmly established as the Hot Club had hoped. The first concert had succeeded largely because the club members had made a point of bringing their families and friends. The second gathering, however, proved that without such special efforts, their project might not proceed. Nevertheless, the Hot Club persisted in organizing concerts, and over time the members were able to rent and fill larger venues, including the hall at L'École Normale de Musique, where they gave regular concerts throughout the rest of the 1930s.

The third concert given by the Hot Club, still in the Montparnasse basement, drew Charles Delaunay, son of the modernist artists Robert and Sonia Delaunay.[31] He had begun listening to Charlestons on the portable phonograph player that his parents had used at their parties in the 1920s. When a record seller asked Delaunay to create some drawings for advertisements, he also let the young artist listen to a few records. Delaunay quickly found himself attracted to American jazz music, but none of his friends shared his interests despite his best efforts to introduce them to jazz. At first, Delaunay felt isolated in his appreciation for the music. Inspired by a radio broadcast, he went to La Boîte à Musique to purchase the record he had heard, once he overcame his fear that the clerk might make fun of his tastes. Fortunately, the clerk happened to be Levy-Alvarez. He not only recommended several other records to Delaunay but also invited him to come to the next Hot Club concert, which Delaunay happily did. On hearing the music, Delaunay later wrote, "I was paralyzed by emotion, I was no longer on the ground." He thus embarked on his "new religion" of being a jazz fan.[32] Delaunay soon became one of the leaders of the Hot Club, editing its magazine in the late 1930s and authoring the extremely influential *Hot Discography* (1936), the first published listing of hot jazz records. Delaunay would further help to define and lead the French hot jazz community in the years to come.

From its earliest days, the Hot Club actively reached outside of Paris in order to draw people from all over France into its organization. "We ask those of our members who live in the provinces," proclaimed an unsigned editorial in *Jazz-Tango-Dancing*, "to help publicize the club and to win as many adherents as possible."[33] Soon, branches of the Hot Club throughout France—in Marseilles, Bordeaux, Nancy, Lille, and Cannes—conducted their own local activities, although the numbers remained small. Auxenfans presented a "plan of action" for local Hot Clubs in one issue of *Jazz-Tango*, describing how "3 or 4 active amateurs with a small collection of hot records" could attract others to the organization. They should organize record concerts and offer commentary on the music being played. The Paris office would provide assistance in the selection of records and with the commentary. Branches could also gather local musicians and organize performances on the condition that only hot music would be played. The result of such activities, these guidelines suggested, would be new converts to hot jazz. "The new recruits brought to these musical gatherings," Auxenfans concluded, "will not delay in joining the Movement and in taking an active part in the publicity."[34]

The centralized institution of the Hot Club provided individual listeners throughout France with access to hot music through concerts, recordings, and publications, thereby working to overcome the Hot Club's lingering fear that hot jazz would remain obscure. The Hot Club always believed in the power of the music to convert listeners to their cause and therefore wanted to disseminate it as widely as possible. But they also sought to craft people's understanding of the music by supplying information about jazz, and they were able do so through this growing network of local branches. Panassié and others gave lectures in cities across France. The Paris office sent informational material about various recordings almost as if conducting a correspondence school in jazz studies. In doing so, the Hot Club was creating a subculture of fans with an institutional affiliation, membership rites, and rituals of listening and performing that bound together fans throughout the country. It provided the basis for a community of listeners who could gather at concerts or around record players and share their common interests. Without self-conscious efforts to gain and educate audiences, the Hot Club argued, the music would have been subjected to the whims of the marketplace. Many listeners might not have discovered hot music without the Hot Club's efforts, they believed, because hot records still did not sell widely on their own—even though, apparently, Ellington and Armstrong had sold enough records to be able to attract an audience by the time of their concerts. Instead, the network of people and ideas that they created began to fix hot jazz in French musical culture by cultivating a willing group of adherents who were sure to tell others.

For all the Hot Club's efforts, its most permanent and influential creation was a band that bore its name. Even today, the mention of jazz in France usually brings to mind the names Django Reinhardt and Stéphane Grappelli, the leaders of the Quintet of the Hot Club of France; the Hot Clubs that remain in France today are devotees of their music at least as much as of American hot music. The idea of a French hot band had been discussed for some time before the Quintet's creation. As early as March 1933, Léon Fiot, musician and editor of *Jazz-Tango-Dancing*, wrote that "our idea is to form an orchestra of hot jazz composed only of the best French musicians, and of course they will be devoted to hot music."[35] But later that year, the first band to perform live, on the radio, and in recording sessions under the sponsorship of the Hot Club was the Hot Club Orchestra, composed of American players and starring Freddie Johnson, Arthur Briggs, and Big Boy Goodie. Nevertheless, the Hot Club was always on the lookout for talent, and when a friend told Nourry about a guitarist named Django Reinhardt living on the outskirts of Paris, Nourry went to meet him.

Born in 1910, Reinhardt grew up amid the gypsy caravans that continued to crisscross Europe.[36] According to friends, in many ways he never left that world behind, often taking to the road and living by his own schedule regardless of having been hired to play at a certain performance. Reinhardt had shown an early passion for music. By the age of ten, he was begging his mother for a guitar, but he did not have one until two years later when a neighbor gave it to him. Watching the other musicians in his encampment, Reinhardt memorized the movements of the players and then practiced what he had seen at home, quickly learning to play guitar with no formal training. Performing in the dance halls and *bals-musettes* around Paris, Reinhardt began to make a name for himself. He even attracted the attention of Hylton, who asked Reinhardt to join his band. But a fire in his caravan in November 1928, only a few days after Hylton's offer, badly burned Reinhardt's left hand and seemed to put an end to his career. Struggling back from his injuries, he taught himself to play the guitar again, now with a damaged hand. Reinhardt's more thorough immersion in jazz came when he encountered the experienced musician Mougin in a Montmartre nightclub shortly after the accident and joined Mougin's band. Later, traveling in the south, Reinhardt met the artist Emile Savitry, who played a few hot records for him—Joe Venuti, Ellington, and Armstrong—and the music supposedly stirred Reinhardt to tears with his head in his hands.

Back in Paris, Reinhardt visited the club La Croix du Sud in Montparnasse one evening with some friends. There he heard Ekyan's band, which included a young violinist named Stéphane Grappelli. When Grappelli saw the gypsies in the audience, they stood out from both the high-society crowd and artists, and he thought that they might have been gangsters. Still, the tallest one looked like someone that he had seen playing guitar in the streets. Reinhardt, the tall man, approached the stage and signaled that he wanted to speak with Grappelli. With some apprehension, Grappelli stepped backward to have a word with the stranger. Once they spoke, Grappelli and Reinhardt quickly recognized their common musical interests, and during a break Reinhardt played for Grappelli. Reinhardt wanted to start a band with himself and Grappelli, but Grappelli was hesitant to leave his steady job with Ekyan. In the nights to come, though, the two men continued to talk about jazz and their favorite records as Reinhardt visited La Croix du Sud and Grappelli journeyed to Reinhardt's trailer, where they practiced together.

Grappelli had come to La Croix du Sud after many years of musical study and performing.[37] He was born in 1908, but his mother died just a few years later, leaving her husband as their son's only caregiver. The elder Grappelli, an Italian immigrant to France, lived the bohemian lifestyle of a would-be intellectual—Stéphane later called him "the first 'hippie' that I ever knew"—and made his living poring over texts in the library as a freelance translator.[38] Meanwhile, Grappelli spent parts of his youth in Montmartre hanging around the *tabacs* where musicians played cards and waited for someone to hire them.[39] But he had his first real experiences with music as a student in a school opened by the American expatriate dancer Isadora Duncan in order to introduce children to art, music, and dance. After World War I, Grappelli began his formal musical training, eventually enrolling in the Conservatory in Paris in 1920, and he played in cafés and cinemas while going to school.

As he told the story, Grappelli's introduction to jazz came in a store near the cinema in which he was performing. One of the gadgets for sale was a

U.S.-made proto-jukebox, and when Grappelli put in his money, he heard Mitchell's Jazz Kings. "I was absolutely hypnotized by that kind of music," he remembered. "I used to go every day to listen to the same tune."[40] The Montmartre nightclubs provided Grappelli with another way to hear this new music, which he began to play until his violin was stolen in 1925. Once he got a new instrument, Grappelli performed at one of the dance schools that flourished thanks to the continued fashion for dancing. There he met Mougin, who was also playing for the dance students, and Grappelli took his first steps toward jazz improvisation by learning from the more experienced Mougin. Mougin introduced him to the other up-and-coming young French jazz players, including Brun, Vauchant, and Ekyan. Grappelli played with them and others on Saturday and Sunday nights at the Association des Étudiants dances in the Latin Quarter. "We set out to play tangos," Grappelli recalled of these sessions, "and ended up playing jazz. That's where I began to embellish"—in other words, to play hot.[41] Through contacts from these dances, Grappelli soon joined many others— including Brun, Mougin, Vauchant, Ekyan, and saxophonist Alix Combelle—in Grégor's band, in which he played piano, only switching to violin at Grégor's insistence.

The famous Quintet was not far away. Reinhardt had already begun to play in concerts organized by the Hot Club as early as 1934, but he was still not well-known. Hot Club cofounder Bureau misspelled his name as "Jungo" in a review of the concert in *Jazz-Tango* and expressed surprise at this guitarist's talents. As Bureau observed, "This is a very curious musician whose style resembles no one else's. This white guitarist proceeds by [playing a series of] small, strange phrases that are bizarrely constructed, in a way that draws on an extraordinary imagination. . . . We now have a great improviser in Paris."[42] Later, when some scheduled trumpeters did not show up for a gig sponsored by the Hot Club, Nourry drove around Paris looking for replacements. He returned with Django and his brother Joseph. As these musicians became better known, jazz fans like those in the Hot Club soon hoped to promote them to wider audiences. "The idea of a group with Django as its leader was already in the air," explained Charles Delaunay in his biography of Reinhardt. "Pierre Nourry had discussed the project with Emile Savitry and Django, who dreamed of playing with a string ensemble."[43] And Nourry and the Hot Club were also eager to attach their name to a band with only French musicians.

Later that year, Reinhardt and Grappelli were both performing in a band directed by Louis Vola at L'Hôtel Claridge along with most of the other great French jazz players of the day. One day when Reinhardt was playing by himself backstage, Grappelli came and joined him in an impromptu jam session. "He asked me to play a little riff that he'd just put together," Grappelli said of the occasion. "The effect pleased both of us and we went on to play some more tunes."[44] The next day during the intermission, Reinhardt and Grappelli were again jamming backstage to the tune "Dinah" when Roger Chaput and then Vola joined them. After numerous rehearsals at Bricktop's, and with the subsequent addition of Django's brother, the original Quintet of the Hot Club of France was born.[45]

The musicians initially doubted their marketability as a band, and their long efforts to gain a recording contract demonstrated ongoing reluctance on the part of the music industry to accept them. After cutting some audition records with Odéon, the company executives returned a less than promising verdict: "The administrative committee has agreed that the records your band has made are far too modern."[46] Despite such hurdles, the Quintet went on to an astounding success not only in recordings but in live and broadcast concerts around the world. "I was a little dubious about giving the name of the Hot Club de France to the group," Nourry later admitted, adding:

> Stéphane was none too keen on it; Django, on the other hand, was agreeable; and all in all, I don't think there's been any cause to regret it. The title probably helped to launch the band, but the quintet has paid back its debt a hundredfold, for if the name of the Hot Club doesn't count for very much today, that of the Quintet of the Hot Club de France is still known the world over.[47]

By promoting hot music, one might think that the Hot Club was working at cross-purposes with other French bands like Ventura's and Grégor's, for example. After all, hot jazz musicians and fans approached the music in very different ways from many others, especially when it came to the issue of jazz's racial and national identities. Ventura and Grégor, as we have seen, tried to create what they called a Latin style of jazz based on French songs, thereby de-emphasizing both the blackness and Americanness of jazz. By contrast, the Hot Club closely associated itself with black American musicians. Despite these differences, however, both groups of French jazz fans were still working toward the common goal of building a French jazz community and making jazz a part of the repertoire of French musicians. Most important, both groups proudly hoped to increase the popularity of jazz music by the fact that French musicians were playing it. French musicians, they asserted, were just as talented as Americans of any color. In some ways, the Hot Club went further than Ventura and Grégor in its claims about the abilities of French musicians to bring jazz into the French musical mainstream. Whereas Ventura and Grégor removed the racial component of jazz to make it seem more French, the Hot Club suggested that even race was not a barrier to the musical talents of the French. Black musicians were not the only ones who could play hot music, they argued. Instead, the Hot Club and the Quintet believed that the French could do so too. Making this point also served to take musical talent out of the realm of being an innate racial quality and placed it more in the category of being a learned ability of which the French were more than capable.

HUGUES PANASSIÉ AND *LE JAZZ HOT*

Even before the Hot Club and the Quintet began to promote hot music, Panassié had already been working to convince people of its superiority through his seemingly endless writing. Panassié was one of the French jazz community's chief philosophers and polemicists, and one of the individuals most dedicated to securing the place of jazz in France's entertainment repertoire. Panassié's writings explained hot jazz to readers who did not know much about it or rarely distinguished between the different styles of jazz. His books and articles, presented with an irrepressible passion for the music, made him one of the most significant jazz critics of the age—not just in France but anywhere—and his work made a profound impression on many other fans and critics around the world.[48] As a leader of the jazz community in Paris in the 1930s, Panassié not only influenced what people meant when they referred to jazz but also shaped how they heard and thought about it.

Although Panassié spent much of his time away from Paris after 1933, he remained a leader among jazz fans by hosting radio programs, giving public lectures, and writing letters to record companies in hopes of convincing them to release previously unavailable records to the French marketplace. He also eagerly participated in and perpetuated the rituals of the nascent French jazz community by going to clubs, organizing jam sessions, helping to found a record label, preparing recording sessions, and listening to and discussing records with others. One U.S. jazz fan remembered just such a gathering in Panassié's cramped hotel room in Montmartre:

Eight people completely filled it. M. Panassie [*sic*] sat beside a small non-electric victrola, putting on records, first calling out their English titles in a language I could not understand. . . . M. Panassie went into a frenzy of movement, jerking his whole body in time to the records, playing every solo in pantomime, smiling a particularly delighted and charming smile that I seldom saw him without.[49]

Born in Paris in 1912, Panassié grew up in the Aveyron region in the south of France among the western foothills of the Massif Central.[50] His father, Louis, was a government engineer who discovered one of the world's largest deposits of manganese on an official mission to the Caucasus and soon became wealthy from the mining venture. As a child, Louis Panassié had dreamed of owning a castle in his native Aveyron. On his return there in 1900 from a twenty-year stay in Georgia, he bought and renovated Le Château du Gironde with his newfound wealth. Partly in Paris and partly in these aristocratic surroundings, Hugues Panassié spent his childhood with his two half sisters, but he also lived in the nearby town of Villefranche-de-Rouergue, where he went to school, played rugby and other sports, and listened to classical music with his friends.[51]

The image of Panassié growing up in a castle provides a useful symbol with which to understand certain aspects of his later life and thought. In many ways, he was a very conservative figure. A devout Catholic, Panassié spent time in his youth among the circles influenced by Charles Maurras, the nationalist and monarchist leader of L'Action Française, until Maurras's excommunication by the pope. Panassié also participated in several demonstrations against the democratic government of the Third Republic. On one occasion in 1932, while handing out pamphlets on behalf of one royal pretender's claim to the throne of France, he was expelled from a cinema after engaging in a brief row with a young communist.[52] In part, Panassié was skeptical of democratic society because it represented the growing power of the largely uneducated masses and their whims of fashion. Closely related to this skepticism was a related critique of mass culture's influence that he saw—along with its consumerist ethos—as a corrupting influence on France. More important, it was a danger to the jazz that he elevated as pure art. Much of the jazz that was performed for large audiences—namely, the popular dance music of the 1920s—lacked any real sense of taste and artistry, he argued, because it was bland and homogenized. And when musicians appeared to give in to the commercial pressures of the marketplace to please undiscerning listeners and merely to sell records, Panassié unleashed a biting criticism to chastise those he saw as traitors to the pure values of the art of jazz that he sought to uphold.

Panassié did not begin his love of jazz through hot music, however, but through the popular dance music that he would later come to ridicule. He discovered that sort of jazz when he was quite young during a family vacation to the resort of Saint-Raphaël, where he took a few dance lessons. "This teacher taught me the tango, the one-step, the fox-trot, the Charleston, this last dance very new at the time," he later recalled, and he practiced his dancing with the girls he met there.[53] But not long afterward, in 1926, at the age of fourteen, Panassié's life changed dramatically. A few days after a smallpox vaccination, he contracted polio and was rushed to Paris for treatment. One leg was restored, but the other was not. Panassié was no longer able either to play the rugby that he enjoyed or dance the new steps that he had so recently learned. While recovering after the onset of his illness, Panassié asked his father for a saxophone like the ones he had seen the band playing at Saint-Raphaël just a few months before. "The saxophonist and his saxophone fascinated me," recalled Panassié, but the music did not draw him to the instrument at first as much as the look of the saxophone. "The sound of the instrument was not displeasing, certainly, but it was above all the eye that attracted me," he remarked.[54] Hugues's father, obliging his son's wish, purchased the instrument and also found him a teacher, the well-known French jazz saxophonist Christian Wagner. "Wagner came and gave me lessons and I made progress," Panassié remembered. "But the really important thing was that he brought me records and said to me, 'Since you are interested in jazz, here is what you should listen to; you don't know anything good.' "[55] Until that time, Panassié's only knowledge of jazz had come from the popular bands of the day like Hylton's, Whiteman's, and their French counterparts. Now Wagner introduced Panassié to the hot music that he would come to champion for the rest of his life.

When in Paris, Panassié still heard the popular "commercial" bands, as he later called them, playing in the orchestral style. But these bands grew tiresome and dissatisfying to him, especially once he became aware of the new generation of French musicians influenced by hot music. By listening to Brun, Mougin, Vauchant, and others as well as by talking with them about jazz, Panassié continued his musical education. He recounted his meetings with several of these influential early players in his memoir of the era, *Douze années de jazz* (Twelve years of jazz) (1946). During 1928 and 1929, as he told the story, Panassié visited the dance hall Washington on a regular basis. There, he began listening to Brun, Mougin, and the drummer Maurice Chaillou, who were performing there in alternating sets with a tango orchestra. Brun, Panassié commented, "hardly knew two or three Louis Armstrong records and was entirely under the influence of Bix [Beiderbecke] and Jimmy MacPartland, the two most renowned white clarinet players of the day." Mougin had been inspired by Beiderbecke too, he wrote, and "is probably the best jazz pianist France has produced." Chaillou had learned much from Dave Tough when the Chicago drummer had visited France. These French players had studied American records and live performances, and now taught the music to French enthusiasts like Panassié. While the tango band was performing and the jazz players were sitting off to the side, Panassié talked with them about their musical preferences. "Who do you like better? Bix or Red Nichols?" he inquired, to which Brun sharply replied, "A thousand times Bix! There is no comparison! Red Nichols is worthless." "Do you know Louis Armstrong's records?" Brun then asked Panassié. "They may be a little crazy but I love them!" Panassié described this back-and-forth exchange as one of the best places to learn about the music that, at the time, he was just discovering, and it constituted an important practice in the life of the growing jazz community. Brun "corrected my errors, constantly put me back on the right road," he admitted. In moments like these, along with jam sessions in clubs and gatherings in people's homes to listen to records, Panassié and others in Paris learned the intricacies of hot jazz.[56]

One of the most significant influences on Panassié was his friendship with the American clarinetist Milton "Mezz" Mezzrow. Mezzrow, one of the Chicago-style jazz players, was performing in 1929 at L'Ermitage Moscovite, a club owned and staffed by Russian émigrés, which Mezzrow described as "loaded up with slick-haired gigolos who pranced the tango and the Charleston with American dowagers and collected their fees after each whirl like they'd just turned in an honest day's work."[57] Panassié—who Mezzrow portrayed as "a studious young chap, all eyes and ears for our music, animated as a Disney cartoon"—rushed to meet Mezzrow and asked the musician to give him saxophone lessons. Mezzrow accepted the offer in large part because he was so taken with Panassié's excitement for the music:

> I liked this kid's enthusiasm, so I went over to see him one day, lugging my records and horns along. I found him living in a great big house where he had a special study lined with shelves and shelves of records. When he got straight on my version of *My Blue Heaven* I played the second harmony sax

part along with him, and that got him steamed up some. Then I let him hear those records, and all excited, he ran into the foyer and shouted for his whole family to come down and listen.[58]

Mezzrow and Panassié remained lifelong friends and collaborators in their efforts to publicize hot jazz.

Panassié met other musicians in this way by drawing them into his fraternity with his passion and initiative. By doing so, he also quickly expanded his own influence and reputation among jazz musicians as an enthusiastic fan and sympathetic critic. He was a regular in the clubs and a friend of many of the French jazz musicians who played in them. When Sam Wooding's band came to town, for example, the musicians gathered at Panassié's home between concerts and listened to records.[59]

Panassié had contributed two articles to Grégor's *La Revue du jazz* and a few essays to other musical journals when, in 1930, Mougin asked if he would be interested in writing for the newly formed magazine *Jazz-Tango*, although like all of the contributors he would have to do so without pay. There, Panassié found the first regular outlet for his thoughts about jazz music. He wrote articles about Armstrong and the differences between black and white musicians, for instance. He also compiled a regular "Review of the Press" under the pseudonym "Ache-Pé"—the French phonetic equivalent of his initials, H. P.—in which he excerpted articles about jazz from various publications and explained to his readers why these other critics were either totally ignorant of jazz or, less frequently, why they understood the music about which they were writing. But Panassié quickly became conscious that he was only writing for a select few since *Jazz-Tango* "was hardly read outside the professional milieu." In spite of his desire to enlarge the audience for jazz and his growing belief that such an expansion could happen, he concluded that "the number of 'amateurs' that were prepared to know and appreciate real jazz music by reading *Jazz-Tango* must not have been more than two or three hundred in all of France."[60] And regardless of the benefits of a magazine like *Jazz-Tango*, Panassié thought that it was more of an organ for the particular interests of musicians than a means for spreading the music to new listeners.

By the early 1930s, Panassié was an essential point of connection between jazz players, fans, and critics in Paris. In these years, a number of well-known American musicians—like Sam Wooding, Muggsy Spanier, and Fats Waller—came to Paris, and Panassié heard them all. He helped to create the Hot Club de France in 1932, and was at the center of all the early efforts to organize and publicize their concerts. In his autobiography, he told the story, for example, of Nourry, Delaunay, and himself hanging up posters around Paris for a concert, and then, to attract attention to the signs, standing back and looking up at them inquisitively in hopes that passersby would see them and do the same.[61] But in June 1933, Panassié left Paris and returned to his family's castle in the Aveyron. There, he wrote the book that launched him into the forefront of jazz criticism, not only in France, where he was already known among jazz fans, but in the United States as well.[62]

The twenty-two-year-old Panassié broke ground with *Le Jazz hot* (1934) because it was the first attempt by a French author, and perhaps any author, to define hot jazz music in a systematic way. The Belgian poet Robert Goffin had published *Aux frontières du jazz* two years earlier, but Goffin's remarks were largely based on anecdotal observations of the bands he heard. While Panassié was also writing a work of opinion, he claimed to be providing detailed analyses of each performer in a more "scientific" fashion, believing that he was bringing greater clarity and definition to this often misunderstood musical form. "Goffin approaches jazz through his personal impressions of it in a rather subjective way," Panassié asserted, "while in this book I propose to give in a strictly objective way that information which is indispensable for an exact knowledge of real jazz, especially hot jazz."[63] Most French critics were merely dilettantes as far as he was concerned. However, he believed that since he had come to understand this music, he could now help the rest of France to do so as well.

For Panassié, the need to begin with definitions arose from the substantially unique character of hot music itself. He never satisfactorily defined hot jazz, perhaps because of the very nature of his subject matter and the limits of the written word to adequately convey musical experience; he did acknowledge the "insurmountable difficulties" of getting at the complicated musical elements it entailed.[64] Yet for him, attempting to define this music as a way of setting it apart from all others became of paramount concern. The "very form of jazz," he wrote, "is entirely different" from every other musical form. "It is not surprising, then, to find critics who are quite expert in classical music entirely at sea when they speak of jazz."[65] Instead, critics ignorant of the true nature of jazz merely repeated their "catalog of errors" and, in the process, served to promote the popular forms of dance music that people had for so long been labeling, incorrectly he argued, as jazz.[66]

According to Panassié, jazz music represented a fundamental rupture in the stream of European musical style, and it demanded both a new kind of listener and a different critical audience to appreciate it. The question that the new, modern jazz audience must ask itself is whether the music "swings." "Where there is no swing," Panassié explained, "there can be no authentic jazz."[67] Panassié attempted, largely in vain, to describe this quality of the music. Swing "is a sort of 'swinging' of the rhythm and melody which makes for great dynamic power," he said.[68] It is syncopation and balance, he suggested, and therefore not necessarily inherent in the melody but in how it is played. Quoting an article by Mougin, Panassié agreed that swing "is the swinging between the strong beat and the weak beat—or beats—in a measure."[69] Such definitions were clearly tautological, but Panassié insisted that anyone acquainted with swing could recognize it objectively. Nevertheless, he quickly pointed out its subjective nature and the fact that "such a way of playing cannot be acquired by conscientious study."[70] "Swing is 'a gift'—" he remarked, "either you have it deep within yourself, or you don't have it at all."[71] On this basis, Panassié dismissed bands such as Hylton's—a recurring foil in his book—that lacked the fundamental component of swing. "An orchestra like Hylton's," he quipped, "does not, please notice, make *bad* jazz; it is not jazz at all." And he excluded the "symphonic style" of Gershwin and others from "real" jazz as only "distantly related to hot music."[72]

No music could be real jazz if it did not swing, but there was more than one way for a band to do so. Real jazz could be played straight or hot. To play "straight" meant "playing the piece just as it is written, without modifying it." Straight performances were tied to the notes on the page, yet they could be done in a swinging style. To play hot "means to play with warmth, with heat," and was based on variations of melody and intonation that were improvised anew with each performance.[73] Although both hot and straight were still real jazz because both were based on swing, Panassié elevated hot music as the ultimate form. It came from the personalized interpretation of a composition given to it by each musician rather than merely playing the notes as they appeared on the page. Hot jazz, he said, came from the musician's soul.

Panassié emphasized the importance of improvisation to hot jazz precisely because it shifted the traditional balance between composer and performer, thus producing another distinction between jazz and art music. In "classical" pieces, Panassié maintained, the composer expressed a creative vision through the written notes. But in jazz, hot performers themselves were the artists on display since they were the ones creating and re-creating a tune each time they played it. Hot, straight, and swing are hardly drawn from the vocabulary of traditional art music. These musi-cological neologisms represented a new critical language to accompany a new, modern musical form. And they were subjective qualities that could not easily fit within the older categories but instead represented the turn of modern aesthetics to the interior realm of the artist. As Panassié said, one knows swing because it is "a gift."

The origin of both swing and hot was clear to Panassié, and it was particularly significant to his conception of jazz and the aesthetic values it represented. Like many others who appreciated it, Panassié attributed swing, the cornerstone of real jazz, to black American musicians; he also referred to it as "Negro swing."[74] Throughout *Le Jazz hot* and in his other writing, Panassié constructed jazz as a projection of the black psyche. Unlike the music played by the predominantly white U.S. dance bands or French musicians like Grégor and Ventura, he depicted real jazz as some-thing transcendent and spiritual precisely because of its origins with black Americans. Unfortunately, his explanations of why black people were so good at making music were rarely more concrete than an insistence on innate racial qualities. Just as Ernst-Alexandre Ansermet had observed in 1919 of the Southern Syncopated Orchestra, for Panassié too there was a uniquely black way of playing, and it was far superior to the way that whites normally performed. Jazz may have been a radical break in Euro-pean music for Panassié, but it was simply a continuation of the black musical tradition, from slave songs to religious music to jazz. "It is that ex-pression of sadness, of the melancholy of the soul of the oppressed Negro, which gives swing music its intensely moving accent," he claimed.[75] From the rhythmic syncopation to the vibrato of certain notes, jazz had emerged from the spirit of black American artists, and white musicians, he sug-gested, should aspire to its high standard. The whites who recognized the true quality of jazz, like Mezzrow, had already assimilated the style of black music, he believed. To make the point, Mezzrow, a Jew, identified himself as "Negro" on his passport. But, Panassié noted, such whites were the only ones with the "courage" to recognize the value of black music because of the racial prejudice in the United States that Panassié often denounced.[76] If only whites would realize what they were missing, he lamented, and embrace the emotion and spirit of black musicians, they could play real jazz too.

In *Le Jazz hot*, Panassié's racial construction appeared to be double-edged at times. Black American performers were unpolished and, he suggested, less musically perfect. The hot style created by blacks was perfected by white musicians, who brought a "more orderly, more subtle, and more sophisticated" style to jazz. Whites focused and directed black "heat" and passion without eliminating "that wild Negro spontaneity" that Panassié treasured. "Few things," Panassié remarked, "have been as fruitful as this particular collaboration by two races."[77] Armstrong—Panassié's archetypical hot jazz musician as well as personal friend, musical hero, and author of an introduction to *Le Jazz hot*—illustrated the desired balance of the so-called primitive and civilized in a great jazz performance. Panassié contended that Armstrong began his career with a rather ragged musical style, but improved over time. However, "What I imply by 'refinement' [of Armstrong's performance] is not, I hasten to say, any perversion of that native, savage simplicity in Louis' playing," he added.[78] In Armstrong's music, the "savage" of the black style existed in tandem with a "serene" polish.[79] Whether the "shortcomings" of black American musicians resulted from the lack of training or a racial quality, Panassié did not intimate; his exact meaning when he referred to white culture as "superior" is unclear in the text.[80] Still, he was not ambiguous about his love for the spirit of African American music or his firm conviction that it was the purest sort of hot jazz.

Despite these initial comments about the relative contributions of black and white musicians to real jazz, by 1942 Panassié had reconsidered his original words and wrote in *La Véritable musique du jazz* (The real jazz) even more enthusiastically about the black culture from which jazz came. "Since jazz is a music created by the black race, it is very difficult and, in fact, almost impossible for a white man to get to the heart of it at first shot," he apologized.[81] Becoming familiar with jazz at first mainly through white musicians, "I did not realize until some years after the publication of my first book that, from the point of view of jazz, most white musicians were inferior to black musicians."[82] Although the differences between these two books appeared stark at times, the overall shift of attitude was not surprising. Panassié did not contradict his earlier love of the blackness of the music but rather pushed it further as he proceeded by steps toward a fuller embrace of African American culture. Much of the revision in his views instead centered on his reassessments of specific hot musicians, both white and black, and a refinement of the definitions of the music he loved.

Real jazz was not only black, though, because Panassié also envisioned it outside the mass consumerism represented by the successful dance bands whose music he deplored. Indeed, these two qualities were linked. Looking beyond the relative few in France who, he believed, could appreciate hot music, Panassié saw only those people who listened to jazz casually as a new form of dance music or music hall diversion, not critically and studiously as he did. As a popular music, most jazz was performed by bands interested in making money, and they played to suit the audience's tastes. Yet the sort of music played by the big, frequently white bands was not, according to Panassié, real jazz because it did not incorporate swing. "In fact," he argued many years later, "all this jazz that flourished in dancing was nothing more than a commercialized, saccharinized pseudo-jazz done for white tastes and had only a very superficial relationship with the music of black Americans."[83]

Panassié explicitly connected white music with mass consumerism and, by extension, black music with a noncommercial, art for art's sake expression. Such a view inverted the attitudes of those who had criticized black jazz in the 1920s for eroding the artistic ethos of old Montmartre because of the new music's commercialism. To make the link between black and noncommercial music, Panassié had to overlook the fact that jazz had been commercially successful in the first years of the 1920s precisely because black American musicians performed it. And black jazz was still making money in the 1930s, as press reactions to Ellington's 1933 concerts revealed. Nonetheless, in Panassié's distinction between white and black jazz, once again Hylton took the brunt of his criticism, especially on the issue of moneymaking. Hylton had the resources to produce good music if he wanted to, Panassié claimed, but "Hylton doesn't want to—his interest is 'commercial,' and he is content to produce, under the name of jazz, music which pleases the public." Driven by the whims of popular taste that Panassié believed to be ill informed about musical quality, "all this represents only commercial exploitation of music by musicians who make concessions to get more money."[84]

For Panassié, real jazz was played for its own sake, not for profit. This characterization was somewhat impractical and insensitive given the struggles of French musicians, who often seemed to be barely surviving in the business, especially during the depression. Mougin, a working musician, frequently complained in *Jazz-Tango* about having to bow to the demands of the marketplace, but he nevertheless acknowledged the necessity of doing so in order to survive. Still, for Panassié the purist, jazz was not a commodity to be traded but an experience to be treasured. He thought that audiences demanded the less challenging sounds of popular jazz, the music that Robert Goffin had described as a compromise between real jazz and "the prejudices of the bourgeois public."[85] Or as Panassié simply put it, musicians "were obliged to act . . . in order to please their clientele."[86]

For Panassié, real jazz instead represented freedom from the mass market that threatened to dilute jazz. The culture of American blacks was communal, he said, based on personal connections and oral memory passed down through generations, not revolving around impersonal, cash relationships.[87] He described jazz players' jam sessions as a forum that embodied such values. There, musicians could "practice the music that they loved with complete freedom, which they couldn't do with the large orchestras of 'commercial' jazz."[88] The fickle tastes of the masses shaped jazz in a consumer society and watered it down to meet popular tastes, but in the privacy of the jam session, musicians could play and improvise as freely and with as much variety and personalized passion as they wished. "Here is the music in its most natural state," Panassié wrote adoringly, "delivered from all dressing-up, from all artifice, from all refinement (in the bad sense of the word)."[89] Real jazz represented a liberty for the individual musician, who could craft an expression of his own inner self through the improvisational character of the music.

Panassié's dislike for mass culture and his rejection of the market's influence on artistic creation were not unique. He was part of a larger interwar critique of mass production, mass consumption, and mass entertainment as these developments shaped various aspects of life in France— much to the disdain of observers, who deplored their potential consequences. As we have seen, because mass culture was often understood both as an imported influence and something that challenged older French conceptions of good taste, discontent was frequently expressed in the discourse about America; the United States was the best example of a mass society and, many believed, the harbinger of further change to come to France.[90] Panassié shared much with commentators like Duhamel, Aron and Dandieu, and the critics of mechanical music discussed earlier, who attacked the United States and the values for which it stood. They attacked mass culture for lowering the standards of French consumers because mass-produced items reduced style and craftsmanship into what could merely be produced most cheaply and easily by machines. In spite of developments made since the war to expand industrial production, in the 1930s, France was still an important producer of luxury goods made by skilled artisans that connoted high quality. By contrast, Americans supposedly all lived in houses that looked remarkably similar and were filled with the same shoddy goods. Items bought at the new prix uniques stores were believed to be inferior merchandise, much of them also allegedly foreign imports.[91] Critics also charged mass culture with robbing the French of the refined pleasures of life, such as their cuisine. If food were thoroughly Americanized in its production, it would lose the subtlety of its flavor, which the French had always savored. Bread in the United States, remarked one gastronomic critic, "resembled nothing so much as a ball of cotton caught in a downpour."[92] In the realm of entertainment, lower prices for mass amusements like U.S. films meant that more people could attend, but it also entailed pandering to the uncultivated sensibilities of people, critics asserted, in order to draw larger audiences. Unlike fellow critics of mass culture, though, Panassié did not spend his time condemning the United States; in fact, he rarely spoke of it per se. After all, he did not see jazz as an American music but rather a black music. His criticisms of mass culture were instead specifically directed at the "pseudo" jazz that was a corrupted form of real jazz.

Above all, many believed that a mass culture would rob the French of their individuality—one of their most prized cultural characteristics. "In this age of Henry Ford, France may seem out of date," wrote political economist André Siegfried. "Nevertheless it is in the individuality of the worker, if only it can survive, that lies our true personality."[93] Individual artisans who tastefully made goods, he feared, could easily be reduced to cogs in a large and impersonal production machine. In the process of such changes, French taste—ineffable as it was—was in danger of being subjected to the "tyranny of the majority" dreaded since Tocqueville's time. Panassié's elitism fits with these sorts of critiques, particularly given his general distaste for democratic principles. "The democrat's logic makes a person submit himself entirely to the law of numbers," Panassié remarked in an interview late in his life, speaking broadly of politics and society. "But, the law of democracy being that the majority is always right, how could this majority deceive itself? All of this is ridiculous to the point of discouraging refutation."[94]

Against the tendency toward homogenized, mass entertainment, Panassié held up the individual jazz musician as an echo of France's artisan past. For him, the talents and tastes of individual artists still mattered just as they had in France for centuries. The popular dance band style of jazz that had been masquerading under that name, he argued, was to be deplored because it merely pandered to the whims of audiences in the marketplace just like mass-produced goods. Instead, he turned to real jazz, a music that was based on artisanship, skill, and craft, and that was outside the mass marketplace, he believed. Panassié looked to the older aesthetic project that valued taste and quality over profit and quantity.

Panassié was using jazz to remember what, according to many critics, was being lost in the emerging age of mass culture in the 1920s and 1930s. For many, the changes of the early twentieth century demanded a re-evaluation of France's place in a world where mass-produced goods easily crossed national boundaries. But unlike many conservatives who believed that the French character was rooted in France's own self-contained popular traditions and folklore, Panassié rediscovered them in a music from far away. He heard elements of a simpler French past in jazz music. Indeed, in an interview toward the end of his life that summarized much of his earlier writing, Panassié spoke of the parallels between (in many ways stereotypical) black American and French societies as they became clear to him on a visit to New York in the 1930s:

> I discovered thus with *Noirs* a society that takes itself much less seriously than ours, which freely teases itself with nicknames, people much less sensitive than us, not taking a tragic view of life. . . . And when I arrived in New York the first time, I was struck by the contrast between the white city and the black city: on the white side, people rushed around with their business, anxious, knocking you over almost to such a degree that they were brusque; in Harlem, by contrast, relaxed people, people strolling around as in Paris. . . . This black American society, totally different from the white, is in the final analysis less distant from the French. A French person who goes there, without bizarre preconceived ideas, would feel more at home in Harlem than in the white part of town (where there are no cafés, something very important).[95]

Panassié spoke of a kind of human interaction that was missing in modern life, but that he found in a romanticized conception of African American society. He envisioned the real jazz that emanated from this world as somehow connected to his own cultural tradition. The whites who had not assimilated the spirit shared by real jazz were the detached, alienated people he observed rushing around New York, while Harlem represented for Panassié a reminder of a more sociable way of life in France that was threatened by dramatic economic and cultural change in the 1920s and 1930s. Or perhaps it was an alternative way of preserving the old spirit of the cafés and relaxed French culture alongside the modern demands of life in the early twentieth century. In either case, real jazz could link the French past to its future.

Making this link between past and future has often been a function of the kind of nostalgia in which Panassié indulged, but he was not alone. As described earlier, for much of jazz's history in France, commentators had portrayed it as nostalgic. They did not generally say that the music made them feel nostalgic, rather that the music itself expressed the emotion. As the chronicler of Paris André Warnod wrote in his book *Les Bals de Paris* of a jazz band: "But suddenly, in the roar of the machines come to life, a moan rises, a high-pitched nostalgic song, . . . it evokes distant lands that one has never seen. Invitation to impossible voyages."[96] Usually, French writers linked this sentiment to the black musicians who were playing jazz, thereby suggesting that these artists were communicating a sense of loss for an older, African culture through their music—"a tragic nostalgia of exiled slaves," as one observer put it.[97] But by the 1930s, the object of the nostalgia in jazz began to include a French past. Critic Fortunat Stowski, for example, said in a 1926 article that he heard in jazz "several old French songs or some of the elegant tunes from the seventeenth and eighteenth centuries that were preserved . . . until the time of our grandmothers." When he heard jazz in the United States, Stowski stated with longing that "it led me back under the skies of France, in a slightly hazy countryside where I heard, in the distance, a melody from another time."[98] Ventura's jazz-style chansons also evoked nostalgia in some listeners, as we have seen. Panassié's ideas were another attempt to link the sound of jazz with a conception of a France that was dead or dying. And for him, the music promised the possibility of recapturing that past.

SPREADING HOT MUSIC

Although Panassié wanted to protect hot music from the dangers of popular taste, he did not wish to keep the music all to himself. He believed that if only people heard this music in its purest form, they would come to love it too. Skeptical of the masses of uneducated listeners, he nevertheless wanted to teach them what good music was all about and elevate them along with the music. At the same time, although hot music had been created by black musicians, Panassié wanted French performers to learn to play it and, by so doing, recapture something of French society that was being lost.

Using the definitions laid out by Panassié in his book and elsewhere to clarify the distinctions between hot jazz and other kinds of music, the Hot Club acted to shape public tastes. Previously, the Hot Club argued, only a few had understood hot music. Audiences were still divided between those who liked it and those who preferred "Hyltonesque" music.[99] "For the good professional musicians," noted Hot Club's cofounder Auxenfans, "this 'hot' movement must create an audience capable of appreciating them" because that audience did not yet exist.[100] The group continued to organize concerts, often featuring the Quintet of the Hot Club. Panassié explained hot jazz in radio broadcasts and gave public lectures in Paris, the provinces, and abroad. The Hot Club also established a club room where members could gather, listen to records, and discuss hot music. Such a setting fulfilled Auxenfans's vision of "having the public in hand, and plunging it in a powerful atmosphere that would fill it entirely and leave it with a durable and precise impression [of the music]."[101] The Hot Club did not think that the changes they desired would happen overnight, but they did believe in the power of their music to win new fans. "We have not pretended," maintained Panassié, "that people will understand it automatically by our explanations. No. We only wish to introduce them to it, to give others the *possibility* of appreciating and loving it."[102] Once people had the opportunity, the Hot Club thought that they would recognize the music's inherent beauty.

To further the cause of educating the public, *Jazz-Tango* reported Dutch critic J. B. van Praag's 1933 proposal to create an academy of jazz centered in Brussels or Paris that would engage in research related to the history and musical techniques of jazz.[103] Grégor had already proposed a "Jazz Conservatory" in an article that was reprinted in the first issue of *La Revue du jazz*, but unlike Grégor's idea, van Praag's excluded all forms of music that were not hot.[104] The Hot Club de France seconded the idea as a worthy project because of its desire to identify jazz exclusively with hot music. An academy would help "to define jazz, to fix it as one fixes a language," declared Auxenfans, "and having constructed a doctrine on a sound and solid base, then to diffuse it widely."[105] Although no such academy was created, the idea nevertheless demonstrated the importance that hot fans assigned to their task. Music critics who had written about jazz had been unable, in the Hot Club's view, to distinguish good music from bad, and they left the public confused. Now, the Hot Club believed it would set the public straight.

Panassié was not the only significant figure in the Hot Club, nor was his book the only attempt to define real jazz. In 1936, Delaunay released his *Hot Discography*, which is often identified as the first discographical listing of any sort. By cataloging, grouping, and labeling records as well as offering information about each recording session, this book quickly became a standard reference work for any serious jazz collector. It was also revised in several later editions in order to remain current. Delaunay began this endeavor, he recalled, simply by wanting to keep track of the records he owned. He soon started a record exchange service—*"une bourse aux disques"*—for the readers of *Jazz-Tango*.[106] Information about the personnel of many recordings was sketchy because the record companies had not always kept track of the sessions, and the details could be recovered only from the memories of musicians who were present. Delaunay persisted in talking to performers as they came through Paris to learn what he could. "The nights we spent at Freddy Johnson's, around his Victrola, listening to records," Delaunay remembered, for instance, "gave us many discoveries."[107]

Delaunay's book highlighted two important points. First was the significance of records for the spread of hot jazz in France. On a record, audiences could hear a musician before he had ever crossed the Atlantic. For Panassié they proved crucial to his first book, which he wrote largely based on listening to records. Recorded music figured as a central aspect of Panassié's notion of the jazz aesthetic itself since "the record is the only medium there is for preservation of tonal improvisations which, without records, would be lost forever."[108] Art music could be written down and played identically each time, but because hot jazz was improvised, each performance was a unique artifact from a specific place and time.[109] Delaunay's *Hot Discography* reinforced the importance of recordings by solidifying their prominent role in the jazz culture and applying a logic to their collection. Second, Delaunay's book furthered the cause of defining real jazz as only music that had swing and preferably only the jazz that was hot. Commercial music could not be allowed to eclipse hot music, Delaunay and others held, and an authoritative listing of good jazz music would help to educate audiences by teaching them how to listen and buy wisely. "To earn money [for hot music], the public must be won over, and it lets itself be bought thanks to Publicity, the modern machine for manufacturing audiences," Delaunay asserted in 1939, criticizing the music industry that only sought profits.[110] Whether they sought profits or not, Delaunay and Panassié were just as much a part of "manufacturing" audiences, only ones more to their liking, and *Hot Discography* was a crucial element in doing so.

Another important figure advancing the cause of hot music at the same time as Panassié and Delaunay was Jacques Canetti. An Eastern European immigrant to France, Canetti got a job writing for the British magazine *Melody Maker* and working at the radio station Poste Parisienne. In these jobs, he could pursue his love of jazz music through the records with which he came into contact. In 1933, Canetti organized the concerts that brought Ellington to Paris.[111] Like Panassié and the members of the Hot Club, Canetti believed in hot music and worked to make it more accessible to larger audiences by releasing American hot records once he began to work in the record industry. Writing in *Jazz-Tango-Dancing*, he called for fans of hot music to "fight against the detractors of 'hot' jazz," and he longed for the day when a French band would play in this style so that the French would truly come to know it.[112] In February 1933, not long after the Hot Club offered its first program in the basement of a Montparnasse record store, Canetti, with access to more resources, organized an evening of hot jazz performances at the Cinéma Falguière. The program included three short films of jazz performances—featuring Bessie Smith, Armstrong, and Ellington—some live performances, his own commentary on the music, and a public discussion led by Panassié. Panassié's talk, accompanied by Mougin on the piano, did not go well, and the pair was dropped from future programs.

Tension between Panassié and Canetti began to grow. According to Panassié, Canetti was not a purist, and Panassié thought that Canetti's concerns were too commercial in nature. Canetti soon became Panassié's nemesis because he represented to Panassié much that was wrong with the music business—primarily the fact that it *was* a business—and a battle started to brew between the two men. Canetti wrote a critical review of *Le Jazz hot* in *Jazz-Tango* that, despite often favorable observations, charged Panassié with having "a polemical tone" as well as establishing "arbitrary comparisons and classifications between different musicians."[113] Most important, a few months earlier Canetti had become embroiled in a business affair with Armstrong that went bad. Canetti had been acting as Armstrong's manager during his European tour in 1934–1935. When Armstrong left Europe unexpectedly in January 1935 due to problems with his lip, however, Canetti charged the trumpeter with violating their contract and costing him money.[114] Canetti decided to write about his experiences in the *Melody Maker* and *Jazz-Tango*. He publicly attacked Armstrong, thus incurring Panassié's anger. The details of this "Armstrong-Canetti affair," as Panassié dubbed it, are less important than its result: causing

Panassié to end his collaboration with *Jazz-Tango*, the "journal that had become his [Canetti's] fief."[115] Panassié and the other members of the Hot Club now decided to publish their own journal, *Jazz-Hot*, which began in March 1935 and lasted in its first run until the war.

Jazz-Hot expanded the French jazz community further by disseminating information about hot music to fans throughout the country. Once *Jazz-Tango* ceased publication in 1936, *Jazz-Hot*, edited by Delaunay and filled with frequent contributions from Panassié, became France's preeminent journal devoted to the music and helped to define it more thoroughly. *Jazz-Hot* was also a major forum for publicizing French musicians, especially the Quintet of the Hot Club, by keeping readers up-to-date on their recordings and appearances. Panassié reviewed the newest record releases from the United States and Europe. Offering his judgments on which recordings were good and bad along with which were worth buying also reinforced his status as an arbiter of taste. The magazine and Hot Club sponsored prizes for the best record of the year as well as a contest for amateur jazz players. *Jazz-Hot* announced club appearances in France, radio broadcasts, record concerts, and where to take jazz lessons, all in the hopes of spreading hot music to as many listeners as would hear it. Advertisements told fans which shops could provide recordings, and classified ads offered rare records and the names of bands seeking jobs. In spite of its fear of commercialism in music, the Hot Club still saw a limited marketplace as instrumental to its goals and worked to create one.

The project of disseminating hot music advanced again in 1937 when Delaunay and Panassié started a new record label called Swing. The Hot Club had already been rereleasing older recordings and lobbying record companies to issue American hot records in France, but now they planned to make their own new recordings. Delaunay approached a few companies without success, but finally found the French firm Pathé-Marconi willing to work with them in the venture and take care of the technical details, thereby leaving the artists and repertoires to Delaunay and Panassié.[116] The first recordings, released in November 1937, were of Coleman Hawkins and His All-Star "Jam" Band, which combined the talents of the American Benny Carter and two leading French saxophonists, Ekyan and Combelle. Other discs in the first Swing Records catalog featured the Quintet of the Hot Club, Ekyan, Dicky Wells and His Orchestra, and Teddy Weatherford. Such a grouping of artists on one label demonstrated Panassié and Delaunay's desire to place black American performers and French hot musicians on equal terms.[117]

The work of Swing Records took Panassié to New York in the fall of 1938 to direct what became known as the "Panassié sessions." Panassié received an enthusiastic reception on the trip, indicating that many Americans were taking French jazz critics seriously. Staying with his friend Mezzrow in Harlem, Panassié contacted Tommy Ladiner, who Mezzrow remembered as "a great New Orleans trumpet player who'd been completely lost from sight for years."[118] Others like Frankie Newton, Zutty Singleton, and Mezzrow himself also answered Panassié's request to participate in these recordings. During the trip, Panassié met many American critics and musicians, including Whiteman, who organized a luncheon in his honor. Count Basie improvised a tune during a recording session and called it the "Panassié Stomp." Later, Jimmy Lunceford honored the Frenchman with a song titled "Le Jazz Hot," with the subtitle "Dedicated to Hugues Panassié."[119] Panassié also broadcast his views about jazz on U.S. radio and gave a talk at Yale University, home of the Yale Hot Club. This group, and the larger United Hot Clubs of America, was led by Marshall Stearns, who was on his way to becoming an important jazz scholar in the United States.[120] Stearns and his colleagues had based their own organizations on the model established by the Hot Club de France.

Panassié recorded his experiences in the United States in *Cinq mois à New York* (Five months in New York) (1947). The most vivid passages in his book are of his time among African Americans. After eating red beans and rice, he remarked, "I came back to life."[121] He loved the casual, friendly atmosphere of Harlem that seemed to him like life in France, and he embraced the "incredible vitality of this black race in the United States."[122] Panassié was constantly bewildered, however, by U.S. prejudice toward blacks—a view that he did not share. The poor treatment of blacks further reinforced his skepticism of democracy, which in his eyes, acted like the marketplace to degrade standards and replicate prejudices. "Here are the values of the great 'American democracy,'" he quipped sarcastically. "Everyone is equal, yes, but on the condition that they don't have black skin."[123] Meanwhile, all of his positive sentiments about blacks were confirmed in the drama of a throat infection. After difficulty breathing, Panassié was treated by a black doctor, who saved his life when he, according to Mezzrow, "stuck his fingers down Hugues' throat and pulled out a thick string of phlegm that was as long as a footrule, I swear."[124]

The story of the Hot Club and its activities further helps to explain how jazz became a part of the musical life of France between the wars. But another part of the Hot Club's history involved the creation of an international jazz community that transcended national borders. Just as Panassié and the Hot Club shared hot music with France and encouraged the French musicians who played it, they also wanted to bring it to others throughout Europe. Panassié may have been at the heart of the jazz world on his trip to Harlem, but by the late 1930s jazz had clearly expanded to other places as well, just as the Hot Club had hoped.

Before the Hot Club, some ways of talking about the international character of jazz came from motives unrelated to the fans' love of this music. Rather, they had emerged as a set of responses both to the economic crises of the 1930s and the theory that jazz was dying because of dwindling audiences. In the midst of arguments to close French borders to foreign musicians, non-French players wanted to guarantee their ability to still perform in France. "An international organization," wrote one Belgian musician in *Jazz-Tango*, "channeling workers from nation to nation would be more effective in this difficult period" because it would unite everyone in the common [economic] struggle.[125] Another international vision came from the French musician Gottlieb, whose "Call to the Friends of Jazz" ran in several issues of *Jazz-Tango*. Responding directly to various press articles that had proclaimed the death of jazz because of the depression and changing tastes of audiences, Gottlieb proposed an "International League of the Friends of Jazz" with a goal to "promote the diffusion of jazz everywhere it would be possible to understand it." "The friends of jazz are many," he concluded, "more numerous than one supposes," and with such an international organization, the fans of jazz could demonstrate just how alive and well the music truly was.[126] But these efforts were sporadic and unsuccessful. The Hot Club instead became the preeminent voice for jazz as a music that knew no borders, less for economic reasons than for musical ones.

The Hot Club de France conceived of itself as an international organization right from the start, and it was soon at the center of a movement of hot appreciation that included the United Hot Clubs of America and similar groups in other countries. "The Hot Club is open to amateurs of all nationalities," proclaimed the founding statement in *Jazz-Tango*. "Local Hot Clubs are anticipated in the provinces and abroad."[127] Regular reports

The Discovery of Hot Jazz 187

from throughout France and around the world soon emphasized the growing global community of hot jazz. As the voice of the Hot Club from 1935 until 1940, *Jazz-Hot* carried news stories and reports from around Europe and beyond in addition to its coverage of American jazz affairs. The magazine was published bilingually in French and English with a group of regular contributors from across Europe and the United States, again stressing the international vision of its founders and continuing transatlantic traffic of hot jazz musicians.

On the Hot Club page of *Jazz-Tango* for February 1933, readers found a reprint of Article IV of the Hot Club's statutes, the section on "Foreign Hot Clubs." With the goal of "international cooperation," clubs outside of France were encouraged to follow the organizational scheme of the Paris headquarters and remain in contact with the Paris office, thus ensuring Paris's leadership. "Despite the necessary autonomy, there must be a correlation of views and actions between the Foreign Hot Club and the H.C. de Paris," the statutes declared, consisting of correspondence, the publication of news from the Paris office in local newsletters, and a regular congress of delegates from the various Hot Clubs.[128] The headquarters had an obligation to ensure the proper interpretation and understanding of the music as it sought to enlighten others about hot jazz. Foreign Hot Clubs also meant those in the French colonies and other territories outside of Europe, including branches in Egypt, Algeria, Morocco, and Senegal; *Jazz-Tango* regularly listed bands that were performing in these locations. By April 1933, the international Hot Club movement already numbered twenty-one affiliates, and its leaders predicted more to come.[129]

The global vision of jazz was enshrined not only in the Hot Club's charter but also in an attempt to form an International Federation of Hot Clubs (IFHC) in 1935. This group named Panassié as its president, yet the primary voice was its secretary general, Marshall Stearns, the president of both the Yale Hot Club and United Hot Clubs of America. Writing in *Jazz-Hot*, which became the IFHC's chief outlet, Stearns stated that the group's motto would be "Dedicated to the universal progress of swing music," and that it would produce new records, organize concerts, and propagate this music throughout the world.[130] Working within the structures of the music business by trying "to influence record companies" to release records that met the IFHC's standards would be crucial.[131] Panassié, for example, wrote many letters to record companies urging them to release certain hot records in France, rerelease older recordings, or make new ones with certain musicians, although his efforts produced mixed results.[132] Despite their good intentions, nothing much ever seemed to come of the IFHC. Although the masthead of *Jazz-Hot* always stated that it was the official organ of the IFHC, few issues carried any information about the organization, which soon appeared to drop from sight. A 1936 letter from Panassié to Stearns mentions how the IFHC "has not yet shown much activity."[133] Even after World War II, Delaunay still wrote of the IFHC as a would-be organization with hopes to "bring about peace and understanding between men of good will" through a common music.[134] Despite its apparent failure, at the very least the impetus to reach across the Atlantic and beyond the boundaries of what most people have traditionally considered the major American centers of jazz in the United States points to the fact that this music cannot be understood within the United States alone, because it was not understood that way at the time either by musicians or fans.

By the late 1930s, the importance of Paris as an international hub of the jazz world was reconfirmed independently of the Hot Club and its efforts. The 1937 International Exposition featured numerous jazz bands in the Exposition City itself, and the various nightclubs and music halls around Paris hosted many more. British jazz critic Leonard Feather, writing in the *Melody Maker*, remarked, "I have just spent a week in Harlem—but it only took me a few hours to get there and back: Lenox Avenue was called the rue Pigalle and the bands worked for francs instead of dollars."[135] The Cotton Club revue, featuring a band led by Teddy Hill and numerous dancers, played Les Ambassadeurs and Le Moulin Rouge during the exposition.

If no one had noticed this continued broadening of the jazz community by early 1939, Delaunay made the point quite clear in at least one article. *Jazz-Hot* regularly ran a feature called "News from America," but as the editor of the magazine, Delaunay used the tardiness of the information for this column one month to make a crucial statement about how big the jazz world was becoming. "The long heralded news from America didn't show up in time for this issue.... But anyway, our readers are getting a bit fed up with this eternal 'News from America,'" he wrote, since "it's always the same sort of stuff." Instead, *Jazz-Hot* would use this column to "reenact right here before you, some unforgettable moments in the select establishments of the Ville Lumière (Paris)."[136] The "News from Paris" column ran until the magazine's end the following year.

Creating an international jazz community seems to work against the value of making jazz French. Yet it might also be viewed as an attempt to situate a growing national French jazz community in a leadership role within an emerging international jazz culture based on a music that knew no borders even if its listeners still did. French fans, like those in the Hot Club, saw themselves in the forefront of promoting this worldwide community, and that gave them a pride of place as being the first among equals. In this international endeavor, French hot musicians and fans simultaneously expressed two identities—as both French people and jazz fans—which were not thought to be contradictory as they had seemed to so many in the 1920s because jazz had become part of French music. Rather, they demonstrated the ability of French musicians to create a local expression of a global musical enterprise.

When World War II broke out, the situation changed for French jazz fans as both the Nazi and Vichy regimes attacked jazz as a foreign music. The openness that had allowed jazz into French culture was under assault by those who envisioned a more restricted "France for the French." Jazz was, once again, a symbol of decadence and could have no place in a France restored to "moral order."[137] Jazz, however, survived the war and in many ways even thrived during it. And by the end of the conflict, it had become even more a part of French entertainment than ever.

9

EPILOGUE

In spite of the best efforts of the Hot Club de France and others, hot jazz remained the pleasure of only a small percentage of the French people before World War II. Although it is impossible to measure the popularity of this music, there were most likely only a few hundred people who considered themselves "serious" hot fans; Delaunay assessed the number of prewar subscribers to *Jazz-Hot*, on five continents, at around fifteen hundred.[1] Many more people undoubtedly heard hot music on the radio, on records, at the cinema, or in the dance halls, but would not have thought of themselves as aficionados of the sort that belonged to the Hot Club or read its magazine. Others remained fans of jazz more broadly defined—the peppy dance music that was still widespread and was now influencing French songwriters like Charles Trénet and Johnny Hess, who incorporated jazz elements into their work.

OCCUPATION AND LIBERATION

When World War II erupted, the fortunes of jazz began to change, often for the better. As historian Ludovic Tournès points out in his history of jazz in France, jazz was never banned by either the Nazis or the southern French collaborationist Vichy government, but instead continued to be performed throughout the war.[2] Historian Julian Jackson likewise notes that "German cultural policy in occupied Paris was comparatively relaxed" as the Nazis pursued a "bread and circuses" approach to distracting the French population.[3] Nevertheless, at the beginning of the occupation, Delaunay closed the Hot Club headquarters for over a year. En route back to Paris later, he recalled encountering a poster in Dijon advertising a concert with some of France's biggest names in jazz. After finding these musicians, who were, of course, friends of his, he realized "the sudden vogue for shows and the taste for jazz that had seized the French."[4] Everywhere in France, it soon seemed, jazz was popular. Its sound filled theaters, nightclubs, and clandestine dance halls throughout the war. By 1943, the International Conservatory of Jazz was founded in Paris, and as the director of the Conservatoire Nationale put it, "Jazz has entered into our customs."[5]

Jazz also became a central part of the wartime countercultural aesthetic of the Zazous, teenage hipsters whose name was derived from the sound of scat singing, like that of Cab Calloway, and attributed to songwriter Hess.[6] The men among these young rebels usually sported long hair and a version of the American zoot suit or other outlandish dress; the women wore lots of makeup, platform shoes, and short skirts.[7] Linking jazz—which flourished in secret dance halls and dancing schools—with resistance to the occupation, the Zazous defied authority and challenged the conservative mores of the day. Going against the grain in occupied France, whether in dress or musical taste, brought trouble, and right-wing protofascist groups like the Jeunesse Populaires Françaises attacked the Zazous, beat them, and cut their hair.[8] In spite of such conflict, however, many young fans continued listening to jazz.

The Hot Club's response to the wave of enthusiasm for jazz was twofold. First, they organized concerts, including a Festival of Jazz in December 1940 with France's most famous jazz musicians, in order to promote the music and also educate newfound listeners, many of whom, as Delaunay put it, "naturally fell upon the white orchestras, whose polish and exhibitionism were more attractive than the old [black] Masters."[9] The Hot Club, as the self-appointed arbiter of the jazz aesthetic in France, again sought to mold the tastes of listeners toward what it believed to be good music. New branches of the Hot Club opened up during the war, and Swing Records continued to press new sides. Although *Jazz-Hot* stopped publishing, a short bulletin circulated clandestinely, according to Delaunay, "which guided, if only a little, all the members scattered throughout the country."[10] And these new fans were no longer largely city dwellers. "After the fall of France," he remembered, "small towns of three or four thousand . . . could draw a thousand enthusiasts at each monthly concert." By 1941, claimed Delaunay, "I was able to lecture on hot music in farm villages."[11]

According to many fans, one of the chief reasons for jazz's ability to remain on the French musical scene during the war was a strategic turn in the Hot Club's activities. It began to promote jazz as essentially French rather than American or black. "All our outside propaganda—that is to say our public concerts, our programmes and press articles," Delaunay explained, "were devoted solely to the defense of jazz as an intrinsically French art, proving that our musicians had not developed from America at all, and giving as an example Django Reinhardt and the new quintet he had just formed."[12] Even though jazz was not forbidden, French jazz fans in the occupied zone still had to be somewhat careful about how they promoted a music that the Nazis had banned within Germany because they saw it as both "Negro-Jewish-American" and "modernist," neither category fitting into the aesthetic culture that Adolf Hitler wanted to cultivate. Frequently, U.S. titles would be translated into French in order to disguise the music's true origin. "Saint Louis Blues" therefore became "La Tristesse de Saint Louis" and "Honeysuckle Rose" was renamed "Chèvrefeuille."[13] Not all Germans were opposed to jazz, though, and Delaunay suggested that jazz records sold well early on since Germans, "long deprived of jazz, stampeded the French record shops."[14] Changing song titles was a kind of accommodation similar to that which a wide variety of writers and artists made during the war in order to continue working in relative comfort. French artistic life continued to exist, even in the occupied zone. Writers, for example, often modified story lines or phrases in books or plays to which the Nazis might object.[15] Yet in many ways, calling jazz French and translating song titles was not so much an adaptation to the Nazis as simply the conclusion of a longer process of absorbing jazz into the French musical repertoire that had been proceeding throughout the 1920s and 1930s.

Under the leadership of Delaunay, himself of Jewish heritage, the Hot Club became actively involved in the Resistance movement, not only on a cultural level but a political one too.[16] Delaunay had read *Mein Kampf* early on, he recalled, and deduced the consequences for both jazz and France more broadly. During the war, the headquarters of the Hot Club de France on rue Chaptal became a meeting place for British soldiers who had parachuted into France and were now disguised as Frenchmen, and they mingled with the club members and listened to records. Hot Club members kept Allied agents informed of the underground meeting places that changed from night to night. In October 1943, the Gestapo arrested British soldiers in the club along with Hot Club leaders and took them to Fresnes Prison. According to one account, one of the Hot Club's secretaries was killed in an extermination camp; Delaunay himself was interrogated for five and a half hours.[17]

Making sense of the enthusiasm for jazz during the war years is difficult because, as always, various groups responded differently. Jazz served as a necessary diversion in a difficult time, just as it had during and after the First World War. For many, jazz was also a form of resistance to the Nazi occupation and the cultural revolution of the Vichy government. For the Zazous, for instance, jazz provided a form of resistance just as it did for the

"Swing kids" of Germany who listened to jazz precisely because it was taboo under Hitler's regime.[18] The response of the rest of the French population to jazz is more difficult to interpret. Exactly why they would turn to jazz during the war is not entirely clear, and measuring the degree to which they really did so is difficult, despite the claims of Delaunay and others.

But numerous reports of its popularity indicate at least one conclusion: for many listeners by the time of the war, jazz was no longer "away from home." Rather, it had found a new home in France and had penetrated deeply enough into the popular consciousness to be meaningful during wartime. Jazz had become French—at least French enough to inspire many people to turn to it as a means of asserting their independence from the German invaders. Reinhardt and other French performers enjoyed tremendous success during these years. "Without American films, cut off from the 'climat américain,'" Delaunay suggested, "the young people of France suddenly realized that jazz was really their music."[19] The Hot Club's promotion of jazz as a purely French music was, in part, a front for the sake of the Nazi and Vichy regimes. Yet by the 1940s, there was an important element of truth to such a description of the music as being French, regardless of the Germans' presence, because of the efforts of fans, musicians, and critics during the preceding two decades.

The war also helped Delaunay and others to realize further that jazz was a worldwide music, even while it had new, national meanings in France. Groups throughout Europe and elsewhere emerged that paralleled the developing French jazz community. This international network even came to Delaunay's aid during the war. In order to complete an updated edition of his *Hot Discography*, he relied on information given to him by Swedish and Swiss groups along with a German officer. Despite being cut off from the United States and elsewhere, "the grapevine," remarked one *Downbeat* reporter, "was sufficiently effective for Delaunay to learn the personnel of all the records made by Duke Ellington up through 1942!"[20] Mezzrow also experienced the far-flung jazz community firsthand. "Wherever I went," he said, "merchant seamen, soldiers and sailors from many different countries, and writers and critics and artists and students and fellow musicians too, would drop around to say 'hello'" and talk about his music. Panassié organized jazz fans around the world to write to Mezzrow after his release from prison in 1942, and Mezzrow received much correspondence, including "a whole gang of letters from other guys in Hot Clubs all over the world."[21] Letters received by *Down-*

beat, one of the chief U.S. jazz magazines, from European correspondents revealed a self-conscious connection among fans around the world regardless of nationality. One German, writing from France in 1947, asked the *Downbeat* editors to put him in touch with "an American hot jazz fan who would like to correspond with me." From Hamburg, another German fan wrote asking for issues of the magazine and "any enthusiastic fan—jockey, collector, musician or whatever he might be—who's got the goodwill to help a lot of young Germans serving the same thing he does." Scrawled on the top of this letter, someone at *Downbeat* noted: "We sent him some copies. How about a pen pal mention?"[22] Jazz fans the world over shared a love of music that transcended national boundaries even as each nation created its own jazz community.

The war had not brought all jazz fans and musicians together, however. Soon after the liberation of France, jazz bands struck up openly again, but old arguments about musical style continued. The Mouvement de la Libération Nationale sponsored a Franco-American concert at Le Palais de Chaillot featuring the "symphonic jazz" of Robert Bergmann, who performed Gershwin's *Rhapsody in Blue* along with works played in the Whiteman and Hylton style. Later in October, the Hot Club organized a concert at the École Normale de Musique where, "for the first time in Paris since the liberation of the capital," commented one reporter, "American musicians played with their French colleagues."[23] But there, black American musicians and French players performed hot music, unlike the symphonic jazz of the other concert. The old split between different kinds of music called jazz persisted. However the jazz world soon experienced a new schism that shattered the tight-knit French hot jazz community.

THE COMMUNITY FRAGMENTS

Once France was reunited following the liberation, the Hot Club could resume its activities without fear of censorship. But even if the country was whole again, the Hot Club ceased to be so fortunate. This wing of the French jazz community fragmented beyond repair in the 1940s, producing two separate institutions, each with its own leader: the Hot Club de France, still led by Panassié, and the Hot Club de Paris under Delaunay's directorship. The reasons and terms of this split are difficult to determine fully because each side told the story to his own advantage, but there seem to have been two main issues at stake.

First, Delaunay suggested that the activities of each man during the war had taken them down separate paths. Panassié remained in the unoccupied zone writing and sometimes traveling to Switzerland to lecture, while Delaunay stayed in occupied Paris directing the Hot Club, organizing concerts, and participating in the resistance. Delaunay accused Panassié of sitting out the war, "surrounded by his courtesans . . . frozen in his provincial hole."[24] After the war, a clash of personalities between the two created a hostile atmosphere within the Hot Club. There were disputes over *Jazz-Hot* that had begun again in 1945 as Panassié accused Delaunay of censoring his articles. Problems arose over Swing Records, too, with Panassié claiming that Delaunay stopped recording sessions that he had arranged.[25] Finally in 1947, the general assembly of the Hot Club de France voted Delaunay out of office as the secretary general and replaced him with a Panassié loyalist.

Second, whatever the internal politics of the Hot Club may have been, they were coupled with a growing difference of opinion about the direction in which jazz music itself was heading. In both Europe and the United States throughout the 1940s, jazz fans took sides over the question of bebop and whether this music could be considered jazz alongside New Orleans–style and swing music from the 1920s and 1930s. For "modernists," bop was a new and welcome development, but for the "fundamentalists"—soon dubbed "moldy figs" by the other camp—bop was not jazz because it departed from the black, folk, and blues origins of the music in favor of a more experimental and avant-garde sound. Musicians and critics soon created firm encampments and used the jazz press to argue their cases, often berating the views of the opposite side. British critic Leonard Feather employed a bitter wartime metaphor in one article, alleging that "just as the fascists tend to divide group against group and distinguish between Negroes, Jews, Italians, and 'Real Americans,' so do the Moldy Figs try to categorize New Orleans, Chicago, swing music, and 'the real jazz.' "[26] These divisions emerged within France, too, particularly when Delaunay moved to the side of modern jazz while Panassié remained firmly entrenched within the fundamentalist camp. The international community that many had dreamed of was in jeopardy as a result of the split. Panassié himself was sometimes the target of attacks. Eddie Condon, smarting from having been left out of Panassié's list of the best guitar players, quipped famously, "How come the French cats are telling us how to play jazz? Do I tell Panassié how to jump on a grape?"[27] One author called the Hot Club de France an organization "whose purpose before the war seemed to be nothing more than to make confusion more confounded," and he quoted another critic who decried Panassié's first book as "without doubt the worst book I ever read in my life."[28]

Jazz had come full circle by the 1940s with a new series of debates over how this music would be defined as musicians, critics, and audiences lent their support to one style or another. Jazz was still a contested term some thirty years after its beginnings, although for different reasons and among different people. The debate over the definitions of jazz was now internal to a jazz community of fans, critics, and musicians rather than one that pitted an older musical establishment against a new musical form. Those who would seek to redefine jazz would try to do so from within the jazz world itself.

But if definitions of the music were largely internal to jazz experts, neither the discussions about the larger cultural significance of jazz nor the controversies about whether it fit within France's national identity were over. As many in France worried about their increasingly Americanized culture after World War II, new criticisms could be leveled against jazz as part of the growing influence of popular culture from the United States—an issue that now took on greater importance in light of the cold war, decolonization, and France's diminishing place as a global power. And a new generation of critics, musicians, and fans would seek to "make jazz French" in the postwar years partly as a way to negotiate between American culture and their desire to retain some sense of their identity as a nation with creative powers.[29]

CODA

In this book, I have argued that between the world wars, jazz music became an important part of French entertainment for a variety of reasons, from tax policies and entrepreneurship to the significance of performance venues like music halls to its embrace by the avant-garde of the 1920s. By the 1930s, one of the most critical factors in this transformation was a group of fans, musicians, and critics who incorporated jazz into the French consciousness. They turned it from a foreign music into a sound that emanated from French bands (sometimes performing French compositions) that were supported by French organizations like the Hot Club de France and the journal *Jazz-Tango*. Although many detractors lamented the changes that jazz seemed to be introducing into the country, some fans heard in the music a way of recapturing French traditions or adapting them to the modern age. Foreign influences, new communications technology, a burgeoning mass culture, changes in urban living, and a new relationship with the United States were all remaking France between the wars. Yet France was also resilient and flexible, able to graft new trends onto old customs.

One pressing question remains: why such adaptation to the challenges of modern life could still take place after the devastation of World War I. The fact that many listeners believed that jazz was simply incompatible with an authentic French culture because it had come from without fits well with the exclusivist understanding of the nation that was common in the interwar period. But the reception of jazz in Paris during these years also suggests that many people did not entirely accept the xenophobia and integral nationalism for which this era is notorious. Instead, many retained a more cosmopolitan outlook.

Tracing the history of cosmopolitanism in France is difficult because there is no coherent body of literature on the topic. It is an idea whose fortunes have advanced and receded with events over the course of French history, just as have those of xenophobia.[30] Certainly, Paris has long enjoyed a reputation as one of the world's most cosmopolitan cities due to its accessibility and hospitality to people from around the world. It has been a home for exiles and expatriates of nearly every sort—from Karl Marx to Gertrude Stein, among many others—in part because it has provided an atmosphere of relative liberty to think, write, and share ideas. Historian Lloyd Kramer described the pull of Paris for a wide variety of individuals in the mid–nineteenth century, although his words could apply to the twentieth century too. As he put it, "The city offered something for everybody: elegance and privilege for aristocrats, a market for merchants, intrigue for diplomats, contacts and ideology for revolutionaries, an audience for writers and artists, jobs for laborers."[31] Cultural institutions like the café also supplied a space for conversation and discovery between people from around the world, especially in the twentieth century.

Closely connected to the history of cosmopolitanism is the issue of whether elements of France's culture could originate outside of France's borders. Influential scholars like historian Fernand Braudel have argued against such a position. France's culture coincided with its political boundaries, he asserts, and it had been established over the *longue durée* of history so that one can speak of a relatively definitive France by the early modern period.[32] In response to Braudel, historian Gérard Noiriel has reminded us of the fact that foreigners have contributed immensely to France's politics, art, music, literature, philosophy, and entertainment throughout its history.[33] Taking issue with the way that Braudel depicted French nationhood in essentialist terms, Noiriel has shown how French culture has long absorbed the contributions of foreigners who have moved there and how immigrants have assimilated characteristics thought to be traditionally French. Others historians have filled out the picture as well. Gary Cross and Nancy Green, for instance, have demonstrated the complex interrelationships between French and immigrant laborers who traveled to France and remained, thereby adding to the diverse texture of French life.[34] Similarly, French historian Pascal Ory has remarked on France's ability

> to take seriously activities elsewhere deemed trivial, a characteristic of France that is likely to provoke puzzlement or irony abroad. In the twentieth century this tendency can be seen at work in the role that France has played in bestowing respectability on the "minor arts" of "popular culture." From film to comic books, from the Surrealist Revolution to "hot jazz," France has taken the fore in promoting the notion that there are no limits to conceptualization and that the intellect ennobles whatever it touches.[35]

Although one may question the implicit notion that no other nation takes popular culture as seriously as France, Ory helpfully points out France's history of directing critical attention to many different art forms. He also makes clear that the objects of such intellectual activity were not solely French because critics in France also saw value in examining other cultures.

France's tradition of defining the national community in cultural rather than ethnic terms, as Noiriel and Rogers Brubaker have both maintained, was one reason why this cultural give-and-take between foreigners and the French was possible.[36] Immigration policy under the Third Republic was one political example of this ongoing cultural cosmopolitanism in the 1920s and 1930s. The Republic offered anyone from outside France the opportunity to become a French citizen as well as culturally French by assimilating the norms of French society—learning the language, for one. This sort of openness was not without its limitations, and it points to the fact that cosmopolitanism is not necessarily the same as multiculturalism. Republican elites assumed that there was already a relatively unified cultural entity called France that they were working to complete through their educational policies along with the building of roads and railroads.[37] Their Republican nation was thought to be superior to all others, particularly to the people in the colonies who were in need of French "civiliza-tion."[38] And the promise of becoming French came, at least in theory, at the expense of abandoning much of one's former identity—a view that revealed a certain contradiction between the Republican belief in the indi-vidual and the requirement to sacrifice one's individual roots.[39] But if one were willing to meet such criteria, the doors of the nation were believed to be open to all. As Noiriel has suggested, that openness to immigrants produced cultural changes that the Republic might not necessarily have forseen.[40]

Cosmopolitanism, reflected both in immigration policies and the ability of French musicians to make jazz their own, has in actuality been an ongoing aspect of how many in France have defined their nation through-out the nineteenth and twentieth centuries. A legacy of the Enlightenment and one (although certainly not the only) component of the French revolu-tionary tradition, cosmopolitanism reaffirmed the belief in the universal equality of humanity over a more provincial chauvinism that claimed "France for the French." It suggested the dignity of all peoples and their ability to peacefully coexist.[41] Cosmopolitanism did not necessarily work against nationalism. Rather, it offered another view of the nation and an alternative to the growing exclusionary nationalism of the interwar years that sought to narrow the definition of what was truly French. It paral-leled, in the cultural sphere, elements of the Third Republic's political agenda, even while contributing to the "culture wars" of the era that ultimately helped to weaken the government since, clearly, not everyone embraced cosmopolitanism as part of France's heritage.

I suggest looking at the French acceptance of jazz against the backdrop of a persistent—although not total—cosmopolitanism that offered a way to adapt foreign cultures to French society in the modern age. Indeed, one should note that immigrants or their children were often at the center of the French jazz community—Grégor, Reinhardt, and Grappelli, to name a few. Cosmopolitanism enabled a set of creative responses to the many tensions of the early twentieth century. Jazz was an imported music to be sure, but not one that was incomprehensible, threatening, or unable to be brought into French entertainment. For many audiences in the 1920s, and especially for French jazz players in the 1930s, the "true" France did not exclude foreigners but rather encouraged a blending of French customs with imported influences. One writer in the widely read magazine *L'Il-lustration* put it this way regarding foreigners in Montparnasse:

These people who have come from all over the world feel perfectly at home [here]; and we accept them among us with an amused indulgence. . . . We accept many things with an ease that one hardly sees among other people. And to explain this ability, there is a reason that does not make us blush and that we hold as one of our highest principles: our immense love of liberty.[42]

Likewise, the French musicians who took up jazz seriously did not express merely a fashionable interest in things outside Europe that passed away with other fads, nor was it a temporary escape to exoticism. Instead, they demonstrated a willingness to look beyond the borders of France and bring a new music into their own culture. This cosmopolitanism was possible because French culture was not fixed or timeless but resilient and flexible, even after the turmoil of World War I. A more historically accurate portrait of the true France in the 1920s and 1930s was, in fact, one that had already been shaped by many foreign influences, and jazz came to play its part in adding to French culture by introducing a new sound for the new century that many listeners came to take as their own.

In light of this story, one might reconsider the much discussed américanisation that has altered France profoundly in the years since World War II, but that began in the 1920s and 1930s with jazz, among other imports.[43] The United States has certainly exerted an important influence over European life throughout the twentieth century, thereby creating a culture of movies, restaurants, and music shared by people the world over. Any visitor to Paris can eat at McDonald's, see the latest Hollywood films (in French or English), or visit the many jazz clubs around the city. But the presence of such phenomena does not necessarily make Paris any less French, nor does it imply an inevitable triumph of mass culture over the small-scale artisan craft for which Paris is still famous. The French may not be aesthetic arbiters for the rest of the world but they are for themselves. The Americanization model of cultural change is only another name for the modernization theses that historians have rejected as too teleological and simplistic.

Recently, Benjamin Barber offered a vision of the dark side of Americanization through a critique of the dual tensions of "Jihad" and "McWorld" in the post–World War II era, whose roots one could also begin to see in the 1920s and 1930s. Barber argues that the world is becoming more homogeneous through the spread of global (usually U.S.) cultural products (McWorld) and is simultaneously breaking up into smaller identity groups that seek to define themselves at the expense of others (Jihad). These two processes are related, Barber claims, because Jihad is an emotional and fearful response to McWorld's increasing intrusion into unique local cultures and traditions. At the same time, McWorld taps into people's need for emotional identification by creating identities under the rubric of corporate brand names and selling these new identities to individuals in the form of cultural products. Both of these processes, Barber argues, are antithetical to democracy because they undermine notions of tolerance, diversity, and civic participation in a common destiny. The nation-state, the traditional guarantor of democratic values, is assaulted by both Jihad and McWorld.[44]

In many ways, the spread of jazz from the United States to France provides one early piece of evidence for Barber's contention. Large U.S. record companies driven by the desire for profit exported recordings and promoted bands throughout France and the world. The response by many was to reject jazz as an alien infringement on the sort of music that was seen as truly French and retreat into an inward-looking view of the nation. But the story of jazz also involved many grassroots efforts on the part of French musicians and fans who sought to spread jazz themselves. As the case of jazz in interwar France highlights, cultural transmission has not always been "top-down," as Barber imagines it, nor was it always driven by corporate interests. Furthermore, the impulse to exclusion and nativism was not the only way to define French national identity during the 1920s and 1930s. Its antithesis, cosmopolitanism, was still at work. Nor does adaptation necessarily lead to homogenization. Perhaps the impulse to make jazz French—a process that lay somewhere between Jihad and McWorld—even provided a piece of fertile ground for a democratic culture that would resurface after the interlude of Vichy by preserving and adapting a vision of a more open, flexible society.

Since the transmission of cultural products is not always a top-down process, one must take into account that these products frequently change when they cross borders, both in meaning and content, and that French audiences have brought their own understandings to music, film, television, and other forms of entertainment just as audiences in any country. Such differences in understanding lie at the heart of the process of making jazz French that I have tried to demonstrate. Consumers are not merely passive recipients of information but act on what they see and hear in order to make sense of it. Some scholars, notably the Frankfurt School and their followers, have treated consumption as something imposed by a culture industry in order to homogenize individuals into a compliant mass of purchasers.[45] The case of jazz in interwar Paris, however, seems to support the conclusions of others who show how consumption can be a creative act that allows for a dialogue between consumers and products.[46]

Finally, the story of jazz in interwar France points to a larger process related to those above that has defined the twentieth century: globalization. Attempting to map the complex transformations that accompany the creation of a worldwide culture, scholars like Arjun Appadurai, James Clifford, and Marshall Sahlins have outlined the ways in which people interpret global products in light of their own experiences in order to reimagine their identities—including (but not limited to) national identities that seem to be under assault from the expansion of global capitalism. "The globalization of culture is not the same as its homogenization," Appadurai reminds us, "but globalization involves the use of a variety of instruments of homogenization (armaments, advertising techniques, language hegemonies, and clothing styles) that are absorbed into local political and cultural economies, only to be repatriated as heterogeneous dialogues of national sovereignty, free enterprise, and fundamentalism."[47] To his list of the instruments of homogenization, one might add phonographs, films, and radios. But as Appadurai suggests, the outcomes are far from certain since homogenization is not a guaranteed product of globalization. Instead, the results are often new debates about national identity that take into account the range of cultural flows that cross boundaries and become part of new national traditions. Sahlins puts it this way: "The world is also being re-diversified by indigenous adaptations to the global juggernaut. In some measure, global homogeneity and local differentiation have developed together, the latter as a response to the former in the name of native cultural autonomy."[48] And new, nonnational identities can emerge too. The movement of cultural products helps "stitch together languages, traditions, and places in coercive and creative ways, articulating embattled homelands, powers of memory, styles of transgression, in ambiguous relation to national and transnational structures," writes Clifford.[49] In that vein, one might see the Hot Club de France as the site of a new identity bridging a global network of jazz fans and musicians with national aspirations for a French jazz community through a common language of music: one could be both French and a jazz fan at the same time, with one foot in each culture, yet without fear of self-contradiction. Put another way, jazz music, which helped to inaugurate the first century of global media and international communication, underwent a parallel process of "localization" by which French musicians and audiences made it their own.

APPENDIX

Histories of Jazz in Interwar France

Among students of jazz in the United States, few French names have been placed within the canon of great performers from the 1920s and 1930s. Only Django Reinhardt and Stéphane Grappelli regularly appear in histories of jazz by American scholars. Instead, when considering the interwar period France has been more famous for its jazz critics, particularly Hugues Panassié and Charles Delaunay, and sometimes Belgian critic Robert Goffin. As a result, accounts of the 1920s and 1930s by jazz studies scholars and jazz historians make few references to personalities beyond this short list of names. Jazz in France has also gone largely unexamined by French historians, who often only mention the craze for jazz as one aspect of the 1920s or discuss Josephine Baker, rather erroneously, as a symbol of the entire phenomenon of jazz in France.

Nevertheless, some important works have laid a foundation for the study of this subject. Chris Goddard's *Jazz away from Home* (1979) is one of the most widely known accounts of jazz in interwar France. Goddard offers many insights about the musicians and bands performing in London and Paris, and provides a basic—although often highly anecdotal—narrative about jazz in the 1920s that serves as a good starting point for discussion. Goddard, however, does not try to place the music within the larger context of French history, and he ends his examination before French musicians began to take up jazz as a music of their own in the 1930s.

Other than Goddard's book, one of the most interesting works on jazz in the interwar period is William H. Kenney's article "Le Hot: The Assimilation of American Jazz in France, 1917–1940" (1984). Kenney, a well-known historian of jazz in the United States, maintains that French musicians of the 1930s "nationalized" jazz by adapting the American form of the music to French tastes and, in the process, "created their own '*école française de jazz*'" (5). My argument follows some of the basic lines of inquiry laid down by Kenney, especially the question of how a music "assimilates" into another culture and how that process of adaptation works with national identity. Kenney also begins to outline the dissemination of jazz in France, describing the significance of both the Hot Club de France and French musicians in making jazz a part of French popular culture.

In the end, though, Kenney's answers are more purely musical than historical. Musicians translated jazz into French forms, he argues, by substituting stringed instruments for the brassy sounds of the saxophone and trumpet. Whether the French musical tradition can be reduced to the centrality of strings seems a dubious claim, but more important, he overlooks the ways in which music is perceived and interpreted by audiences in being defined as national. His account also lacks a broad range of primary sources with which to tell the whole story of jazz in France. It is therefore skewed toward emphasizing the Hot Club and the music that it supported at the expense of other French musicians who were popular in the 1920s and 1930s.

Several other studies have paved the way for an examination of jazz in interwar France as well. Michael Haggerty's Harvard dissertation research was published in a special issue of *Jazz Magazine* in Paris in January 1984. Haggerty offers a brief outline of the reception of jazz along with a series of sketches of important musicians and intellectuals who became fans of the music. He has also collected an impressive array of visual sources—from photos to publicity posters to cartoons—that demonstrate the many ways in which jazz became a part of French entertainment and popular culture. Likewise, Ron Welburn's "Jazz Magazines of the 1930s: An Overview of Their Provocative Journalism" in *American Music* (1987) and A. David Franklin's article "A Preliminary Study of the Acceptance of Jazz by French Music Critics in the 1920s and 1930s" in *Annual Review of Jazz Studies* (1988) help to put authors like Panassié and Delaunay into a larger perspective.

More recently, jazz has become a subject of much greater interest to French historians, and a new wave of analysis has reopened the music to greater scrutiny. Ludovic Tournès's *New Orleans sur Seine: histoire du jazz en France* (1999) is a wonderfully readable and extensively researched grand narrative of the incorporation of jazz music into the mainstream of French popular culture. Tournès shows that this assimilation has taken place in three stages, which he labels "diffusion," "acculturation," and "legitimation." He takes the reader inside the organizations and institutions that spread jazz to French listeners, from the Hot Club de France to the Orchestre nationale de jazz created in 1986, which marks the culmination of both the process he describes and his book. Given the controversy surrounding the potentially shocking qualities of this music, one of the most surprising aspects of Tournès's book, however, is its clean, simple story that eliminates most traces of struggle concerning jazz's reception in France. One might think after reading this book that the French welcomed jazz with open arms and never doubted that they had made the right choice. More recently, *La France du jazz: musique, modernité, et identité dans la première moitié du XXe siècle* (2002) by Denis-Constant Martin and Olivier Roueff offers an overview of the history of jazz in France during the first part of the century and begins to interpret it against larger cultural questions, including some of the same ones that I have used here (the foreignness of jazz and jazz as a symbol of modernity). Their book also provides a useful collection of primary sources from the critical writing on jazz by French authors during the 1920s and 1930s.

Other French historians are exploring jazz in the interwar period too. Matthew F. Jordan's dissertation "Jazz Changes: A History of French Discourse on Jazz from Ragtime to Be-Bop" (1998) is an excellent account of jazz in France in the 1920s and 1930s. Jordan not only outlines much of the controversy surrounding jazz but also takes up the question of how it became a permanent part of French entertainment. He explores the rich discourse surrounding the music and its potential threats to French cultural traditions as well. In the process, Jordan discovers how debates about jazz gradually shifted to assume that this music was no longer outside the French tradition. By World War II, he asserts, the French had come to accept jazz as a given. I agree with Jordan's basic point even as his focus on the discourse surrounding the music sometimes removes the jazz that he discusses from a firm grounding in its historical context, and there is not always a clear sense in his account of why the music became such a touchstone of the complex debate that he portrays at each historical moment.

Concentrating on the immediate post–World War I period, Seth Schulmans's essay "Pleasures of the Primitive: A Cultural Genealogy of the Jazz-Band in Post–World War I Paris" (1998) is a superb illustration of the connections between the controversies surrounding jazz and the psychological effects of battle. See also his dissertation, "The Celebrity Culture of Modern Nightlife: Music Hall, Dance, and Jazz in Interwar Paris, 1918–1930." (2000) Elizabeth Vihlen takes up the story of jazz in the post–World War II era in her dissertation, "Sounding French: Jazz in Postwar France" (2000), and her article "Jammin' on the Champs-Elysées: Jazz, France, and the 1950s" (2000).

Beyond these works that most directly discuss jazz in France, studies by French historians become increasingly fragmented and touch on jazz incidentally or as only one part of a larger story. Some historians have examined jazz musicians as part of the history of African Americans in Paris. The best example is Tyler Stovall's book *Paris Noir: African Americans in the City of Light* (1996), which provides an extremely thorough, readable analysis. In particular, he describes the critical role that jazz played in helping to create an African American expatriate community in Paris. He also underscores the important association in the minds of French audiences of jazz with black American performers. Because Stovall's focus is on African Americans, he does not pay as much attention to the French audiences who listened to jazz or the French musicians who started to perform it. Consequently, he overlooks the shift that took place from the popularity of "black" jazz to the success of "white" jazz in the mid-1920s, along with the ways in which this transformation in the music's image made it more widely acceptable to Parisian audiences. Also exploring jazz within the context of African American history are Craig Lloyd's biography *Eugene Bullard: Black Expatriate in Jazz-Age Paris* (2000) and William A. Shack's book *Harlem in Montmartre: A Paris Jazz Story between the Great Wars* (2001). Both provide interesting discussions of the interwar period, also focusing on performers rather than audiences. These books can be examined in relation to Stovall's work as well. Lloyd's biography deepens the story of the cabaret owner Bullard during his time in Paris and extends it to cover his earlier and later life in the United States. By contrast, Shack's work condenses many of the events and personalities depicted in Stovall's book. He also adds some new details of his own, although without really supplying any new interpretive insights.

More broadly, Charles Rearick's book *The French in Love and War: Popular Culture in the Era of the World Wars* (1997) places jazz within the larger context of the entertainment of the 1920s and 1930s, but only mentions it in passing. In many ways, his work forms a crucial backdrop to research on jazz because he demonstrates that it was not the only noteworthy popular musical form of the 1920s—unlike the Americans, the French rarely if ever called it the Jazz Age.

Historians are not the only scholars now interested in jazz in France. Jody Blake's *Le Tumulte Noir: Modernist Art and Popular Entertainment in Jazz-Age Paris, 1900–1930* (1999) is an intriguing exploration of the impact of jazz music on the visual artists of the interwar era. Blake, an art historian, reconstructs the basic story of jazz music in 1920s Paris in order to show the many reactions it evoked from artists at the time. Modernist painters could not help being influenced by this prominent musical phenomenon, Blake argues, and they often frequented jazz clubs and listened to jazz records. Blake's attention to this aspect of the cultural context of modernist art is important and richly described. The story she tells is one in which jazz began in the 1920s as an explosion of exoticism in France, and ended by being tamed and controlled by a formalist reaction in the 1930s. There is evidence for such a narrative, but only if one excludes popular sentiment and influential jazz critics outside the art world in the 1930s like Panassié, who continued to celebrate the blackness of the music. Blake writes about a particular group of elites—painters, composers, and authors—who had little impact on jazz music or its reception beyond how they appropriated it into their own work. It is at this juncture that the interlocking worlds of art and popular entertainment in her story depart ways. Popular attitudes toward jazz were often more complex than she claims. Also, from an art historical point of view, Petrine Archer-Straw carefully documents the complicated fascination of the Parisian avant-garde art world with an international "black culture," including jazz, in *Negrophilia: Avant-Garde Paris and Black Culture in the 1920s* (2000). Doing so helps to situate jazz within a larger theoretical literature on the role of racial and cultural representation throughout the arts.

Philosopher Bernard Gendron takes up the linkages between the Parisian avant-garde and jazz in his book *Between Montmartre and the Mudd Club* (2002), set in the context of a larger set of questions about fluid cultural hierarchies and aesthetic theories. His discussion of jazz is firmly situated in a broader conceptualization of the history of modernism as expressed in the French tradition of popular entertainment in Montmartre.

Musicologists and music historians have also started to look at French jazz. "La Musique pour tout le monde: Jean Wiéner and the Dawn of French Jazz" (1998), a dissertation by Denise Pilmer Taylor, is a very good account of one crucial figure in French jazz during the 1920s. More broadly, Nancy Perloff's book *Art and the Everyday: Popular Entertainment and the Circle of Erik Satie* (1991) offers important insight into the connections between the avant-garde musicians Les Six and jazz by revealing how their efforts to create a new musical aesthetic led them to explore various aspects of popular culture including jazz. Glenn Watkins's *Pyramids at the Louvre: Music, Culture, and Collage from Stravinsky to the Postmodernists* (1994) shows the many connections between a modernist music like jazz with other art forms, both musical and visual—what Watkins calls "the assemblage and rearrangement of a rich parade of cultural loans involving textures, timbres, temperaments, and generative procedures ranging from the banal to the esoteric" (3). Both Watkins and Perloff demonstrate the uses to which many musicians put jazz in their attempts to break apart traditional cultural hierarchies in order to reinvent music and art in the interwar era.

NOTES

INTRODUCTION

1   Reprinted in Serge Dillaz, *La chanson sous la IIIe république (1870–1940)* (Paris: Tallandier, 1991), 169 (my translation).

2   The issues I address here are not the only developments that one might categorize as part of the debates about modern life in the 1920s and 1930s, but rather some of those that have emerged from the documents I examined relating to jazz. Other historians have described various attempts by people in interwar France to confront changes that can also be considered part of modern life. Mary Louise Roberts's book *Civilization without Sexes: Reconstructing Gender in Postwar France, 1917–1927* (Chicago: University of Chicago Press, 1994) captures this sense of cultural upheaval by demonstrating that it penetrated down to the level of gender roles and relationships. Robert Wohl's classic *The Generation of 1914* (Cambridge: Harvard University Press, 1979) outlines the various reactions of writers and intellectuals to the experience of the Great War along with the accompanying confusion at being, as he puts it, "wanderers between two worlds." Modris Eksteins's *The Rites of Spring: The Great War and the Birth of the Modern Age* (New York: Anchor Books, 1989) also grapples with how people tried to make sense of the modern age in the years just before and immediately after World War I.

3   Steven Kern describes the new perceptions of movement beginning in the late nineteenth century in *The Culture of Time and Space, 1880–1918* (Cambridge: Harvard University Press, 1983). See also Matt K. Matsuda, *The Memory of the Modern* (New York: Oxford University Press, 1996). James Clifford has recently contributed to thinking about cultural mobility in *Routes: Travel and Translation in the Late Twentieth Century* (Cambridge: Harvard University Press, 1997), reminding us that not only have individuals long come into contact with other cultures through travel but that travel and mobility can constitute a kind of cultural identity. Marshall Berman also depicts the sense of instability and change associated with modernity in his classic *All That Is Solid Melts into Air: The Experience of Modernity* (New York: Simon and Schuster, 1982). Eksteins describes the French fascination with Lindbergh in *Rites of Spring*, 242–47.

4   See Tyler Stovall, "The Color Line behind the Lines: Racial Violence in France during the Great War," *American Historical Review* 103 (June 1998): 737–69; and "Colour-Blind France? Colonial Workers during the First World War," *Race and Class* 35 (October 1993): 35–55.

5 See Michael Marrus, *The Unwanted: European Refugees in the Twentieth Century* (New York: Oxford University Press, 1985); and Robert H. Johnston, *New Mecca, New Babylon: Paris and the Russian Exiles, 1920–1945* (Kingston, Ontario: McGill-Queen's University Press, 1988). In the early 1930s, France briefly accepted Jews fleeing Nazi Germany, although the policy did not last long. See Vicki Caron, "The Politics of Frustration: French Jewry and the Refugee Crisis in the 1930s," *Journal of Modern History* 65 (June 1993): 311–56, and *Uneasy Asylum: France and the Jewish Refugee Crisis, 1933–1942* (Stanford, Calif.: Stanford University Press, 1999).

6 For discussions of the variety of ways in which foreigners were treated in interwar France, see Gérard Noiriel, *The French Melting Pot: Immigration, Citizenship, and National Identity*, trans. Geoffrey de Laforcade (Minneapolis: University of Minnesota Press, 1996); Ralph Schor, *L'Opinion française et les étrangers en France, 1919–1939* (Paris: Publications de la Sorbonne, 1985); Gary Cross, *Immigrant Workers in Industrial France: The Making of a New Laboring Class* (Philadelphia, Pa.: Temple University Press, 1983); Eugen Weber, *The Hollow Years: France in the 1930s* (New York: W. W. Norton, 1994); and Alec G. Hargreaves, *Immigration, "Race," and Ethnicity in Contemporary France* (London: Routledge, 1995).

7 Jane F. Fulcher, *French Cultural Politics and Music: From the Dreyfus Affair to the First World War* (New York: Oxford University Press, 1999).

8 There is a growing literature on Franco-American cultural interaction and particularly the question of américanisation, including: Paul A. Gagnon, "French Views of the Second American Revolution," *French Historical Studies* 2 (1962): 430–49; David Strauss, *Menace in the West: The Rise of French Anti-Americanism in Modern Times* (Westport, Conn.: Greenwood Press, 1978); Tony Judt, *Past Imperfect: French Intellectuals, 1944–1956* (Berkeley: University of California Press, 1992); Richard F. Kuisel, *Seducing the French: The Dilemma of Americanization* (Berkeley: University of California Press, 1993); Jean-Philippe Mathy, *Extrême-Occident: French Intellectuals and America* (Chicago: University of Chicago Press, 1993), and *French Resistance: The French-American Culture Wars* (Minneapolis: University of Minnesota Press, 2000); Kristin Ross, *Fast Cars, Clean Bodies: Decolonization and the Reordering of French Culture* (Cambridge: MIT Press, 1995); Ludovic Tournès, "L'Américanisation de la culture française, ou la rencontre d'un modèle conquérant et d'un pays au seuil de la modernité," *Historiens et géographes* (July/August 1997): 65–79; Shanny Peer, *France on Display: Peasants, Provincials, and Folklore in the 1937 Paris World's Fair* (Albany: State University of New York Press, 1998); Marjorie Beale, *The Modernist Enterprise: French Elites and the Threat of Modernity, 1900–1940* (Stanford, Calif.: Stanford University Press, 1999); and Stephen L. Harp, *Marketing Michelin: Advertising and Cultural Identity in Twentieth-Century France* (Baltimore, Md.: Johns Hopkins University Press, 2001). For other views of U.S. influence on Europe, see Richard Pells, *Not Like Us: How Europeans Have Loved, Hated, and Transformed*

American Culture since World War II (New York: Basic Books, 1997); and Mary Nolan, *Visions of Modernity: American Business and the Modernization of Germany* (New York: Oxford University Press, 1994).

9 James H. Smiley, "American Goods as a Leavening Agent in the Living Standards in Foreign Countries," *Proceedings of the Institute of International Relations* 5 (1930): 97–99.

10 See Anson Rabinbach, *The Human Motor: Energy, Fatigue, and the Origins of Modernity* (Berkeley: University of California Press, 1992); Ellen Furlough, "Selling the American Way in Interwar France: *Prix Uniques* and the Salons des Arts Menagers," *Journal of Social History* (spring 1993): 491–519; and Beale, *The Modernist Enterprise*.

11 On Paris as a modern city, see Vanessa Schwartz, *Spectacular Realities: Early Mass Culture in Fin-de-Siècle Paris* (Berkeley: University of California Press, 1998); Berman, *All That Is Solid Melts into Air*; David Jordan, *Transforming Paris: The Life and Labors of Baron Haussmann* (New York: Free Press, 1995); Michael B. Miller, *The Bon Marché: Bourgeois Culture and the Department Store, 1869–1920* (Princeton, N.J.: Princeton University Press, 1981); and T. J. Clark, *The Painting of Modern Life: Paris in the Art of Manet and His Followers* (Princeton, N.J.: Princeton University Press, 1984).

12 See Tyler Stovall, "Paris in the Age of Anxiety, 1919–39," in *Anxious Visions: Surrealist Art*, ed. Sidra Stich (New York: Abbeville Press, 1990), 201–21; and Barnett Singer, "Technology and Social Change: The Watershed of the 1920's," in *Proceedings of the Fourth Annual Meeting of the Western Society for French History* (1977): 321–29. Singer also points to the limits of technological change as well as its impact.

13 See Furlough, "Selling the American Way"; Miller, *The Bon Marché*; and Jerrold Seigel, *Bohemian Paris: Culture, Politics, and the Boundaries of Bourgeois Life, 1830–1930* (New York: Penguin, 1986).

14 Herrick Chapman makes the link between these concepts in his review article "Modernity and National Identity in Postwar France," *French Historical Studies* 22 (spring 1999). Although Chapman is primarily discussing books from the post–World War II era, the story of jazz in the interwar period demonstrates that this connection can be made even earlier in the century.

15 Chris Goddard, *Jazz away from Home* (London: Paddington Press, 1979). See the appendix for a fuller discussion of Goddard's book and its place in the literature on jazz in France.

16 See also Ludovic Tournés, *New Orleans sur Seine: histoire du jazz en france* (Paris: Fayard, 1999). Several other works on jazz in Europe help to further illustrate the wider popularity of the music beyond the United States, including Michael H. Kater, *Different Drummers: Jazz in the Culture of Nazi Germany* (New York: Oxford University Press, 1992); S. Frederick Starr, *Red and Hot: The Fate of Jazz in the Soviet Union, 1917–1980* (New York: Oxford University Press, 1983); Jim Godbolt, *A History of Jazz in Britain, 1919–1950*

(London: Quartet Books, 1984); and Uta G. Poiger, *Jazz, Rock, and Rebels: Cold War Politics and American Culture in a Divided Germany* (Berkeley: University of California Press, 2000). On jazz beyond Europe, see for example, E. Taylor Atkins, *Blue Nippon: Authenticating Jazz in Japan* (Durham, N.C.: Duke University Press, 2001).

17 Others have written about the ways in which French composers—like Debussy, Satie, Milhaud, and others—absorbed jazz techniques into their works to alter or invigorate European art music. On this subject, see, for example, Nancy Perloff, *Art and the Everyday: Popular Entertainment and the Circle of Erik Satie* (Oxford: Clarendon Press, 1991); Glenn Watkins, *Pyramids at the Louvre: Music, Culture, and Collage from Stravinsky to the Postmodernists* (Cambridge: Harvard University Press, 1994); Jack Sullivan, *New World Symphonies: How American Culture Changed European Music* (New Haven, Conn.: Yale University Press, 1999); and Bernard Gendron, *Between Montmartre and the Mudd Club: Popular Music and the Avant-Garde* (Chicago: University of Chicago Press, 2002).

18 Weber, *The Hollow Years*. Another similar title is William Wiser's *The Twilight Years: Paris in the 1930s* (New York: Carroll and Graff, 2000).

19 Herman Lebovics, *True France: The Wars over Cultural Identity, 1900–1945* (Ithaca, N.Y.: Cornell University Press, 1992), xiii. See Robert O. Paxton, *Vichy France: Old Guard and New Order, 1940–1944* (New York: Columbia University Press, 1982).

20 Lebovics, *True France*, 190.

21 Romy Golan, *Modernity and Nostalgia: Art and Politics in France between the Wars* (New Haven, Conn.: Yale University Press, 1995), x.

22 Martha Hanna, *The Mobilization of Intellect: French Scholars and Writers during the Great War* (Cambridge: Harvard University Press, 1996).

23 Michael B. Miller, *Shanghai on the Metro: Spies, Intrigue, and the French between the Wars* (Berkeley: University of California Press, 1994), 5. See also Roberts, *Civilization without Sexes*.

24 Peer, *France on Display*; Beale, *The Modernist Enterprise*; and Harp, *Marketing Michelin*. See also Chapman, "Modernity and National Identity in Postwar France." Olivier Barrot and Pascal Ory's collection *Entre deux guerres: la création française entre 1919–1939* (Paris: Editions François Bourin, 1990) also gathers essays on a wide range of popular culture in the 1920s and 1930s to demonstrate that French artists and intellectuals remained active and productive even in the wake of war. Likewise, historians such as Charles Rearick in *The French in Love and War: Popular Culture in the Era of the World Wars* (New Haven, Conn.: Yale University Press, 1997) and Daniel J. Sherman in *The Construction of Memory in Interwar France* (Chicago: University of Chicago Press, 1999) add to an understanding of the interwar years as complex and variegated.

25 Rearick, *The French in Love and War*.

26 Golan, *Modernity and Nostalgia*, ix.

27 Articles and books from the time period reveal much of this continued diversity in meaning. For a discussion of the many—often dubious—meanings of the word's origins and definitions, see also Alan P. Merriam and Fradley H. Garner, "Jazz—The Word," *Ethnomusicology* (September 1968): 373–96.

1 THE ARRIVAL OF JAZZ

1 See Henry Blumenthal, *American and French Culture, 1800–1900: Interchanges in Art, Science, Literature, and Society* (Baton Rouge: Louisiana State University Press, 1975); Harvey Levenstein, *Seductive Journey: American Tourists in France from Jefferson to the Jazz Age* (Chicago: University of Chicago Press, 1998); and Jean-Philippe Mathy, *Extrême-Occident: French Intellectuals and America* (Chicago: University of Chicago Press, 1993).

2 Seth Schulman makes this argument well in "Pleasures of the Primitive: A Cultural Genealogy of the Jazz-Band in Post–World War I Paris," *Proceedings of the Western Society for French History* 26 (1998): 354–61.

3 Samuel Taylor Moore, *America and the World War: A Narrative of the Part Played by the United States from the Outbreak to Peace* (New York: Blue Ribbon Books, 1937), 141–42.

4 Joseph Delteil, *The Poilus: An Epic,* trans. Jacques LeClerc (New York: Minton, Balch, and Company, 1927), 114.

5 Moore, *America and the World War*, 141.

6 *Wine, Women, and War: A Diary of Disillusionment* (New York: J. H. Sears, 1926), 31.

7 Delteil, *The Poilus*, 114.

8 Sam M. Lewis, "Mighty" Joe Young, and Walter Donaldson, "How 'Ya Gonna Keep 'Em Down on the Farm (After They've Seen Paree?)" (New York: Watson, Berlin, and Snyder, 1919); see also Levenstein, *Seductive Journey*, 233.

9 See Frank Freidel, *Over There: The Story of America's First Great Overseas Crusade* (New York: Bramhall House, 1964); see also Levenstein, *Seductive Journey*.

10 Levenstein, *Seductive Journey*, 221–24.

11 Cited in Alan Williams, *Republic of Images: A History of French Filmmaking* (Cambridge: Harvard University Press, 1992), 82.

12 Richard Abel, *French Cinema: The First Wave, 1915–1929* (Princeton, N.J.: Princeton University Press, 1984), 10.

13 Williams, *Republic of Images*, 81.

14 See Victoria de Grazia, "Mass Culture and Sovereignty: The American Challenge to European Cinemas, 1920–1960," *Journal of Modern History* 61 (March 1989): 53–87.

15 Tyler Stovall, *Paris Noir: African Americans in the City of Light* (Boston: Houghton Mifflin, 1996), 18.

16 Michel Fabre, *From Harlem to Paris: Black American Writers in France, 1840–1980* (Urbana: University of Illinois Press, 1991), 2.

17 Cited in Stovall, *Paris Noir*, 18; and Michel Fabre, *La Rive noire: de Harlem à la Seine* (Paris: Lieu Commun, 1985), 49.

18 Fabre, *From Harlem to Paris*, 2.

19 See Stovall, *Paris Noir*.

20 See Nancy Perloff, *Art and the Everyday: Popular Entertainment and the Circle of Erik Satie* (Oxford: Clarendon Press, 1991).

21 On James Reese Europe, see Samuel B. Charters and Leonard Kunstadt, *Jazz: A History of the New York Scene* (Garden City, N.Y.: Doubleday, 1962); and Reid Badger, *A Life in Ragtime: A Biography of James Reese Europe* (New York: Oxford University Press, 1995).

22 Cited in Charters and Kunstadt, *Jazz*, 65.

23 Charters and Kunstadt, *Jazz*, 65–66.

24 See Egino Biagioni, *Herb Flemming: A Jazz Pioneer around the World* (Alphen aan den Rijn, Netherlands: Micrography, 1977).

25 Cited in Badger, *A Life in Ragtime*, 194.

26 Badger, *A Life in Ragtime*, 163.

27 Charles Welton, "Filling France Full of Jazz," *World Magazine*, 30 March 1919, excerpted extensively in Emmett J. Scott, *Scott's Official History of the American Negro in the World War* (New York: Arno Press, 1969), 303.

28 Cited in Badger, *A Life in Ragtime*, 193.

29 Cited in Scott, *Scott's Official History*, 308. Another account of black American musicians in France during World War I can be found in Addie W. Hunton and Kathryn M. Johnson, *Two Colored Women with the American Expeditionary Forces* (1920; reprint, New York: AMS Press, 1971).

30 Robert Goffin, *Jazz: From the Congo to the Metropolitan*, trans. Walter Schaap and Leonard G. Feather (Garden City, N.Y.: Doubleday, 1946), 69.

31 Cited in ibid.

32 Goffin, *Jazz*, 69.

33 Darius Milhaud, "Les Ressources nouvelles de la musique," *L'Esprit nouveau*, July 1924 (a slightly different version of this article appeared as "The Jazz Band and Negro Music," *Living Age*, 18 October 1924, 169–73); Jean Cocteau, "Cock and Harlequin," in *A Call to Order*, trans. Rollo H. Myers (New York: Henry Holt, 1923); and Jacques-Charles, *Cent ans de music-hall* (Geneva: Editions Jeheber, 1956), 186.

34 Perloff, *Art and the Everyday*, 53.

35 Le Masque d'Enfer, "La Potinière: une grande générale de guerre," 13 December 1917, R018454, Bibliothèque de l'Arsenal.

36 Cocteau, "Cock and Harlequin," 13–14.

37 René Wisner, "Soirée Parisienne," 14 December 1917, R018454, Bibliothèque de l'Arsenal.

38 Programs from Casino de Paris, R018516, Bibliothèque de l'Arsenal.

39 *Pionniers du jazz français: Paris 1906–1931*, LP recording, Pathé 1552551, SD3071232, Bibliothèque Nationale, Département Audiovisuel.

40 See Jacques Hélian, *Les Grands orchestres de music hall en France: souvenirs et temoignages* (Paris: Filipacchi, 1984).

41 Cited in Hélian, *Grands orchestres*, 36.

42 Hélian, *Grands orchestres*, 33.

43 Cited in Hélian, *Grands orchestres*, 37.

44 Hélian, *Grands orchestres*, 37.

45 Ibid., 41–42.

46 Cited in Chris Goddard, *Jazz away from Home* (New York: Paddington Press, 1979), 261–62.

47 Ibid., 272.

48 Biographical information on Vauchant compiled from Goddard, *Jazz away from Home*; and Charles Delaunay, *Delaunay's Dilemma: de la peinture au jazz* (Mâcon: Editions W, 1985).

49 Ted Gioia, *The History of Jazz* (New York: Oxford University Press, 1997), 45.

50 See William Howland Kenney, *Chicago Jazz: A Cultural History, 1904–1930* (New York: Oxford University Press, 1993), chap. 2.

51 Gioia, *History of Jazz*, 46.

52 Goddard, *Jazz away from Home*, 23.

53 Ibid., 22.

54 James Lincoln Collier, *The Making of Jazz: A Comprehensive History* (New York: Dell Publishing Company, 1978), 73.

55 For a broad overview, see Jack Sullivan, *New World Symphonies: How American Culture Changed European Music* (New Haven, Conn.: Yale University Press, 1999), 191–237.

56 See Marc A. Wiener, "*Urwaldmusik* and the Borders of German Identity: Jazz in Literature of the Weimar Republic," *German Quarterly* 64 (1991): 475–87; Peter Jelavich, *Berlin Cabaret* (Cambridge: Harvard University Press, 1993); and Michael H. Kater, *Different Drummers: Jazz in the Culture of Nazi Germany* (New York: Oxford University Press, 1992).

57 Sam Wooding, "Eight Years Abroad with a Jazz Band," *Etude*, April 1939, 233.

58 On Weill and Krenek and their relationship to jazz, see Susan C. Cook, *Opera for a New Republic: The Zeitopern of Krenek, Weill, and Hindemith* (Ann Arbor, Mich.: UMI Research Press, 1988); and Sullivan, *New World Symphonies*.

59 Maxwell Philpott, "Jazz in a Desert City," *Jazz-Hot*, May/June 1935, 17–19.

60 See Goddard, *Jazz away from Home*; and Collier, *The Making of Jazz*.

61 See Jim Godbolt, *A History of Jazz in Britain, 1919–1950* (London: Quartet Books, 1984).

62 Goddard, *Jazz away from Home*, 23.

63 Cited in ibid., 32.

64 Ibid., 32, 52.

65 Ernst-Alexandre Ansermet, "Bechet and Jazz Visit Europe, 1919," trans. Walter Schapp, in *Frontiers of Jazz*, ed. Ralph de Toledano, 3d ed. (Gretna, La.: Pelican, 1994), 112. Ansermet's article has also been reprinted in Robert Gottlieb, ed., *Reading Jazz: A Gathering of Autobiography, Reportage, and Criticism from 1919 to Now* (New York: Pantheon, 1996).

66 Ansermet, "Bechet and Jazz," 115.

67 Ibid. The idea that jazz is more a way of playing than a specific repertoire of songs is not surprising; Ansermet's connection of that style with black Americans and racial characteristics is the significant cultural point.

68 Maurice Mairgance, "Un jazz célèbre en 1844," *Ami du peuple du soir*, 22 August 1929.

69 "Un jazz nègre dans un mariage mystique du seizième siècle," *Comœdia*, 8 · April 1931.

70 "Du blanc et du noir dans le jazz," *Musique et instruments*, 10 August 1928, 1047.

71 P. Pompilio, "Analyze documentaire," *L'Artiste musicien de Paris*, October 1926, 296–97.

72 André Demaison, "Jazz William's," *Jazz: l'actualité intellectuelle*, 15 March 1929, 175–77.

73 André Salmon, "Negro Art," trans. D. Brinton, *Burlington Magazine* 1920, 164; see also Phyllis Rose, *Jazz Cleopatra: Josephine Baker in Her Time* (New York: Vintage, 1989).

74 Cited in Rose, *Jazz Cleopatra*, 45.

75 See Brett A. Berliner, "The 'Exotic' Black African in the French Social Imagination in the 1920s" (Ph.D. diss., University of Massachusetts at Amherst, 1999). For a discussion of the ambiguities in Maran's novel, see Stovall, ·*Paris Noir*, 32.

76 See, for example, Paul Gaultier, "Du jazz-band au roman nègre," *Revue politique et littéraire (Revue bleue)*, 21 January 1922.

77 Salmon, "Negro Art," 164.

78 Ibid., 165.

79 Jean Laude, *La Peinture française (1905–1914) et l'art nègre* (Paris: Editions Klincksieck, 1968), 535. On race and images of Africans in France, see Berliner, "The 'Exotic' Black African"; Dana Hale, "Races on Display: French Representations of the Colonial Native, 1886–1931" (Ph.D. diss., Brandeis University, 1998); Brent Edwards, "Black Globality: The International Shape of Black Intellectual Culture" (Ph.D. diss., Columbia University, 1998); Jan Nederveen Pieterse, *White on Black: Images of Africa and Blacks in Western Popular Culture* (New Haven, Conn.: Yale University Press, 1995); Petrine Archer-Straw, *Negrophilia: Avant-Garde Paris and Black Culture in the 1920s* (London: Thames and Hudson, 2000); Elizabeth Ezra, *The Colonial Unconscious: Race and Culture in Interwar France* (Ithaca, N.Y.: Cor-

nell University Press, 2000); and Bernard Gendron, *Between Montmartre and the Mudd Club: Popular Music and the Avant Garde* (Chicago: University of Chicago Press, 2002).

80 One all-female band named Les Ingénues featured harp, tuba, accordion, drums, banjo, cello, and piano, but it did not appear to promote itself as a jazz band. See advertisement in *Sud*, 1 March 1929, 20, R0585, Bibliothèque de l'Arsenal.

81 Advertisement for La Neige des Cevennes. My thanks to Christian Senn for calling this to my attention.

82 Charles Rearick, *The French in Love and War: Popular Culture in the Era of the World Wars* (New Haven, Conn.: Yale University Press, 1997), 91–92. For a discussion of these fears outside the context of jazz, see Mary Louise Roberts, *Civilization without Sexes: Reconstructing Gender in Postwar France, 1917–1927* (Chicago: University of Chicago Press, 1994), chap. 5.

83 Mary Louise Roberts, "Samson and Delilah Revisited: The Politics of Women's Fashion in 1920s France," *American Historical Review* 98 (June 1993): 657–84.

84 "Robes à danser," *Femina*, 1932 (month unclear from microfilm), 39.

85 The word *jazz* itself has a long, confusing, and contested history that includes possible French origins (some believed that it came from the verb *jaser*, which means "to gossip"). See Alan P. Merriam and Fradley H. Garner, "Jazz—The Word," *Ethnomusicology* (September 1968): 373–96.

86 These magazines can be found in Bibliothèque de l'Arsenal, 4° Rk19759 and Ro 4° 16449, respectively.

87 Advertisement for Etablissements Jules Piano in *Musique et instruments*, 10 February 1925, 122.

88 Irving Schwerké, *Kings Jazz and David (Jazz et David, Rois)* (Paris: Irving Schwerké, 1927), 34.

89 Cited in André Cœuroy and André Schaeffner, *Le Jazz* (Paris: Editions Claude Aveline, 1926), 118. In their book, Cœuroy and Schaeffner reprinted the responses that they had elicited from a survey of composers, critics, and intellectuals. They originally published these responses in *Paris-Midi* in 1925.

90 Ibid., 119.

91 Cited in Goddard, *Jazz away from Home*, 16.

92 Emile Vuillermoz, "Rag-time et jazz-band," 6 October 1918, R0585, Bibliothèque de l'Arsenal.

93 Michel Leiris, *Manhood: A Journey from Childhood into the Fierce Order of Virility*, trans. Richard Howard (New York: Grossman, 1963), 108.

94 Cited in Cœuroy and Schaeffner, *Jazz*, 126.

95 Ibid., 132.

96 Claude Gay, "Le jazz," *Vie Marseillaise*, 7 August 1930.

97 Sem, *La Ronde de nuit* (Paris: Arthème Fayard, 1923), 28.

98 Marcel Espieu, "Au rhythme infernal du jazz," *Avenir*, 18 February 1926.

99 Cited in Goddard, *Jazz away from Home*, 16.

100 Cocteau, "Cock and Harlequin," 13.

101 "Le jazz du peuple," *Musique et instruments*, 10 October 1929, 1397.

102 "Le jazz est né d'une invention française," 16 June 1926, R0585, Bibliothèque de l'Arsenal.

103 A.-M. de Bodisco-Carsaguene, "Une enquête sur le jazz," *Européen*, 1 January 1930.

104 Cited in Cœuroy and Schaeffner, *Jazz*, 126.

105 Paul Le Flem, "Le jazz serait-il français?" *Comœdia*, 25 January 1926.

106 On instruments, see Milhaud, "The Jazz Band and Negro Music"; Leiris, *Manhood*; and Goddard, *Jazz away from Home*. On the saw as a jazz instrument, see François Oswald, "La reine du jazz," *Paris-Midi*, 4 July 1927.

107 Cited in Cœuroy and Schaeffner, *Jazz*, 119.

108 André Warnod, *Les Bals de Paris* (Paris: Editions Georges Crès, 1922), 292.

109 Gustave Fréjaville, "L'orchestre du Dr Moreau," *Débats*, 9 July 1927. Gothas were a type of German bomb used during World War I, and Gotha was also the German city where airplanes were made.

110 Cited in Cœuroy and Schaeffner, *Jazz*, 118.

111 Cited in André Mauprey, "Le jazz peut-il rendre fou?" *Jazz-Tango*, August 1931.

112 Jacques Yvel, "Aimez-vous le jazz?" *Soir*, 1 April 1927.

113 Jacques Janin, "Le jazz, lumière de l'occident? Les nouveautés de la «nationale»," *L'ami du peuple du soir*, 26 March 1929.

114 A. Jeanneret, "Le nègre et le jazz," *La Revue musicale*, 1 July 1927, 26.

115 R0585, Bibliothèque de l'Arsenal.

116 Cited in Cœuroy and Schaeffner, *Jazz*, 125.

117 Cited in R0585, Bibliothèque de l'Arsenal.

118 Yvel, "Aimez-vous le jazz?"

2 THE SPREAD OF JAZZ

1 "Note sur les principales danses modernes," in *Les Spectacles à travers les ages*, Claude Berton et al. (Paris: Aux Editions du Cygne, 1932), 358.

2 R. de Givrey, "La verité sur la danse?" R013017, Bibliothèque de l'Arsenal.

3 Charles Rearick, *Pleasures of the Belle Epoque: Entertainment and Festivity in Turn-of-the-Century France* (New Haven, Conn.: Yale University Press, 1985), 70.

4 Ibid., 70–71; and Jerrold Seigel, *Bohemian Paris: Culture, Politics, and the Boundaries of Bourgeois Life, 1830–1930* (New York: Penguin, 1986), 215–41.

5 Rearick, *Pleasures of the Belle Epoque*, 71.

6 See Rearick, *Pleasures of the Belle Epoque*; Charles Rearick, "Song and Society in Turn-of-the-Century France," *Journal of Social History* 22 (fall 1988): 45–63; and Bernard Gendron, *Between Montmartre and the Mudd Club: Popular Music and the Avant-Garde* (Chicago: University of Chicago

Press, 2002). On the creation and expansion of other kinds visual entertainment in the fin de siècle, see Vanessa Schwartz, *Spectacular Realities: Early Mass Culture in Fin-de-Siècle Paris* (Berkeley: University of California Press, 1998).

7   Jules Bertaut, *Paris: 1870–1935*, trans. R. Millar (London: Eyre and Spottiswoode, 1936), 256.

8   Georges de Wissant, "Le théâtre se meurt! Autant l'achever tout de suite," *Paris*, 5 January 1923.

9   Additional information on taxes gleaned from references in the trade journal *Musique et instruments*, 10 May 1920; on complimentary tickets, see "Duel over Tax," *Variety*, 25 October 1923, 2.

10 Jean Millot, "La taxe sur les spectacles en France," *Comœdia*, 24 February 1928.

11 *Musique et instruments*, 10 September 1920.

12 Bricktop with James Haskins, *Bricktop* (New York: Atheneum, 1983), 138.

13 On changing tax conditions throughout the 1920s, see Millot, "La taxe sur les spectacles en France." On the situation in the provinces, see Paul Gordeaux, "La grève générale du spectacle aura-t-elle lieu le 15 février," *Echo*, 2 January 1923.

14 Millot, "La taxe sur les spectacles en France."

15 "Banish Cafe Musicians," *Variety*, 9 July 1920, 2.

16 E. G. Kendrew, "In Paris," *Variety*, 30 July 1920, 2.

17 "Paris Vaudevillians File New Minimum Scale Basis," *Variety*, 16 July 1920, 2.

18 "Musique d'hier et d'aujourd'hui," *Radio magazine*, 9 September 1928, 2.

19 "Un Record," 23 February 1918, Ro18454, Bibliothèque de l'Arsenal.

20 de Wissant, "Le théâtre se meurt!"

21 "Huge Amusement Trust Aims to Corrupt World in Paris," *Variety*, 9 January 1920, 4.

22 René Dumesnil, "Les Concerts Symphoniques," *Le Correspondent* (1924), 700.

23 Bertaut, *Paris*, 275.

24 See Jean-Jacques Becker and Serge Bernstein, *Victoire et frustrations, 1914–1929* (Paris: Editions du Seuil, 1990), 359.

25 Historian Louis Chevalier also describes the nouveaux riches in his book *Montmartre du plaisir et du crime* (Paris: Editions Robert Laffont, 1980).

26 See Harvey Levenstein, *Seductive Journey: American Tourists in France from Jefferson to the Jazz Age* (Chicago: University of Chicago Press, 1998), chaps. 15–18.

27 On French views of the United States as a consumer society, see chapter 4 of this book. On prix uniques stores and advertising, see Ellen Furlough, "Selling the American Way in Interwar France: *Prix Uniques* and the Salons des Arts Menagers," *Journal of Social History* (spring 1993): 491–519; Marjorie Beale, *The Modernist Enterprise: French Elites and the Threat of Modernity, 1900–1940* (Stanford, Calif.: Stanford University Press, 1999); Stephen L. Harp, *Marketing Michelin: Advertising and Cultural Identity in Twentieth-*

Century France (Baltimore, Md.: Johns Hopkins University Press, 2001); and Levenstein, *Seductive Journey*.

28 Claude Berton et al., *Les Spectacles à travers les ages* (Paris: Aux Editions du Cygne, 1932), 358.

29 On nostalgia, see Matt K. Matsuda, *The Memory of the Modern* (New York: Oxford University Press, 1996). See also Ingrid Elizabeth Fey, "First Tango in Paris: Latin Americans in Turn-of-the-Century France, 1880–1920" (Ph.D. diss., University of California, Los Angeles, 1996).

30 Bertaut, *Paris*, 272.

31 Advertisement for La Neige des Cevennes.

32 G. George, "La Théorie du shimmy," *La Danse*, September 1921.

33 "La Vie à Paris," *La Moniteur Franco-Américain*, February 1925, 49–52.

34 Jean Laporte, *Musiciens de Pigalle, ou, cinquante ans de musique: mémoires* (Paris: Editions de Bruyère, 1985), 8.

35 Hervé Lauwick, "Comment on danse un danse nouvelle," *Intransigeant*, 18 January 1920.

36 Frank J. Gibbons, "A Survey of America's Music," *Metronome*, September 1923, 88.

37 Paul Specht, "Yankee Jazz Abroad," *Jacobs' Orchestra Monthly*, October 1927, 9.

38 Julian Street, *Where Paris Dines* (London: William Heinemann, 1929), 141.

39 Ibid., 142.

40 Jules Bertaut, *Les Belles nuits de Paris* (Paris: Editions Jules Tallandier, 1956), 145.

41 Francis de Miomandre, "Au Dancing," *Europe Nouvelle*, 23 May 1920.

42 On musicians leaving the stage, see André Warnod, *Les Bals de Paris* (Paris: Editions Georges Crés, 1922), 294.

43 Ibid., 296.

44 Ibid.

45 Ibid., 19–20.

46 Ibid., 296–97.

47 Ralph Nevill, *Days and Nights in Montmartre and the Latin Quarter* (New York: George H. Doran, 1927), 42.

48 Ibid.

49 Sisley Huddleston, *Back to Montparnasse: Glimpses of Broadway in Bohemia* (Philadelphia, Pa.: J. B. Lippincott, 1931), 48.

50 Léon Werth, *Danse, danseurs, dancings*, 5th ed. (Paris: F. Rieder, 1925), 109.

51 Ibid., 110–11.

52 Warnod, *Les Bals de Paris*, 6–7.

53 Werth, *Danse*, 112.

54 For a firsthand account of Le Bal Nègre by the Antillean musician Ernest Léardée, see Jean-Pierre Meunier and Brigitte Léardée, *La biguine de l'oncle Ben's: Ernest Léardée raconte* (Paris: Editions Caribéennes, 1989).

55 George F. Paul, "The Gayest Dance in Gay Paree," *Abbot's Monthly*, August 1931, 6.

56 Ibid., 60.

57 Marcel Pays, "Un bal nègre," *Information*, 23 July 1926.

58 Michael Haggerty and Michel Leiris, "Jazz," *Sulfur* 15 (1986): 98.

59 Pays, "Un bal nègre."

60 Paul, "Gayest Dance," 60.

61 Warnod, *Les Bals de Paris*, 300.

62 Leonard R. Berlanstein, *The Working People of Paris, 1871–1914* (Baltimore, Md.: Johns Hopkins University Press, 1984), 127.

63 Warnod, *Les Bals de Paris*, 285.

64 Ibid., 287.

65 Cited in ibid., 289.

66 Sisley Huddleston, *Paris Salons, Cafés, Studios* (New York: Blue Ribbon Books, 1928), 25.

67 Werth, *Danse*, 104–5.

68 Sem, *La Ronde de nuit* (Paris: Arthème Fayard, 1923), 117–18.

69 Henry Lyonnet, "Les Bals Publics de Paris," in *Les Spectacles à travers les âges*, Claude Berton et al. (Paris: Aux Editions du Cygne, 1932), 356.

70 This information is summarized from Roland Gelatt, *The Fabulous Phonograph: From Tin Foil to High Fidelity* (Philadelphia, Pa.: J. B. Lippincott, 1955). The word *phonograph* originally referred to a vertical recording cylinder, and the term *gramophone* applied to a horizontal recording disk. Eventually, phonograph came to mean all manner of talking machines.

71 "Le commerce international et les machines parlantes," *Musique et instruments*, 10 December 1929, 1717.

72 Russell Sanjek, *American Popular Music and Its Business: Volume III, from 1900–1984* (New York: Oxford University Press, 1988), chap. 7.

73 This description of the salon is based on Gelatt, *The Fabulous Phonograph*, 103.

74 See, for example, Harry Alan Potamkin, "The Progress of Mechanical Entertainment in Europe," *Phonograph Monthly Review*, July 1930, 336; and "Recital phonographique," *Musique et instruments*, 10 February 1927, 183.

75 "Les machines parlantes et leur diffusion," *Musique et instruments,* 10 October 1926, 1111.

76 "Musique d'hier et aujourd'hui," *Radio magazine*, 9 September 1928, 2.

77 André Cœuroy and G. Clarence, *Le Phonographe* (Paris: Editions Kra, 1929), 71.

78 Potamkin, "The Progress of Mechanical Entertainment in Europe," 336.

79 Michel Emer, "Soirée hot au Cinéma Falguière," *Jazz-Tango-Dancing*, March 1933, 5.

80 St. Vilmer, "Mon Cœur est un Jazz-Band," *La Cinématographie française*, n.d., Rk 6510, Bibliothèque de l'Arsenal. See also L. C., "Mon Cœur est un Jazz-Band," *Cinéjournal*, 26 April 1929, 8–9.

81 "Les Présentations," *Cinéjournal*, 5 July 1929, 22. See also R03349, Bibliothèque de l'Arsenal.

82 Becker and Bernstein, *Victoire et frustrations*, 382.

83 Cécile Méadel, *Histoire de la radio des années trente: du sans-filiste à l'auditeur* (Paris: Anthropos/INA, 1994), 316–17.

84 For information on radio broadcasting as well as a variety of radio magazines and journals from the period, including *Radio magazine* and *Le Petit radio*, see F21 4700, F21 4701, Archives Nationales. See also *La Parole libre TSF*, Bibliothèque Centrale de la Radio France.

85 René Dumesnil, *La Musique en France entre les deux guerres, 1919–1939* (Geneva: Editions du Milieu de Monde, 1946), 77–78.

86 Etienne Royer, "La musique et la T.S.F.," *La Revue musicale*, August 1924, 158, 159.

87 Lionel Landry, "L'industrialisation de la musique," *La Revue musicale*, 1 March 1928, 123.

88 Ibid., 122.

89 For discussions of américanisation and mass culture, see chapter 4. On the creation of mass culture in the late nineteenth century, see Schwartz, *Spectacular Realities*.

90 On the active interpretation by audiences of cultural products, see, for example, John Clarke, "Pessimism versus Populism: The Problematic Politics of Popular Culture," in *For Fun and Profit: The Transformation of Leisure into Consumption*, ed. Richard Butsch (Philadelphia, Pa.: Temple University Press, 1990).

3 JAZZ AND THE CITY OF PARIS

1 See Jerrold Seigel, *Bohemian Paris: Culture, Politics, and the Boundaries of Bourgeois Life, 1830–1930* (New York: Penguin, 1986).

2 See, for example, Pierre Courthion, *Montmartre*, trans. Stuart Gilbert (Lausanne, Switzerland: Skira, 1956).

3 See Seigel, *Bohemian Paris*; Harold B. Segel, *Turn-of-the-Century Cabaret: Paris, Barcelona, Berlin, Munich, Vienna, Cracow, Moscow, St. Petersburg, Zurich* (New York: Columbia University Press, 1987); and Lisa Appignanesi, *The Cabaret* (New York: Universe Books, 1976).

4 On chansons, see Bettina L. Knapp, "The Golden Age of the Chanson," *Yale French Studies* 32 (1964): 82–98; and Elaine Brody, *Paris: The Musical Kaleidoscope, 1870–1925* (New York: George Braziller, 1987), chap. 5.

5 Segel, *Turn-of-the-Century Cabaret*, 35–48.

6 Cited in ibid., 44.

7 Émile Zola, *Paris*, trans. Ernest Alfred Vizetelly (London: Chatto and Windus, 1922), 218. On this connection between Zola's description and Bruant's cabaret, see Richard Lionel, *Cabaret, cabarets: origines et décadence* (Paris: Plon, 1991).

8 Zola, *Paris*, 219–20.

9 Bricktop with James Haskins, *Bricktop* (New York: Atheneum, 1983), 86.

10 Pierre MacOrlan, *La Lanterne Sourde: Aux Lumières de Paris, Images sur la Tamise, Romantisme de la fin d'un monde* (Paris: Gallimard, 1953), 51–52.

11 Jean Gravigny, *Montmartre en 1925* (Paris: Editions Montigne, 1925), 44.

12 For an excellent account of African Americans in Montmartre, see Tyler Stovall, *Paris Noir: African Americans in the City of Light* (Boston: Houghton Mifflin, 1996), chap. 2. See also William A. Shack, *Harlem in Montmartre: A Paris Jazz Story between the Great Wars* (Berkeley: University of California Press, 2001).

13 Langston Hughes, *The Big Sea: An Autobiography* (New York: Thunder's Mouth Press, 1986), 162.

14 On Bricktop, see Bricktop with Haskins, *Bricktop*. On Bullard, see Craig Lloyd, *Eugene Bullard: Black Expatriate in Jazz-Age Paris* (Athens: University of Georgia Press, 2000).

15 See Stovall, *Paris Noir*.

16 Sidney Bechet, *Treat It Gentle* (New York: Da Capo Press, 1975), 149.

17 See Charles Rearick, "Song and Society in Turn-of-the-Century France," *Journal of Social History* 22 (fall 1988): 45–63; and Knapp, "The Golden Age of the Chanson."

18 Charles Rearick, *The French in Love and War: Popular Culture in the Era of the World Wars* (New Haven, Conn.: Yale University Press, 1997), 69.

19 See Knapp, "The Golden Age of the Chanson"; and Rearick, *The French in Love and War*.

20 "Est-ce l'agonie de la chanson française?" *Comœdia*, 15 November 1926.

21 Georges Millandy, *Lorsque tout est fini . . .* (Paris: Albert Messein, 1933), 280.

22 Gabriel Astruc, *Le Pavillon des Fantômes: Souvenirs* (Paris: Pierre Belfond, 1987), 196.

23 Christiné and Trébitsch, "Ah! La Musique Américaine," 1913, Musée de Montmartre.

24 Robert Forrest Wilson, *Paris on Parade* (Indianapolis, Ind.: Bobbs-Merrill, 1925), 266.

25 See Rearick, "Song and Society."

26 Julian Street, *Where Paris Dines* (London: William Heinemann, 1929), 245–46.

27 Gravigny, *Montmartre en 1925*, 44.

28 Sisley Huddleston, *Paris Salons, Cafés, Studios* (New York: Blue Ribbon Books, 1928), 25.

29 Jean Émile-Bayard, *Montmartre hier et aujourd'hui* (Paris: Jouve, 1928), 155.

30 Charles A. Beard, "The American Invasion of Europe," *Harper's Magazine*, March 1929, 470–79.

31 Wilson, *Paris on Parade*, 275.

32 Pierre MacOrlan, *Montmartre: Souvenirs* (Brussels: Editions de Chabassol, 1946), 151–52.

33 Wilson, *Paris on Parade*, 266.

34 Francis Carco, *The Last Bohemia: From Montmartre to the Latin Quarter*, trans. Madeleine Boyd (New York: Henry Holt, 1928), 104. *Guinguettes* were open-air cafés or dance halls.

35 André Warnod, "Montmartre et ses derniers plaisirs," *Comœdia*, 24 February 1928.

36 Pierre MacOrlan, "Montparnasse," in *My Paris: An Anthology of Modern Paris from the Works of Contemporary French Writers*, ed. Arthur K. Griggs (New York: Dial Press, 1932), 67.

37 Information about La Commune Libre de Montmartre gleaned from the press clippings in R014868, Bibliothèque de l'Arsenal.

38 Cited in Humphrey Carpenter, *Geniuses Together: American Writers in Paris in the 1920s* (Boston: Houghton Mifflin, 1988), 90.

39 Paul Cohen-Portheim, *The Spirit of Paris* (Philadelphia, Pa.: J. B. Lippincott, 1937), 33–43. Cohen-Portheim's depiction is typical of others from the era.

40 Xavier de Hautecloque, "Montparnasse: Carrefour du Monde," *Petit Journal*, 22 December 1929–5 January 1930.

41 Sisley Huddleston, *Back to Montparnasse: Glimpses of Broadway in Bohemia* (Philadelphia, Pa.: J. B. Lippincott, 1931), 47.

42 See Noël Riley Fitch, *Sylvia Beach and the Lost Generation: A History of Literary Paris in the Twenties and Thirties* (New York: W. W. Norton, 1983).

43 Émile-Bayard, *Montparnasse*, 505.

44 Cited in Émile-Bayard, *Montparnasse*, 504.

45 Millandy, *Lorsque tout est fini . . .*, 287.

46 André Warnod, "Montparnasse," *Annales politiques et littéraires*, 6 December 1925, 620.

47 Ibid., 621.

48 "Montparnasse Jazz Is Stilled by Police," *New York Times*, 20 November 1927, 2.

49 Huddleston, *Back to Montparnasse*, 46.

50 Jules Bertaut, *Paris: 1870–1935*, trans. R. Millar (London: Eyre and Spottiswoode, 1936), 281.

51 Huddleston, *Paris Salons*, 29.

52 As Jerrold Seigel has argued, the bohemianism of these years bore less and less similarity to the classical bohemian existence of earlier times. See Seigel, *Bohemian Paris*.

53 See Seigel's discussion of this phenomenon in *Bohemian Paris*.

54 Dominique Bonnaud, "Montmartre," *Les Annales politiques et littéraires*, 6 December 1925, 617–18.

55 Ralph Nevill, *Nightlife: London and Paris—Past and Present* (London: Cassell and Company, 1926), 282; emphasis added.

56 Wilson, *Paris on Parade*, 268.

57 Basil Woon, *The Paris That's Not in the Guide Books* (New York: Robert M. McBride, 1931), 264.

58 Huddleston, *Paris Salons*, 31. Woon describes Zelli throughout *The Paris That's Not*.

59 Woon, *The Paris That's Not*, 245.

60 Ralph Nevill, *Days and Nights in Montmartre and the Latin Quarter* (New York: George H. Doran, 1927), 49.

61 On Zelli's, see Woon, *The Paris That's Not*, 231, 245, 247–48.

62 On the rotating bands, see the descriptions by Gene Bullard in P. J. Carisella and James W. Ryan, *The Black Swallow of Death* (Boston: Marlborough House, 1972), 207; and Michel Leiris, *Manhood: A Journey from Childhood into the Fierce Order of Virility*, trans. Richard Howard (New York: Grossman, 1963), 131.

63 Woon, *The Paris That's Not*, 248.

64 Ibid., 173.

65 Ibid., 230, 248–56.

66 On Bricktop, see Bricktop with Haskins, *Bricktop*; and Stovall, *Paris Noir*, 44–45.

67 Robert McAlmon and Kay Boyle, *Being Genuises Together, 1920–1930* (Garden City, N.Y.: Doubleday, 1968), 316–17.

68 Stovall, *Paris Noir*, 46.

69 Bricktop with Haskins, *Bricktop*, 138.

70 Ibid., 102.

71 See Lloyd, *Eugene Bullard*.

72 Sem, *La Ronde de nuit* (Paris: Arthème Fayard, 1923), 122.

73 Nevill, *Days and Nights*, 33.

74 Huddleston, *Back to Montparnasse*, chap. 2.

75 Odette Pannetier, *Plaisirs forcés à perpétuité* (Paris: Editions Prométhée, 1929), 15.

76 Huddleston, *Back to Montparnasse*, 139.

77 Billy Klüver and Julie Martin, eds., *Kiki's Memoirs*, trans. Samuel Putnam, Billy Klüver, and Julie Martin (Hopewell, N.J.: Ecco Press, 1996), 153. See also Pannetier, *Plaisirs*, 15.

78 Cited in Dominique Desanti, *La Femme au temps des années folles* (Paris: Stock/L. Pernoud, 1984), 157.

79 Huddleston, *Back to Montparnasse*, 139.

80 Cohen-Portheim, *Spirit of Paris*, 44.

81 "Le joyeux gala de 'Paris-Montparnasse,'" *Paris-Midi*, 31 May 1929.

82 Wilson, *Paris on Parade*, 195.

83 Paul LeFlem, "Le jazz serait-il français?" *Comœdia*, 25 January 1926.

4 THE MEANINGS OF JAZZ
America, *Nègre*, and Civilization

1   See MacDonald Smith Moore, *Yankee Blues: Musical Culture and American Identity* (Bloomington: Indiana University Press, 1985), 111.

2   *Excelsior*, 20 December 1920, Ro13017, Bibliothèque de l'Arsenal.

3   "Jazz at the Sorbonne," *New York Times*, 20 June 1926, sec. 8, 2.

4   "French Police Stop Jazz Band at Burial," *New York Times*, 18 October 1923, 3.

5   Lucien Farnoux-Reynaud, "L'Époque du Jazz-Band," *Gaulois*, 6 March 1926.

6   Nancy Perloff, *Art and the Everyday: Popular Entertainment and the Circle of Erik Satie* (Oxford: Clarendon Press, 1991), 46.

7   Cited in ibid., 47.

8   Irene Castle, as told to Bob and Wanda Duncan, *Castles in the Air* (New York: Da Capo, 1958), 54.

9   Castle, *Castles in the Air*, 54–55.

10 On the larger presence of British tourists, see "Statistique Touristique," BA2255, folder 158056E1, Paris Police Archive.

11 See Harvey Levenstein, *Seductive Journey: American Tourists in France from Jefferson to the Jazz Age* (Chicago: University of Chicago Press, 1998), 236.

12 Cited in Warren I. Susman, "Pilgrimage to Paris: The Background of American Expatriation, 1920–1934" (Ph.D. diss., University of Wisconsin, 1958), 357–58.

13 See Sisley Huddleston, *Paris Salons, Cafés, Studios* (New York: Blue Ribbon Books, 1928), 30; and Levenstein, *Seductive Journey*, 242.

14 On Fontainbleau, see Elizabeth Hutton Turner, *American Artists in Paris: 1919–1929* (Ann Arbor, Mich.: UMI Research Press, 1988), 31.

15 Walter White, "The Color Line in Europe," *Annals of the American Academy of Political and Social Science* 90 (November 1928), 332.

16 Francis Miller and Helen Hill, *The Giant of the Western World: America and Europe in a North-Atlantic Civilisation* (New York: William Morrow, 1930), 79–80.

17 Paul Morand, "Pourquoi les Américains vivent en Europe," *Annales politiques et littéraires*, 15 January 1930, 55.

18 Susman, "Pilgrimage to Paris," 166.

19 Ibid., 163; and Miller and Hill, *Giant of the Western World*, 57–58.

20 Miller and Hill, *Giant of the Western World*, chap. 3.

21 James H. Smiley, "American Goods as a Leavening Agent in the Living Standards in Foreign Countries," *Proceedings of the Institute of International Relations* 5 (1930): 97–99.

22 André Citroën, "Speeding up the Automobile Industry," *European Finance*, 13 June 1928, 171. See also James M. Laux, *The European Automobile Industry* (New York: Twyane, 1992).

23 Miller and Hill, *Giant of the Western World*, 185. See also Stephen L. Harp,

Marketing Michelin: Advertising and Cultural Identity in Twentieth-Century France (Baltimore, Md.: Johns Hopkins University Press, 2001).

24 Miller and Hill, *Giant of the Western World*, 173.

25 See Marjorie Beale, *The Modernist Enterprise: French Elites and the Threat of Modernity, 1900–1940* (Stanford, Calif.: Stanford University Press, 1999); and Richard F. Kuisel, *Seducing the French: The Dilemma of Americanization* (Berkeley: University of California Press, 1993).

26 Robert Aron and Arnaud Dandieu, *Décadence de la nation française* (Paris: Les Editions Rieder, 1931).

27 For a discussion of the cultural and political implications of these changes, see Paul A. Gagnon, "French Views of the Second American Revolution," *French Historical Studies* 2 (1962): 430–49; and Anson Rabinbach, *The Human Motor: Energy, Fatigue, and the Origins of Modernity* (Berkeley: University of California Press, 1992).

28 Donald Roy Allen, *French Views of America in the 1930s* (New York: Garland Publishing, 1979), 112. I also draw more generally from Allen's discussion of Fordism and Taylorization.

29 Aron and Dandieu, *Décadence*, 227.

30 Ellen Furlough, "Selling the American Way in Interwar France: *Prix Uniques* and the Salons des Arts Menagers," *Journal of Social History* (spring 1993): 501.

31 Georges Duhamel, *America the Menace: Scenes from the Life of the Future* (Boston: Houghton Mifflin, 1931), 106.

32 Ibid., xiv.

33 Susman, "Pilgrimage to Paris," 163–65.

34 Ibid., 164–67.

35 On cowboy dress, seè Ralph Schor, *L'Opinion française et les étrangers, 1919–1939* (Paris: Publications de la Sorbonne, 1985), 161. Michel Leiris also discusses the fascination with dressing in U.S. style clothes in his *Manhood: A Journey from Childhood into the Fierce Order of Virility*, trans. Richard Howard (New York: Grossman, 1963).

36 Modris Eksteins, *The Rites of Spring: The Great War and the Birth of the Modern Age* (New York: Anchor Books, 1989), 242–74.

37 Duhamel, *America the Menace*, 121.

38 Ibid., 104.

39 Paul Claudel, "L'Élasticité Américaine," in *Œuvres en Prose* (Paris: Editions Gallimard, 1985), 1205.

40 André Suarès, cited in Hugues Panassié, *Douze années de jazz: (1927–1938), souvenirs* (Paris: Editions Corrêa, 1946), 67.

41 Jacques Janin, "Le jazz, lumière de l'occident? Les nouveautés de la 'nationale,'" *L'Ami du peuple du soir*, 26 March 1929.

42 Marcel Espiau, "Au rythme infernal du jazz," *Avenir*, 18 February 1926.

43 Richard Abel, *French Cinema: The First Wave, 1918–1929* (Princeton, N.J.: Princeton University Press, 1984), 49.

44　For a general history of the French film industry, see Abel, *French Cinema*. Victoria de Grazia also provides a helpful summary of Americanization in the French film industry and its relationship to changing perceptions of national identity in "Mass Culture and Sovereignty: The American Challenge to European Cinemas, 1920–1960," *Journal of Modern History* 61 (March 1989): 53–87. For additional documentary evidence on protests by French filmmakers, see series F21, boxes 4696, 4697, Archives Nationale.

45　de Grazia, "Mass Culture and Sovereignty," 61.

46　Ibid., 54.

47　Cited in André Cœuroy and André Schaeffner, *Le Jazz* (Paris: Editions Claude Aveline, 1926), 133.

48　Guillaume Apollinaire, cited in Jean-Philippe Mathy, *Extrême-Occident: French Intellectuals and America* (Chicago: University of Chicago Press, 1993), 86.

49　Philippe Soupault, *The American Influence in France* (Seattle: University of Washington Bookstore, 1930), 13–14.

50　Matthew Josephson, *Life among the Surrealists* (New York: Holt, Rinehart, and Winston, 1962), 123.

51　Soupault, *American Influence*, 17. On Soupault's influence, see Josephson, *Life among the Surrealists*, 123.

52　Josephson, *Life among the Surrealists*, 123.

53　Soupault, *American Influence*, 19.

54　Ibid., 20.

55　For a more extensive discussion of Morand's attitudes toward the United States, see Mathy, *Extrême-Occident*, 90–95.

56　Paul Morand, *New York*, trans. Hamish Miles (London: William Heinemann, 1930), 290.

57　Ibid., 303.

58　Ibid., 284.

59　Ibid., 262.

60　Ibid., 19.

61　Ibid., 257.

62　Ibid., 260.

63　André Villeneuve, "Scène de la vie future," *Act Frame*, 5 December 1930.

64　Eksteins discusses the perception that modernism's hopeful qualities were to be found in the United States in *Rites of Spring*, 267–71.

65　For an intriguing collection of essays on the presence of Africans and African Americans in commercial entertainment throughout the nineteenth and twentieth centuries, see Bernth Lindfors, ed., *Africans on Stage: Studies in Ethnological Show Business* (Bloomington: Indiana University Press, 1999).

66　On the history of the cakewalk and ragtime, see Marshall Stearns, *The Story of Jazz* (New York: Oxford University Press, 1956); Marshall and Jean Stearns, *Jazz Dance: The Story of American Vernacular Dance* (New York: Macmillan, 1968); Rudi Blesh and Harriet Janis, *They All Played Ragtime:*

The True Story of an American Music (New York: Alfred A. Knopf, 1950); and Edward A. Berlin, *Ragtime: A Musical and Cultural History* (Berkeley: University of California Press, 1980). Perloff also gives a good summary in *Art and the Everyday*.

67 Perloff, *Art and the Everyday*, 50.

68 "How Sousa Has Bewitched the Parisians with His Band Playing and His Compositions," *San Francisco Chronicle*, 10 June 1900.

69 Concert program from Nouveau Théâtre, 15 rue Blanche, 25 April 1903, box "Théâtres," folder "Théâtre Indépendant," Musée de Montmartre; and "How Sousa Has Bewitched," *San Francisco Chronicle*.

70 See Perloff, *Art and the Everyday*; and Chris Goddard, *Jazz away from Home* (New York: Paddington Press, 1979).

71 *Le Petit Bleu de Paris*, 18 December 1908, B pièce 347 ("coupures de presse"), Bibliothèque de l'Opéra.

72 Gabriel Astruc, *Le Pavillon des Fantômes: Souvenirs* (Paris: Pierre Belfond, 1987), 198.

73 Cited in Perloff, *Art and the Everyday*, 49.

74 Ibid., 49–50.

75 On this influence, see, for example, Glenn Watkins, *Pyramids at the Louvre: Music, Culture, and Collage from Stravinsky to the Postmodernists* (Cambridge: Harvard University Press, 1994); Perloff, *Art and the Everyday*; M. Robert Rogers, "Jazz Influence on French Music," *Musical Quarterly* 21 (1935): 53–68; and Elaine Brody, *Paris: The Musical Kaleidoscope, 1870–1925* (New York: George Braziller, 1987).

76 On French visitors to the United States and their interest in black music in the late nineteenth century, see Jacques Portes, *Fascination and Misgiving: The United States in French Opinion, 1870–1914*, trans. Elborg Forster (Cambridge: Cambridge University Press, 2000), 123–26.

77 Eileen Southern, *The Music of Black Americans: A History*, 2d ed. (New York: W. W. Norton, 1983), 300.

78 Robert Forrest Wilson, *Paris on Parade* (Indianapolis, Ind.: Bobbs-Merrill, 1925), 286.

79 Cited in Michel Fabre, *La Rive noire: de Harlem à la Seine* (Paris: Lieu Commun, 1985), 59.

80 Henry Crowder, *As Wonderful as All That: Henry Crowder's Memoir of His Affair with Nancy Cunard, 1928–1935* (Navarro, Calif.: Wild Trees Press, 1987), 55.

81 Tyler Stovall, *Paris Noir: African Americans in the City of Light* (Boston: Houghton Mifflin, 1996), chap. 2.

82 White, "The Color Line in Europe," 333.

83 Fabre, *La Rive noire*, 59.

84 "Pour Nos Frères de Couleur," *Annales Politiques et Littéraires*, 19 August 1923, 193.

85 Levenstein, *Seductive Journey*, 265; and William A. Shack, *Harlem in Mont-*

martre: A Paris Jazz Story between the Great Wars (Berkeley: University of California Press, 2001), 68.

86 See, for example, Eugene Genovese, *Roll, Jordan, Roll: The World the Slaves Made* (New York: Vintage, 1976).

87 Eric Lott, *Love and Theft: Blackface Minstrelsy and the American Working Class* (New York: Oxford University Press, 1993).

88 Michael Rogin, *Blackface, White Noise: Jewish Immigrants in the Hollywood Melting Pot* (Berkeley: University of California Press, 1996).

89 "Charleston City ouvre aujourd'hui ses portes au Jardin d'Acclimatation," *Le Journal*, 20 May 1927. For numerous press clippings on *Charleston City*, see Ro13021, Bibliothèque de l'Arsenal.

90 René Dumesnil, "Le jazz," *La Femme de France*, 22 March 1931.

91 See Tyler Stovall, "Paris in the Age of Anxiety, 1919–1939," in *Anxious Visions: Surrealist Art*, ed. Sidra Stich (New York: Abbeville Press, 1990). By 1931, there were some fifteen thousand Africans according to French statistics, but whether they were nègre or *arabe* is unclear. African Americans were not distinguished from other Americans. See statistics in Evelyne Cohen, *Paris dans l'imaginaire nationale de l'entre-deux-guerres* (Paris: Publications de la Sorbonne, 1999), 100.

92 On the conflation of African and African American, see Bernard Gendron, "Fetishes and Motorcars: Negrophilia in French Modernism," *Cultural Studies* 4 (May 1990): 141–55; and Petrine Archer-Straw, *Negrophilia: Avant-Garde Paris and Black Culture in the 1920s* (London: Thames and Hudson, 2000).

93 See William B. Cohen, *The French Encounter with Africans: White Response to Blacks, 1530–1880* (Bloomington: Indiana University Press, 1980).

94 See William H. Schneider, *An Empire for the Masses: The French Popular Image of Africa, 1870–1900* (Westport, Conn.: Greenwood Press, 1982).

95 See Tyler Stovall, "The Color Line behind the Lines: Racial Violence in France during the Great War," *American Historical Review* 103 (June 1998): 737–70.

96 See Alice L. Conklin, *A Mission to Civilize: The Republican Idea of Empire in France and West Africa* (Stanford, Calif.: Stanford University Press, 1997).

97 See William H. Schneider, *Quality and Quantity: The Quest for Biological Regeneration in Twentieth-Century France* (Cambridge: Cambridge University Press, 1990); and Conklin, *A Mission to Civilize*, 164.

98 Blaise Pesquinne, "Le blues, la musique nègre des villes; naissance et avenir du jazz," *La Revue musicale*, November 1934, 278.

99 Julien Tiersot, *Chansons nègres: recueillies, traduites, et harmonisées* (Paris: Heugel, 1933), n.p.

100 Emile Vuillermoz, *Musiques d'aujourd'hui*, 5th ed. (Paris: Editions G. Crès, 1923), 210.

101 Dumesnil, "Le Jazz."

102 C. de Valmalete, "Le jazz et ses origines," *Sud*, 1 April 1931.

103 For discussions of nostalgia in the nineteenth century, see Michael S. Roth, "Dying of the Past: Medical Studies of Nostalgia in Nineteenth-Century France," *History and Memory: Studies in Representations of the Past* 3 (1991): 5–29; Alice Bullard, "Self-Representation in the Arms of Defeat: Fatal Nostalgia and Surviving Comrades in French New Caledonia, 1871–1880," *Cultural Anthropology* 12 (1997): 179–212; and George Rosen, "Nostalgia: A 'Forgotten' Psychological Disorder," *Psychological Medicine* 3 (1975): 340–54. Matt K. Matsuda also discusses nostalgia in a similar vein in reference to the tango in his *The Memory of the Modern* (New York: Oxford University Press, 1996), chap. 9.

104 Pesquinne, "Le blues, la musique nègre des villes," 274.

105 Farnoux-Reynaud, "L'Époque du Jazz-Band."

106 Cœuroy and Schaeffner, *Jazz*, 9. Although they seem to suggest that this continuity is the case for every culture, they do not offer any comparison that might help distinguish what they believed to be unique about black musicians.

107 Ibid., 14.

108 André Hoerée, "Le Jazz," *La Revue musicale*, October 1927, 221. Francis Pinguet remarks that Hoerée did not have access to a wide variety of information about jazz with which to make a careful and fully informed judgment. He also comments that *La Revue musicale* was open to a wide range of opinion about jazz, thus explaining how Hoerée's claims could exist there alongside many others that argued for the African roots of jazz. See Francis Pinguet, *Un monde musicale métissé* (Paris: Richard-Masse, 1984).

109 André Schaeffner, "Le Jazz," *La Revue musicale*, 1 November 1927, 76.

110 Robert Goffin, *Jazz: From the Congo to the Metropolitan*, trans. Walter Schaap and Leonard G. Feather (Garden City, N.Y.: Doubleday, 1946), 72.

111 Ibid., 73.

112 Ibid., 76.

113 Robert Goffin, "Jazz-band," *Le Disque vert*, July 1922, 72.

114 Ted Gioia, *The Imperfect Art: Reflections on Jazz and Modern Culture* (New York: Oxford University Press, 1988), 28.

115 Robert Goffin, *Aux frontières du jazz* (Paris: Editions du Sagittaire, 1932), 14.

116 James Clifford, *The Predicament of Culture: Twentieth-Century Ethnography, Literature, and Art* (Cambridge: Harvard University Press, 1988), 167; for a good introductory discussion of Leiris's writing, see chap. 6.

117 Michael Haggerty and Michel Leiris, "Jazz," *Sulfur* 15 (1986): 100.

118 Ibid., 99.

119 Cited in dossier Ro585, Bibliothèque de l'Arsenal.

120 Villeneuve, "Scène de la vie future."

121 Cœuroy and Schaeffner, *Jazz*, 103.

122 Cited in "Le jazz se démode-t-il?" *Intransigeant*, 3 November 1926.

123 Arthur Hoerée, "Le jazz et la musique d'aujourd'hui," *Le Courrier musical et théatral*, 1 December 1928, 671.

124 "La Rentrée de Jack Hylton et ses boys à Paris," *Volonté*, 14 October 1929.

125 Jack Hylton, "Naissance et vie du jazz," *Le Courrier musical et théatral*, 15 March 1932.

126 Dossier R0585, Bibliothèque de l'Arsenal.

127 Gérard Bauer, "Sur le jazz," *Conferencia*, 20 September 1932.

128 Ray Ventura, "Non . . . Le jazz ne meurt pas! Il évolue . . . ," *L'Edition musicale vivante*, September 1931, 9.

129 Miguel Zamacoïs, "La Folie Noire," *Les Annales politiques et littéraires*, 6 December 1925, 592.

130 Georges Pioch, "Progrès vers le simiesque," *Soir*, 5 March 1930.

131 See Schneider, *Quality and Quantity*.

132 Cited in Panassié, *Douze années de jazz*, 66–67.

133 Conklin, *A Mission to Civilize*, 170.

134 Rene Wisner, "C'est un enfer sonore . . . ," *Soir*, 18 June 1926.

135 See Jacques Barzun, *Race: A Study in Modern Superstition* (New York: Harper and Row, 1965); and Tzvetan Todorov, *On Human Diversity: Nationalism, Racism, and Exoticism in French Thought* (Cambridge: Harvard University Press, 1993).

136 On immigration into France, see Gary Cross, *Immigrant Workers in Industrial France: The Making of a New Laboring Class* (Philadelphia, Pa.: Temple University Press, 1983); Schor, *L'Opinion française*; and Gérard Noiriel, *The French Melting Pot: Immigration, Citizenship, and National Identity*, trans. Geoffroy de Laforcade (Minneapolis: University of Minnesota Press, 1996).

137 See Michael Marrus, *The Unwanted: European Refugees in the Twentieth Century* (New York: Oxford University Press, 1985).

138 Statistics on foreign population cited in Schneider, *Quality and Quantity*, 233–34. Schneider is citing figures from Cross, *Immigrant Workers in Industrial France*; and Gary Freeman, *Immigrant Labor and Racial Conflict in Industrial Societies* (Princeton, N.J.: Princeton University Press, 1979).

139 Schor, *L'Opinion française*, 34.

140 See, for example, Robert H. Johnston, *New Mecca, New Babylon: Paris and the Russian Exiles, 1920–1945* (Kingston, Ont.: McGill-Queens University Press, 1988).

141 See Michael B. Miller, *Shanghai on the Metro: Spies, Intrigue, and the French between the Wars* (Berkeley: University of California Press, 1994).

142 For a useful statement of the issue within the context of a broader interpretation, see, for example, Geoffrey Barraclough, *An Introduction to Contemporary History* (London: Penguin, 1967).

143 On *civilisation* as a concept, see Theodore Zeldin, *France: 1848–1945, Volume 2: Intellect, Taste, and Anxiety* (Oxford: Oxford University Press, 1977), chap. 1; Conklin, *A Mission to Civilize*; and Alice Bullard, *Exile to Paradise: Savagery and Civilization in Paris and the South Pacific, 1790–1900* (Stanford, Calif.: Stanford University Press, 2000).

144 See Robert Wohl, *The Generation of 1914* (Cambridge: Harvard University Press, 1979); Eksteins, *Rites of Spring*.

145 Paul Valéry, "La Crise de l'ésprit," in *Œuvres*, vol. 1 (Paris: Gallimard, 1957), 988.

146 Leiris, *Manhood*, 109.

147 Cœuroy and Schaeffner, *Jazz*, 119.

148 Sem, *La Ronde du nuit* (Paris: Arthème Fayard, 1923), 117.

149 For further reflections on the qualities of primitivism perceived to be liberating, see Elazar Barkan and Ronald Bush, eds., *Prehistories of the Future: The Primitivist Project and the Culture of Modernism* (Stanford, Calif.: Stanford University Press, 1995).

150 Henry Malherbe, "Le jazz," *Temps*, 21 August 1929.

151 Espiau, "Au rythme infernal du jazz."

152 Gustave Fréjaville, "L'orchestre du Dr Moreau," *Débats*, 9 June 1927.

153 On the role of taste in French culture and national identity, see Leora Auslander, *Taste and Power: Furnishing Modern France* (Berkeley: University of California Press, 1998); and Pierre Bourdieu, *Distinction: A Social Critique of the Judgement of Taste* (Cambridge: Harvard University Press, 1984).

154 Guy de Teramond, "La Princesse et le jazz-band," *Presse*, 23 April 1926.

155 Cited in Cœuroy and Schaeffner, *Jazz*, 135.

156 André Lénéka, "Le Jazz! On en parle encore!!" *Le Monde théatrale*, 15 September 1929.

157 A. Herbert, "Jazz-band et décadence," *L'Artiste musicien de Paris*, November 1925, 279.

158 de Teramond, "La Princesse et le jazz-band."

159 On changing views of women during the 1920s, see Mary Louise Roberts, *Civilization without Sexes: Reconstructing Gender in Postwar France, 1917–1927* (Chicago: University of Chicago Press, 1994), especially chapter 5 on the pronatalists with references to their attacks on modern dancing.

160 Victor Margueritte, *The Bachelor Girl*, trans. Hugh Burnaby (New York: Alfred A. Knopf, 1923), 108. Another such pronatalist novel that directly portrays jazz music as part of the modern scene is Clément Vautel, *Madame ne veut pas d'enfant* (Paris: Albin Michel, 1924).

161 Espiau, "Au rythme infernal du jazz."

162 Wisner, "C'est un enfer sonore."

163 Jean Cocteau, "Carte Blanche (19): Jazz-Band," *Comœdia*, 4 August 1919.

1 I would again like to emphasize the fact that I am not making an argument about whether musicians in France changed jazz as a musical form but rather how they altered listeners' perceptions. Although I discuss the way in which this modified jazz "sounded," I do so not from a musicological perspective but from the point of view of those listeners who described it in this way and ascribed cultural significance to those changes.

2 Bernard Champigneulle, "Spectacles et Spectateurs," *Mercure de France*, 1 February 1934, 569.

3 Theodore Zeldin, *France, 1848–1945, Volume 2: Intellect, Taste, and Anxiety* (Oxford: Oxford University Press, 1977), 699–700.

4 See Nancy Perloff, *Art and the Everyday: Popular Entertainment and the Circle of Erik Satie* (Oxford: Clarendon Press, 1991), 33; and Jacques-Charles, *Cent ans de music-hall* (Geneva: Editions Jeheber, 1956), 100–101.

5 Joris-Karl Huysmans, *Croquis parisiens, A Vau-l'Eau, Un Dilemme* (Paris: Plon, 1913), 27.

6 Charles Rearick, *Pleasures of the Belle Epoque: Entertainment and Festivity in Turn-of-the-Century France* (New Haven, Conn.: Yale University Press, 1985), 83–84.

7 Ibid.

8 Karl Baedeker, *Paris and Environs with Routes from London to Paris* (Leipzig: Karl Baedeker, 1904), 38.

9 Champigneulle, "Spectacles et Spectateurs."

10 Jules Bertaut, *Paris: 1870–1935*, trans. R. Millar (London: Eyre and Spottiswoode, 1936), 197.

11 Baedeker, *Paris and Environs*, 38.

12 Pierre Bost, *Le Cirque et le music-hall* (Paris: René Hilsum, 1931), 44.

13 Paul Cohen-Portheim, *The Spirit of Paris* (Philadelphia, Pa.: J. B. Lippincott, 1937), 82.

14 For a discussion of the music hall in this era, see most recently Charles Rearick, *The French in Love and War: Popular Culture in the Era of the World Wars* (New Haven, Conn.: Yale University Press, 1997).

15 Bertaut, *Paris*, 197.

16 Jacques Feschotte, *Histoire du music-hall* (Paris: Presses Universitaires de France, 1965), chap. 3.

17 Ibid. On time length, see Maurice Herment, "L'orchestre-jazz," *Candide*, 2 June 1927.

18 P. Gordeaux, "Ambassadeurs—Show of 1928," *Echo*, 23 May 1928.

19 Publicity brochure from Les Ambassadeurs, R015690, Bibliothèque de l'Arsenal. See also Feschotte, *Histoire du music-hall*, 86–87.

20 Jacques-Charles, *Cent ans*, 186–87.

21 See Jacques-Charles, *Cent ans*, chap. 30; Jacques Damase, *Les Folies du music-*

hall: histoire du music-hall à Paris de 1914 à nos jours (Paris: Editions Spectacles, 1960), 105; and R018516, Bibliothèque de l'Arsenal.

22 Dossiers R0585 and 586 at the Bibliothèque de l'Arsenal contain many examples of music hall programs that demonstrate the international character of
entertainment there, as do other dossiers on more specific music halls such as
R015690 on Les Ambassadeurs.

23 Bertaut, *Paris*, 199.

24 Pierre MacOrlan, "Music Hall," *Les Annales politiques et littéraires*, 1 March
1928, 224.

25 "Du nouveau au music-hall," *Petit Journal*, 19 December 1932.

26 "La Boîte à Joujoux," *Intransigeant*, 26 December 1932.

27 Gustave Fréjaville, *Au music hall* (Paris: Aux Editions du Monde Nouveau,
1923), 28.

28 Ibid., 286–87.

29 Robert Goffin, *Aux frontières du jazz* (Paris: Editions du Sagittaire, 1932), 132.

30 Paul Whiteman with Mary Margaret McBride, *Jazz* (New York: J. H. Sears,
1926), 39.

31 Ted Gioia discusses Whiteman's controversial place in jazz history in *The
History of Jazz* (New York: Oxford University Press, 1997), 89–90.

32 Thomas A. DeLong, *Pops: Paul Whiteman, King of Jazz* (Piscataway, N.J.:
New Century, 1983), 96.

33 Irving Schwerké, "Paris Audience Thrilled by Antics of Paul Whiteman's
Jazz Orchestra," *Paris Tribune*, 3 July 1926; reprinted in Hugh Ford, ed., *The
Left Bank Revisited: Selections from the Paris Tribune, 1917–1934* (University
Park: Pennsylvania State University Press, 1972), 221.

34 Cited in Maurice Montabré, "J'adore le jazz . . . ," *Intransigeant*, 12 June 1926.

35 R0586 (possibly *Soir*, 24 June 1926), Bibliothèque de l'Arsenal.

36 For a large number of press articles on Jack Hylton, see R0586, Bibliothèque
de l'Arsenal.

37 Charles Gombault, "Le merveilleux Jack Hylton and His Boys," *Soir*,
8 March 1928.

38 Emile, *Excelsior*, 24 February 1931, R0586, Bibliothèque de l'Arsenal; and
Ray Ventura, "Jack Hylton à l'Opéra," *Jazz-Tango*, 1 March 1931.

39 Lucien Rebatet, "Jack Hylton," 5 January 1936, R0586, Bibliothèque de
l'Arsenal.

40 "Jack Hylton and His Boys," *Petit Marseillaise*, 25 March 1928.

41 G. P., "Jack Hylton et son jazz," *Bavard*, 28 March 1930.

42 Edmond Wellhoff, "Le Jazz et la vie," *Vu*, 14 May 1930.

43 Pierre D., "Jazz-band," *Rumeur*, 30 June 1928.

44 Goffin, *Aux frontières*, 139–41.

45 Paul Le Flem, "Les Waring's Pennsylvanian à la salle Pleyel," *Comœdia*,
9 July 1928.

46 René Bizet, "Jack Hylton and His Boys," *Intransigeant*, 10 October 1929.

47 This same process was at work in the United States, as jazz historian Neil

Leonard has shown in his book *Jazz and the White Americans: The Acceptance of a New Art Form* (Chicago: University of Chicago Press, 1962). See also Kathy J. Ogren, *The Jazz Revolution: Twenties America and the Meaning of Jazz* (New York: Oxford University Press, 1989).

48 Goffin, *Aux frontières*, 145.

49 André Villeneuve, "Scène de la vie future," *Act Frame*, 5 December 1930.

50 For a good discussion among many of *La Revue Nègre*, see Phyllis Rose, *Jazz Cleopatra: Josephine Baker in Her Time* (New York: Vintage, 1989).

51 Cited in Brian Hammond and Patrick O'Connor, *Josephine Baker* (Boston: Bulfinch Press, 1988), 20.

52 Michael Haggerty and Michel Leiris, "Jazz," *Sulfur* 15 (1986): 100.

53 Cited in Rose, *Jazz Cleopatra*, 141.

54 Ibid., 140.

55 Rose, *Jazz Cleopatra*, 151. To view this transformation, see also the articles in Pepito Abatino, ed., *Josephine Baker vue par la presse française* (Paris: Editions Isis, 1931).

56 "Les «Black Birds» au Moulin-Rouge," *Ami du peuple du soir*, 2 June 1929.

57 "Une revue américaine à Paris," *Intransigeant*, 2 June 1929.

58 André Rouveyre, "Théâtre," *Mercure de France*, 1 September 1929, 396.

59 "L'arrivée des Black-birds," *Liberté*, 1 June 1929.

60 P. Loiselet, "Les Black Birds au Moulin Rouge," *Soir*, 12 June 1929.

61 See program for *Blackbirds*, Ro585, Bibliothèque de l'Arsenal.

62 Henry Prunières, "Jazz," *La Revue musicale*, 1 October 1928, 488.

63 Program for *Paris Qui Brille*, Ro18975, Bibliothèque de l'Arsenal.

64 G. de Pawlowski, "'L'Usine à Folies' La Nouvelle revue des Folies-Bergère," *Intransigeant*, 4 April 1931.

65 Glenn Watkins, *Pyramids at the Louvre: Music, Culture, and Collage from Stravinsky to the Postmodernists* (Cambridge: Harvard University Press, 1994), 4–5.

66 For another look at the influence of jazz on avant-garde artists and musicians, see Bernard Gendron, "Jamming at Le Bœuf: Jazz and the Paris Avant-Garde," *Discourse* 12 (fall-winter 1989–1990): 3–27; and *Between Montmartre and the Mudd Club: Popular Music and the Avant-Garde* (Chicago: University of Chicago Press, 2002).

67 The other members of Les Six were Louis Durey, Arthur Honegger, and Germaine Tailleferre.

68 Nancy Perloff, *Art and the Everyday: Popular Entertainment and the Circle of Erik Satie* (Oxford: Clarendon Press, 1991), 1.

69 James Harding, *The Ox on the Roof: Scenes from Musical Life in Paris in the Twenties* (New York: St. Martin's Press, 1972), 78.

70 Darius Milhaud, *Notes without Music*, trans. Donald Evans (London: Dennis Dobson, 1952), 102.

71 Ibid., 118.

72 Ibid., 72.

73 Darius Milhaud, "The Jazz Band and Negro Music," *Living Age*, 18 October 1924, 172.

74 Ibid., 170.

75 Darius Milhaud, "Les Ressources nouvelles de la musique," *L'Esprit nouveau*, July 1924, n.p.

76 Milhaud, "The Jazz Band and the Negro," 171.

77 Cited in John Alan Haughton, "Darius Milhaud: A Missionary of the 'Six,' " *Musical America*, 13 January 1923, 3.

78 See Perloff, *Art and the Everyday*, esp. chap. 4; and Martin Cooper, *French Music, from the Death of Berlioz to the Death of Fauré* (London: Oxford University Press, 1951).

79 Jean Wiéner and Jean Cocteau disagree on the degree to which La Gaya was already well-known.

80 See Maurice Sachs, *The Decade of Illusion: Paris, 1918–1928*, trans. Gladys Matthews Sachs (New York: Alfred A. Knopf, 1933), 16.

81 Ibid., 15.

82 Ibid., 16. For a general description of Le Bœuf, see Harding, *The Ox on the Roof*, 82–85.

83 André Hoerée, "Le jazz," *La Revue musicale*, October 1927, 217.

84 Jean Cocteau, "Cock and Harlequin," in *A Call to Order*, trans. Rollo H. Myers (New York: Henry Holt, 1923), 193.

85 Milhaud, *Notes without Music*, 103; and Jean Wiéner, *Allegro appassionato* (Paris: Pierre Belfond, 1978), 38.

86 Wiéner, *Allegro appassionato*, 83. For a broader discussion of Wiéner's music, see Denise Pilmer Taylor, "La Musique pour tout le monde: Jean Wiéner and the Dawn of French Jazz" (Ph.D. diss., University of Michigan, 1998).

87 Wiéner, *Allegro appassionato*, 83.

88 Cited in ibid., 109.

89 Michael Haggerty and Georges Henri Rivière, "Un mariage d'amour," *Jazz Magazine*, January 1984, 50.

90 Roland-Manuel, "Wiéner et Doucet, ou les plaisirs du jazz," *Revue Pleyel*, July 1926, 11.

91 Daruis Milhaud, *Études* (Paris: Claude Aveline, 1927), 71.

92 Ibid., 72.

93 Robert Brisacq, "Wiéner et Doucet," *Volonté*, 16 May 1929.

94 Haggerty and Leiris, "Jazz," 103.

95 Wiéner, *Allegro appassionato*, 48.

96 Albert Jeanneret, "Musique," *Esprit nouveau* 14 (1923): 1664.

97 Roger Désormière, "Une séance de musique moderne," *Courrier musical*, 1 January 1922; reprinted in Wiéner, *Allegro appassionato*, 60.

98 Wiéner, *Allegro appassionato*, 48.

99 See programs for the "Concerts Wiéner" reprinted in Wiéner, *Allegro appassionato*.

100 Milhaud, *Notes without Music*, 164.

1   Claude Martiau, "Le jazz a vécu," *Radical*, 16 March 1931.

2   Bernard Champigneulle, "Le jazz et l'après-guerre," *Revue Française*, 25 November 1932.

3   Esther Lekain, "Ce que je pense de la chanson française," *Paris qui chante*, February 1931, 3.

4   Cited in "Le jazz se démode-t-il?" *Intransigeant*, 3 November 1926.

5   Cited in Maurice Dabadie, "Après vingt ans de jazz," *Echo Paris*, 29 May 1935.

6   Jean Poueigh, "La débandade du jazz-band," *Volonté*, 30 November 1933.

7   "French Find Our Jazz Too Soul-Disturbing," *New York Times*, 3 February 1929.

8   André Beucler, "Music-Hall," *Jazz*, April 1929, 235.

9   Cited in Maurice Dabadie, "Après vingt ans de jazz," *Echo Paris*, 29 May 1953.

10   Jean Fayard, "Layton et Johnstone et la crise du jazz," *Candide*, 12 February 1931. Russell Sanjek discusses the glut of popular music as the result of films in *American Popular Music and Its Business: Volume III, from 1900–1984* (New York: Oxford University Press, 1988), chap. 9.

11   Cited in Pierre Ramelot, "Le jazz et la crise," *Candide*, 17 February 1927.

12   Henry Malherbe, "Plaidoirie pour le jazz," *Le Temps*, 24 August 1932.

13   *Afro-American*, 26 August 1933, cited in Tyler Stovall, *Paris Noir: African Americans in the City of Light* (Boston: Houghton Mifflin, 1996), 113.

14   Sanjek, *American Popular Music*, 72.

15   Ibid., 118.

16   Cited in Eugen Weber, *The Hollow Years: France in the 1930s* (New York: W. W. Norton, 1994), 36.

17   "Ce que pensent les américains de l'état chaotique du jazz à Paris," *La Revue du jazz*, 7 January 1930, 18.

18   Cited in Ache-Pé, "La revue de la presse," *Jazz-Tango*, 1 March 1931.

19   Cited in Ache-Pé, "La revue de la presse," *Jazz-Tango*, November 1931, 33.

20   Cited in Ache-Pé, "La revue de la presse," *Jazz-Tango*, December 1931, 31.

21   Paul Specht, "Yankee Jazz Abroad," *Jacobs' Orchestra Monthly*, October 1927, 9.

22   I have not found evidence that such players were influenced by the earlier work of Wiéner and Doucet, although it stands to reason that given the duo's popularity, these younger musicians were at least aware of such earlier adapters of jazz. In an interview, Léo Vauchant briefly referred to their playing as "ricky-ticky piano . . . but there were good pianists and very nice" (cited in Chris Goddard, *Jazz away from Home* [New York: Paddington Press, 1979], 271).

23   H. P., "Fats Waller à Paris," *Le Magazin du spectacle*, June 1946, 108.

24 For a good description of Grégor, see Stéphane Grappelli with Joseph Olden-
     hove and Jean-Marc Bramy, *Mon violin pour tout bagage* (Paris: Calmann-
     Lévy, 1992), 57.

25 Ibid.

26 Depiction from *Le Soir*, 10 November 1929, cited in "La revue de la presse de
     la tournée des Gregorians," *La Revue du jazz*, 7 January 1930, 7.

27 Cited in Goddard, *Jazz away from Home*, 224.

28 "L'orchestre Grégor à l'Olympia," *Jazz-Tango-Dancing*, February 1933.

29 "La nouvelle formule du jazz latin va enfin occuper la place qu'elle mérite,"
     Comœdia, 28 February 1930.

30 Jacques Hélian, *Les Grands orchestres de music hall en France: souvenirs et
     temoignages* (Paris: Filipacchi, 1984), 49.

31 Pierre Varenne, "A l'Olympia," *Paris Soir*, 6 June 1930.

32 Hugues Panassié, *Douze années de jazz: (1927–1938), souvenirs* (Paris: Edi-
     tions Corrêa, 1946), 49.

33 Ibid.

34 Cited in Goddard, *Jazz away from Home*, 224.

35 Panassié, *Douze années de jazz*, 51.

36 Benedict Anderson discusses the process of forming community identities in
     print in his influential *Imagined Communities: Reflections on the Origin and
     Spread of Nationalism*, 2d ed. (London: Verso, 1991).

37 La Rédaction, "Notre Programme," *La Revue du jazz*, July 1929.

38 There are several accounts of Ventura's beginnings, including a March 1932
     program found in Bibliothèque de l'Arsenal; see also Pierre Lazareff, "De
     jeunes amateurs Parisiens ont formé un jazz réputé jusqu'en amérique,"
     Paris-Midi, 10 July 1929.

39 On Ventura's band and their other occupations, see Lazareff, "De jeunes
     amateurs Parisiens ont formé un jazz réputé jusqu'en amérique."

40 Titles cited in Hugues Panassié, "Ray Ventura et ses collégians," *Jazz-Tango*,
     April 1931. According to one account, Grégor also began to move in this direc-
     tion as, in 1931, he was "currently preparing a 'History of France' in music
     which will be a happy arrangement of children's rounds" (André Laroche, "La
     rentrée de Grégor et ses Grégorians," *Comœdia*, 4 November 1931).

41 "Ray Ventura et ses collégians," *Jazz-Tango*, December 1930.

42 "Un jazz français: Ray Ventura," *Candide*, 16 April 1931; and "Ray Ventura
     et ses collégians," *Tanagra*, 3 October 1931.

43 Cited in Ache-Pé, "La revue de la presse," *Jazz-Tango*, October 1931.

44 Gérard Bauer, "Sur le jazz: conférence de Gérard Bauer," *Conferencia*,
     20 September 1932, 345.

45 Max Frantel, "Au pays du jazz français par M. Gérard Bauer," *Comœdia*,
     27 November 1932.

46 Bauer, "Sur le jazz," 347.

47 Ray Ventura, "Non . . . le jazz ne meurt pas! Il évolue . . . ," *L'Edition musicale
     vivante*, September 1931, 9.

48 "Les grandes figures du jazz," *Jazz-Tango*, 1 March 1931. Grégor wrote an open letter to Hylton in *La Revue du jazz* expressing his anger over the affair and charging Hylton with taking advantage of his recent hospitalization after a car accident. Musical similarities apparently did not overcome the realities of the music business. See Grégor, "Un scandale," *La Revue du jazz*, 7 January 1930.

49 Henry Prunières, "Jack Hylton," *La Revue musicale*, May 1930, 463.

50 "Les grandes figures du jazz," *Jazz-Tango*, 15 November 1930.

51 "L'Orchestre R. Berson," *Jazz-Tango*, May 1931, 5.

52 See Henry Poisot, *L'Age d'or de la chanson française, 1932–1972: de Mireille à Charles Trénet* (Paris: Editions Saint-Germain-des-Prés, 1972).

53 France Vernillat and Jacques Charpentreau, *La Chanson française* (Paris: Presses Universitaires de France, 1971), 68.

54 Georges Tabet, "Jazz et chanson," *Jazz Magazine*, September 1981, 45–46.

55 Vernillat and Charpentreau, *La Chanson française*, 70.

56 Boris Vian, *En avant la zizique, et par ici les gros sous* (Paris: Union Générale d'Editions, 1966), 174; and Vernillat and Charpentreau, *La Chanson française*, 69.

57 See Noël Balen, *Charles Trénet: le fou chantant* (Paris: Editions du Rocher, 1992); and Richard Cannavo, *Trénet: le siècle en liberté* (Paris: Hidalgo Editeur, 1989).

58 Balen, *Charles Trénet*, 48. See also Ginette Marty, *Johnny Hess: Swing, zazou, et . . . sentimental* (Paris: El-Ouns-Histoire en Chantant, 1997).

59 Pierre Saka, *La Chanson française à travers ses succès* (Paris: Larousse, 1998), 148.

60 Ibid., 148.

61 *Le Matin*, 28 April 1977, 4° SW7070, Bibliothèque de l'Arsenal.

62 For an analysis of *Jazz-Tango*, see Anne Legrand, "Jazz-Tango (octobre 1930–février 1935)" (unpublished manuscript based on a talk for D.E.A d'Histoire de la Musique et Musicologie, Université de Paris IV, Sorbonne, June 1997). I thank Anne Legrand for sharing this manuscript with me.

63 La Direction, "A nos lecteurs," *Jazz-Tango*, 15 October 1930.

64 Cited in Eugen Weber, *The Hollow Years: France in the 1930s* (New York: W. W. Norton, 1994), 33.

65 "Le dancing se meurt," *Volonté*, 14 June 1930.

66 Victoria de Grazia, "Mass Culture and Sovereignty: The American Challenge to European Cinemas, 1920–1960," *Journal of Modern History* 61 (March 1989): 55, 62, 64.

7 NEW BANDS AND NEW TENSIONS
Jazz and the Labor Problem

1 R. Cardinne-Petit, "Les Musiciens français poussent un cri d'alarme," *Le Quotidien*, 16 January 1932; reprinted in *L'Artiste musicien de Paris*, February 1932, 27–29.

2 "Agitation chez les musiciens des établissements de nuits," [police report?], 7 July 1924, F7 13816, Archives Nationales.

3 "France Orders Our Jazz Players Expelled; Acts of Protests by French Musicians," *New York Times*, 31 May 1924, 1.

4 "Vive la chanson française," *La Parole libre TSF*, 19 May 1929, 1.

5 Ch. Coutellier, "Les professionels du jazz protestent contre l'invasion des amateurs marrons étrangers," *Paris-Midi*, 28 September 1929. This article also briefly discusses the 10 percent restriction, which is described as well in "To Oust Americans," *Variety*, 3 March 1922, 2. Walter White also tells of U.S. students paying their way abroad by performing in clubs and restaurants ("The Color Line in Europe," *Annals of the American Academy of Political and Social Science* 90 [November 1928], 335).

6 Letter from the general secretary of the Chambre Syndicale des Artistes Musiciens de Paris et la Région Parisienne to Minister of Interior, 28 December 1926, F7 13909, Archives Nationale.

7 "Too Many Foreign Singers in Paris," *Variety*, 11 June 1920, 2.

8 "Would Limit Foreign Music for France," *Variety*, 5 November 1920, 2.

9 Accounts from the *New York Times* demonstrate that jazz musicians encountered similar reactions in countries like Hungary, Ireland, Bulgaria, and Italy.

10 Thomas A. DeLong, *Pops: Paul Whiteman, King of Jazz* (Piscataway, N.J.: New Century, 1983), 55.

11 "Germans Would Oust American Jazz Bands," *New York Times*, 11 December 1924, 2.

12 M. B. Levick, "Free Trade in Jazz Becomes a Mild Issue," *New York Times*, 28 March 1926, 15.

13 Ralph Schor, *L'Opinion française et les étrangers en France, 1919–1939* (Paris: Publications de la Sorbonne, 1985), 555.

14 Ibid., 597.

15 On immigrant labor, see Gérard Noiriel, *The French Melting Pot: Immigration, Citizenship, and National Identity*, trans. Geoffrey de Laforcade (Minneapolis: University of Minnesota Press, 1996); Gary Cross, *Immigrant Workers in Industrial France: The Making of a New Laboring Class* (Philadelphia, Pa.: Temple University Press, 1983); and Schor, *L'Opinion française*.

16 Cardinne-Petit, "Les Musiciens français poussent un cri d'alarme." In "Rapport morale," August 1932, *L'Artiste musicien de Paris* reported being active in the effort to pass new labor regulations restricting the number of foreigners eligible to work in France.

17 Eugen Weber, *The Hollow Years: France in the '1930s* (New York: W. W.

Norton, 1994), 49. See also Julian Jackson, *The Politics of Depression in France, 1932–1936* (Cambridge: Cambridge University Press, 1985), 25.

18 "Rapport morale," *L'Artiste musicien de Paris*, April 1932, 83.

19 G. Francès, "Application de la loi de protection de la main-d'œuvre nationale," *L'Artiste musicien de Paris*, February 1934, 39.

20 *L'Artiste musicien de Paris*, 1925, passim.

21 "Pourcentage main-d'œuvre étrangere," *L'Artiste musicien de Paris*, March 1932, 60.

22 Reprints from articles in *L'Artiste musicien de Paris*, February 1932.

23 *L'Artiste musicien de Paris*, January 1935, 3; reprint of article from *Petit journal*, 4 January 1935.

24 *L'Artiste musicien de Paris*, December 1931, 425; reprint of "Contre les orchestras étrangers: des musiciens français chômeurs manifestent," *L'Œuvre*, 22 November 1931.

25 *L'Artiste musicien de Paris*, December 1931, 426; reprint of Pierre Regnault, "Les Chômeurs sans secours," *La Liberté*, 4 December 1931.

26 *L'Artiste musicien de Paris*, December 1931, 425; reprint of "Des Musiciens chômeurs ont protesté hier contre les orchestres étrangers," *L'Œuvre*, 24 November 1931.

27 *L'Artiste musicien de Paris*, February 1932, 27–29; reprint of Cardinne-Petit, "Les Musiciens français poussent un cri d'alarme."

28 *L'Artiste musicien de Paris*, December 1931; reprint of article from *Petit Parisien*, 17 December 1931.

29 Maurice Bedouc-Ennouchy, "La Main-d'œuvre étrangère," *Jazz-Tango*, December 1931.

30 Ibid.

31 Ibid.

32 "Marseille," *Jazz-Tango*, 1 February 1931.

33 Louis Dor, "Organisons la corporation," *Jazz-Tango*, June 1931.

34 Stéphane Mougin, "Réponse: de M. Stéphane Mougin," *Jazz-Tango*, May 1931.

35 X, "Réponse d'un musicien Belge," *Jazz-Tango*, May 1931.

36 Stéphane Mougin, "Quelque mots entre nous," *Jazz-Tango-Dancing*, June 1932.

37 See Stéphane Mougin, "Négromanie," *Jazz-Tango*, December 1931, and "Article incompris," *Jazz-Tango*, April 1932.

38 "Compte rendu sténographique de la réunion des musiciens du cinéma," *L'Artiste musicien de Paris*, March 1926, 82.

39 Copy of a 1930 tract from Le Syndicat des Musiciens de la Région Parisienne, F7 13816, Archives Nationales.

40 Statistics in Weber, *The Hollow Years*, 64. See also Cécile Méadel, "Programmes en masse, programmes de masse?: la diffusion de la radio en France pendant les années trente," in *Masses et culture de masse dans les années trente*, ed. Régine Robin (Paris: Editions Ouvrières, 1991), 51–68.

41 Cécile Méadel, *Histoire de la radio des années trente: du sans-filiste à l'auditeur* (Paris: Anthropost INA, 1994), 322.

42 "La musique de danse et la radio," *Jazz-Tango*, June 1931.

43 "A Brief History of the AFM" (http://www.afm.org/about/about.htm?history).

44 Stéphane Mougin, "La dilemme," *Jazz-Tango*, June 1931.

45 Ibid.

46 Stéphane Mougin, "Amis or ennemis?" *Jazz-Tango*, May 1931.

47 Bedouc-Ennouchy, "La Main-d'œuvre étrangère."

48 "Allouche-Tabet," *Jazz-Tango*, 1 February 1931.

49 Stéphane Mougin, "Le monde tel qu'il est," *Jazz-Tango*, October 1931.

8 THE DISCOVERY OF HOT JAZZ

1 Ted Gioia, *The History of Jazz* (New York: Oxford University Press, 1997), 50. Gioia's depiction here is specifically of Oliver's Creole Jazz Band, but it applies more broadly.

2 William Howland Kenney, *Chicago Jazz: A Cultural History, 1904–1930* (New York: Oxford University Press, 1993).

3 On the "New Orleans Diaspora," see Gioia, *History of Jazz*, 45. See also Kenney, *Chicago Jazz*.

4 "Définitions," *Jazz-Tango*, 1 March 1931.

5 Hugues Panassié, "Louis Armstrong," *Jazz-Tango*, 1 February 1931, 7.

6 Henry Prunières, " 'Le Jazz Hot' in Paris," *New York Times*, 4 September 1932, sec. 9, 6. Looking back, jazz critic Boris Vian confirmed this time frame in *Jazz in Paris: Chroniques de jazz pour la station de radio WNEW, New York (1945–1949)* (Paris: Pauvert, 1997). He states that in the late 1920s, "the black influence, at this time, was not as considerable as it currently is: musicians like Eddie Lang and Joe Venuti were much better known than Armstrong and Coleman Hawkins" (30).

7 William Howland Kenney, "Le Hot: The Assimilation of American Jazz in France, 1917–1940," *American Studies* (1984): 10.

8 On race records and their unknown status in France, see Milton "Mezz" Mezzrow and Bernard Wolfe, *Really the Blues* (New York: Random House, 1946), 194–95.

9 Stéphane Mougin, "Le jazz—le hot," *La Revue du jazz*, October 1929, 3.

10 R. D. Darrell, "All Quiet on the Western Jazz Front," *Disques*, September 1932, 291.

11 Emile Vuillermoz, "Duke Ellington et son orchestre," *Excelsior*, 29 July 1933.

12 Madeline Portier, "Duke Ellington et son fameux orchestra," *Comœdia*, 30 July 1933.

13 Jacques Canetti, *On cherche jeune homme aimant la musique* (Paris: Calmann-Lévy, 1978), 27.

14 Henry Malherbe, "A la salle Pleyel: Duke Ellington et son orchestra," *Temps*, 2 August 1933.

15 Carol-Berard, "Duke Ellington à la salle Pleyel," *Echo*, 29 July 1933.

16 G. A., "Musique et spectacles à l'Exposition Coloniale," *La Revue musicale*, November 1931, 349.

17 "A l'Exposition Coloniale de Vincennes," *Paris Music Hall*, 1 July 1931, 15.

18 J. G., "Introduction à la musique nègre," *Quotidien*, 17 May 1931.

19 Stéphen Chauvet, *Musique nègre* (Paris: Société d'Editions Géographiques, Maritimes, et Coloniales, 1929), 9.

20 Stablo-Breval, "Le Maestro MASTER JACK," *Avant-Scène*, 2 November [?] 1934, Ro585, Bibliothèque de l'Arsenal. J. J. Bloch and Marianne Delort, *Quand Paris allait «à l'expo»* (Paris: Fayard, 1980) also identifies jazz as part of the context for the 1925 Exposition des Arts Décoratifs, although the authors do not mention Master Jack by name.

21 Louis Aubert, "La semaine musicale," *Journal*, 1 August 1933.

22 Hugues Panassié, *Douze années de jazz: (1927–1938), souvenirs* (Paris: Editions Corrêa, 1946), 126.

23 Ibid., 129–30.

24 Cited in ibid., 136.

25 Panassié, *Douze années de jazz*.

26 Information on the formation of the Hot Club de France comes from several sources: Panassié, *Douze années de jazz*; Charles Delaunay, *Delaunay's dilemma: de la peinture au jazz* (Mâcon: Editions W, 1985); and *Jazz-Tango*, November 1932 and following. See also Ludovic Tournès, "Les hot clubs: des sociétés au service de la diffusion du jazz," *Cahiers du GHRIS* 6 (1997): 105–220.

27 "Hot Club," *Jazz-Tango*, December 1932.

28 On student dances, see Geoffrey Smith, *Stéphane Grappelli* (London: Pavilion, 1987), 29.

29 Delaunay, *Delaunay's dilemma*, 62.

30 Panassié, *Douze années de jazz*, 98.

31 See Delaunay, *Delaunay's dilemma*.

32 Ibid., 58.

33 "Hot Club," *Jazz-Tango-Dancing*.

34 Jac Auxenfans, "Plan d'action pour les clubs locaux," *Jazz-Tango-Dancing*, March 1933.

35 Léon Fiot, "En faveur du 'jazz hot,'" *Jazz-Tango*, March 1933.

36 Information about Reinhardt, Grappelli, and the founding of the Quintet of the Hot Club of France is available from several sources. I have constructed this account from Charles Delaunay, *Django Reinhardt*, trans. Michael James (New York: Da Capo Press, 1961); Smith, *Stéphane Grappelli*; Panassié, *Douze années de jazz*; and Delaunay, *Delaunay's dilemma*.

37 Biographical information about Grappelli is drawn from Smith, *Stéphane*

Grappelli. See also Stéphane Grappelli with Joseph Oldenhove and Jean-Marc Bramy, *Mon violin pour tout bagage* (Paris: Calmann-Lévy, 1992).

38 Ibid., 13.

39 Ibid., 37.

40 Cited in Smith, *Stéphane Grappelli*, 26.

41 Ibid., 29.

42 Jacques Bureau, "Le concert du Hot-Club," *Jazz-Tango-Dancing*, February 1934.

43 Delaunay, *Django Reinhardt*, 66.

44 Cited in ibid.

45 Generally speaking, other than Reinhardt and Grappelli, the members of the Quintet changed from time to time throughout its history.

46 Cited in Delaunay, *Django Reinhardt*, 68.

47 Cited in ibid., 69.

48 Some jazz historians have argued that Panassié specifically—and the French more generally—paid serious attention to jazz even before American critics. Jazz historian James Lincoln Collier rehearses the literature that has subscribed to this "myth," as he calls it, and then proceeds to reject it. See his *The Reception of Jazz in America: A New View* (New York: Institute for Studies in American Music, 1988), 2–3. Nevertheless, Panassié's impact was significant, even among U.S. critics.

49 Margaret Kidder, " 'Americana' in Paris," *HRS Society Rag*, January 1939.

50 Little has been written on Panassié other than by himself or in articles published about him during his lifetime. One extremely helpful source is a collection of information about and documents by Panassié recently compiled and privately published by Christian Senn and titled *Hugues Panassié: fondateur président du Hot Club de France* (Lausanne, Switzerland, 1995). I would like to thank Christian Senn for sharing his book with me as well as for his correspondence and conversations regarding my own work. Much of this section of biographical material comes from Panassié's own accounts, *Douze années de jazz* and *Monsieur jazz: entretiens avec Pierre Casalta* (Paris: Stock, 1975). See also Ludovic Tournès, *New Orleans sur Seine: histoire du jazz en France* (Paris: Fayard, 1999), 35–58.

51 Some of Panassié's surviving papers and parts of his library are now housed at the Discothèque Municipale in Villefranche-de-Rouergue. My thanks to the staff for their hospitality and assistance.

52 Tournès, *New Orleans sur Seine*, 36.

53 Panassié, *Monsieur jazz*, 33.

54 Ibid., 34.

55 Ibid., 34–35.

56 Panassié, *Douze années de jazz*, 14–17.

57 Mezzrow and Wolfe, *Really the Blues*, 192.

58 Ibid., 194.

59 Panassié, *Douze années de jazz*, 53.

60 Ibid., 65–66.

61 Ibid., 162.

62 Roger Pryor Dodge notes Panassié's popularity in his essay "Consider the Critics," in *Jazzmen*, Frederic Ramsey Jr. and Charles Edward Smith (1939; reprint, New York: Limelight Editions, 1985), 330. See also Neil Leonard, *Jazz and the White Americans: The Acceptance of a New Art Form* (Chicago: University of Chicago Press, 1962), 135–36.

63 Hugues Panassié, *Hot Jazz: The Guide to Swing Music*, trans. Lyle and Eleanor Dowling (New York: M. Witmark and Sons, 1936), xvi. Panassié approved the English translation of his book.

64 Ibid., 4.

65 Ibid., xiv.

66 Ibid., 1.

67 Ibid., 4.

68 Ibid., 4–5.

69 Ibid., 5.

70 Ibid., 8.

71 Ibid., 6.

72 Ibid., 20.

73 Ibid., 22.

74 Ibid., 5.

75 Ibid., 294.

76 Ibid., 28.

77 Ibid., 29.

78 Ibid., 56.

79 Ibid., 60.

80 Ibid., 29.

81 Hugues Panassié, *The Real Jazz*, trans. Anne Sorelle Williams (New York: Smith and Durrell, 1942), vii.

82 Ibid., viii.

83 Hugues Panassié, *La Bataille du jazz* (Paris: Editions Albin Michel, 1965), 65–66.

84 Panassié, *Hot Jazz*, 19–20.

85 Robert Goffin, *Jazz: From the Congo to the Metropolitan*, trans. Walter Schaap and Leonard G. Feather (Garden City, N.Y.: Doubleday, 1946), 145.

86 Panassié, *Douze années de jazz*, 13.

87 Panassié, *Monsieur jazz*, 152–53.

88 Panassié, *Douze années de jazz*, 59–60.

89 Ibid., 61.

90 For discussions of these kinds of critiques, see Paul A. Gagnon, "French Views" of the Second American Revolution," *French Historical Studies* 2 (1962): 430–49; and Ellen Furlough, "Selling the American Way in Interwar

France: *Prix Uniques* and the Salons des Arts Menagers," *Journal of Social History* (spring 1993): 491–519.

91 Furlough, "Selling the American Way," 501. In reality, only a small portion of the goods sold at such stores was foreign in origin, according to Furlough.

92 Cited in Gagnon, "French Views," 444.

93 André Siegfried, *France: A Study in Nationality* (New Haven, Conn.: Institute of Politics/Yale University Press, 1930), 6.

94 Panassié, *Monsieur jazz*, 132.

95 Ibid., 153–54. Panassié makes the same points in his book *Cinq mois à New York* (Paris: Editions Corrêa, 1947), 44–45.

96 André Warnod, *Les Bals de Paris* (Paris: Editions Georges Crés, 1922), 292–93.

97 Lucien Farnoux-Reynaud, "L'époque du jazz-band," *Gaulois*, 6 March 1926.

98 Fortunat Stowski, "Et si le jazz était français," *Paris-Midi*, 20 March 1926.

99 Jac Auxenfans, "Étude sur la technique de la propagande hot," *Jazz-Tango-Dancing*, June 1933.

100 Jac Auxenfans, "Spécial chorus," *Jazz-Tango-Dancing*, February 1933.

101 Auxenfans, "Étude sur la technique de la propagande hot."

102 Hugues Panassié, *Jazz-Tango-Dancing*, January 1934, 30.

103 "Académie de la musique de jazz," *Jazz-Tango-Dancing*, April 1933.

104 Grégor, "Un conservatoire de jazz," *Figaro*, 30 April 1928.

105 Auxenfans, "Étude sur la technique de la propagande hot."

106 Delaunay, *Delaunay's dilemma*, 230.

107 Ibid., 239.

108 Panassié, *Hot Jazz*, 20. Ethnomusicology, an emerging discipline during these years, made the same arguments about the merits of recordings of folk and so-called primitive music from France and around the world. See Miriam Rovsing Olsen, "France," in *Ethnomusicology: Historical and Regional Studies*, ed. Helen Myers (New York: W. W. Norton, 1993).

109 Compositions of art music are, of course, recorded many times under different conductors, orchestras, and soloists, and listeners collect these various recordings precisely because of their variety and individuality. Panassié either does not acknowledge this fact or perhaps was not aware of it at a time when the number of recordings was far fewer than today.

110 Charles Delaunay, "Jazz 1939," *Jazz-Hot*, April/May 1939, 3.

111 Jacques Canetti, *On cherche jeune homme aimant la musique* (Paris: Calmann-Lévy, 1978), 24–25.

112 N. -J. Canetti, "Pour le jazz hot en France," *Jazz-Tango-Dancing*, January 1933.

113 N. -J. Canetti, " 'Le jazz hot': livre de Hugues Panassié," *Jazz-Tango*, January 1935.

114 The story is briefly recounted in the biography of Armstrong by Laurence Bergreen, *Louis Armstrong: An Extravagant Life* (New York: Broadway

Books, 1997), 367–69.

115 Panassié, *Douze années de jazz*, 152.
116 See Delaunay, *Delaunay's dilemma*, 230–31.
117 Swing Records catalog, no. 1, November 1937; see also Hugues Panassié, "How We Recorded for the 'Swing' Label," *Jazz Express*, 1 December 1947.
118 Mezzrow and Wolfe, *Really the Blues*, 292.
119 Panassié, *Cinq mois à New York*, 82.
120 See "Country's Hot Clubs Founded by 'Swing' Devotees at Yale," *New Haven Sunday Review*, 23 February 1936; and Gilbert Millstein, "The Commodore Shop and Milt Gabler," in *Eddie Condon's Treasury of Jazz*, ed. Eddie Condon and Richard Gehman (London: Peter Davies, 1957), 114–15.
121 Panassié, *Cinq mois à New York*, 55.
122 Ibid., 45.
123 Ibid., 94.
124 Mezzrow and Wolfe, *Really the Blues*, 295.
125 X, "Voici la réponse d'un musicien belge," *Jazz-Tango*, April 1931.
126 Gottlieb, "Appel aux amis du jazz," *Jazz-Tango*, June 1931.
127 "Fondation d'un Hot-Club," *Jazz-Tango-Dancing*, November 1932.
128 "Le mouvement," *Jazz-Tango-Dancing*, February 1933.
129 "Le mouvement," *Jazz-Tango-Dancing*, April 1933.
130 Marshall Stearns, "Fondation de la fédération internationale des hot clubs," *Jazz-Hot*, September/October 1935, 3.
131 Marshall Stearns, "Rapport du secrétaire general de la fédération internationale des hot clubs," *Jazz-Hot*, April 1936, 20.
132 Correspondence between Panassié and record companies can be found at the Discothèque Municipale, Villefranche-de-Rouergue, France, and a few letters are located at the Institute for Jazz Studies at Rutgers University, Newark, New Jersey.
133 Correspondence, folder "HP 1936–1974," Institute of Jazz Studies. Dan Morgenstern, the director of the Institute for Jazz Studies, which was founded by Stearns, knew nothing of the International Federation of Hot Clubs when I asked him about it.
134 Charles Delaunay, "As I See It," *Jazz Record*, May 1947, 14.
135 Leonard Feather, "You Can Get to Harlem for £3!" *Melody Maker*, 10 July 1937, 9.
136 Charles Delaunay, "Hot News from Paris," trans. Walter E. Schaap, *Jazz-Hot*, January 1939, 15.
137 See Robert O. Paxton, *Vichy France: Old Guard and New Order, 1940–1944* (New York: Columbia University Press, 1982).

1 Letter to M. le Ministre de l'Information, 30 August 1945, fonds Delaunay, box 72, folder 2, Bibliothèque Nationale de France.

2 Ludovic Tournès, *New Orleans sur Seine: histoire du jazz en france* (Paris: Fayard, 1999), 59–90.

3 Julian Jackson, *France: The Dark Years, 1940–1944* (Oxford: Oxford University Press, 2001), 308.

4 Charles Delaunay, *Delaunay's dilemma: de la peinture au jazz* (Mâcon: Editions W, 1985), 150.

5 Cited in Hervé Le Boterf, *La vie Parisienne sous l'occupation* (Paris: Editions France-Empire, 1997), 216.

6 Article from *Le Matin*, 28 April 1977, 4° SW7070, Bibliothèque de l'Arsenal. See also Ginette Marty, *Johnny Hess: Swing, zazou, et . . . sentimental* (Paris: El-Ouns-Histoire en Chantant, 1997); and Pierre Saka, *La Chanson française à travers ses succès* (Paris: Larousse, 1998).

7 For a description of Zazou dress and culture, see W. D. Halls, *The Youth of Vichy France* (Oxford: Clarendon, 1981), 177.

8 Ibid., 177–78.

9 Charles Delaunay, "France," *Jazz Forum* 1 (1946): 13.

10 Ibid.

11 Cited in Bill Gottlieb, "Delaunay on First Visit to America," *Downbeat*, 26 August 1946, 4.

12 Delaunay, "France." Grappelli remained in England throughout the war, so the Quintet of the Hot Club had to be reformulated without him.

13 For other titles, see Frank Ténot, "Le Jazz en France pendant l'occupation," *Jazz Magazine*, March/April 1978, 18–21.

14 Delaunay, "France."

15 Jackson, *France: The Dark Years*, 300–326.

16 For information on Delaunay's Jewish heritage, I thank Anne Legrand and her work in the fonds Delaunay at the Bibliothèque Nationale de France.

17 Bill Gottlieb, "Delaunay Escapades with Gestapo Related," *Downbeat*, 9 September 1946, 12. See also information in the fonds Delaunay at the Bibliothèque Nationale de France.

18 See Michael H. Kater, *Different Drummers: Jazz in the Culture of Nazi Germany* (New York: Oxford University Press, 1992); and Detlev J. K. Peukert, *Inside Nazi Germany: Conformity, Opposition, and Racism in Everyday Life* (New Haven, Conn.: Yale University Press, 1982). Halls comes to the conclusion that the Zazous and other aspects of youth counterculture were, "in the final analysis, pro-Allied" (*Youth of Vichy*, 178).

19 Delaunay, "France."

20 Gottlieb, "Delaunay Escapades."

21 Milton "Mezz" Mezzrow and Bernard Wolfe, *Really the Blues* (New York: Random House, 1946), 329.

22 Correspondence, "Jazz in France" folder, Institute for Jazz Studies, Rutgers University, Newark, New Jersey.

23 E. Bagge, "Quand l'américain air force embouche le trombone," *Aurore*, 19 October 1944.

24 Delaunay, *Delaunay's dilemma*, 160.

25 For an untitled, typescript document written by Panassié giving his side of the dispute, see Christian Senn, *Hugues Panassié: fondateur président du Hot Club de France* (Lausanne, Switzerland, 1995), 119. It is preceded (115–18) by a similar typescript document by Delaunay titled "Differend Panassié-Delaunay," which can also be found at the Institute for Jazz Studies, Rutgers University.

26 Cited in Ernest Borneman, "The Jazz Cult: II. The War among the Critics," *Harper's Magazine*, March 1947, 269. Borneman's article outlines the general shape of this debate and provides many interesting examples of the vitriol exchanged between the camps.

27 Cited in ibid.

28 Cited in ibid.

29 See Elizabeth Vihlen, "Sounding French: Jazz in Postwar France" (Ph.D. diss., State University of New York at Stony Brook, 2000), and "Jammin' on the Champs-Elysées: Jazz, France, and the 1950s," in *"Here, There, and Everywhere": The Foreign Politics of American Popular Culture*, ed. Reinhold Wagnleitner and Elaine Tyler May (Hanover, N.H.: University Press of New England, 2000), 149–62.

30 For a brief tour through the ebb and flow of these trends, see Gérard Noiriel, "French and Foreigners," in *Realms of Memory, Volume I: Conflicts and Divisions*, ed. Pierre Nora, trans. Arthur Goldhammer (New York: Columbia University Press, 1996), 145–78. See also Yves Lequin, *La Mosaïque France: histoire des étrangers et de l'immigration* (Paris: Larousse, 1988). And for a more thorough discussion of the revolutionary period, see Michael Rapport, *Nationality and Citizenship in Revolutionary France: The Treatment of Foreigners* (Oxford: Clarendon Press, 2000).

31 Lloyd Kramer, *Threshold of a New World: Intellectuals and the Exile Experience in Paris, 1830–1848* (Ithaca, N.Y.: Cornell University Press, 1988), 15.

32 Fernand Braudel, *The Identity of France*, trans. Siân Reynolds (New York: Harper and Row, 1988).

33 Gérard Noiriel, *The French Melting Pot: Immigration, Citizenship, and National Identity*, trans. Geoffroy de Laforcade (Minneapolis: University of Minnesota Press, 1996); and Ralph Schor, *L'Opinion française et les étrangers en France, 1919–1939* (Paris: Publications de la Sorbonne, 1985).

34 Gary Cross, *Immigrant Workers in Industrial France: The Making of a New Laboring Class* (Philadelphia, Pa.: Temple University Press, 1983); and Nancy Green, *Ready-to-Wear and Ready-to-Work: A Century of Industry and Immigrants in Paris and New York* (Durham, N.C.: Duke University Press, 1997).

35 Pascal Ory, "Gastronomy," in *Realms of Memory: The Construction of the*

French Past, Volume II: Traditions, ed. Pierre Nora, trans. Arthur Goldhammer (New York: Columbia University Press, 1997), 467.

36 Rogers Brubaker, *Citizenship and Nationhood in France and Germany* (Cambridge: Harvard University Press, 1992); Noiriel, *The French Melting Pot*.

37 See Eugen Weber, *Peasants into Frenchmen: The Modernization of Rural France, 1870–1914* (Stanford, Calif.: Stanford University Press, 1976).

38 See Alice L. Conklin, *A Mission to Civilize: The Republican Idea of Empire in France and West Africa* (Stanford, Calif.: Stanford University Press, 1997).

39 See Noiriel, *The French Melting Pot*.

40 Vicki Caron also asserts these "countervailing forces" in the 1930s in describing responses to the Jewish refugee crisis in her *Uneasy Asylum: France and the Jewish Refugee Crisis, 1933–1942* (Stanford, Calif.: Stanford University Press, 1999), 5.

41 Noiriel ("French and Foreigners," 151) has pointed out that the universality of revolutionary ideals were not always consistently practiced as, for example, during 1793, when foreigners again became easy scapegoats for political, economic, and military difficulties. Rapport also underscores the ambiguities of these ideas in *Nationality and Citizenship in Revolutionary France*.

42 P. H., "À Montparnasse," *L'Illustration*, 26 March 1932.

43 For some recent reconsiderations of américanisation, see Richard F. Kuisel, *Seducing the French: The Dilemma of Americanization* (Berkeley: University of California Press, 1993), 231–37; Richard Pells, *Not Like Us: How Europeans Have Loved, Hated, and Transformed American Culture since World War II* (New York: Basic Books, 1997); Rob Kroes, *If You've Seen One, You've Seen the Mall* (Urbana: University of Illinois Press, 1996); and Claude-Jean Bertrand, "American Cultural Imperialism—A Myth?" *American Studies International* 25 (April 1987): 46–60.

44 Benjamin Barber, *Jihad vs. McWorld: How Globalism and Tribalism Are Reshaping the World* (New York: Ballentine Books, 1996).

45 See, for example, Theodor W. Adorno, *Introduction to the Sociology of Music*, trans. E. B. Ashton (New York: Seabury Press, 1962), chap. 2.

46 For a useful review of the literature on these different points of view, see John Clarke, "Pessimism versus Populism: The Problematic Politics of Popular Culture," in *For Fun and Profit: The Transformation of Leisure into Consumption*, ed. Richard Butsch (Philadelphia, Pa.: Temple University Press, 1990).

47 Arjun Appadurai, *Modernity at Large: Cultural Dimensions of Globalization* (Minneapolis: University of Minnesota Press, 1996), 42.

48 Marshall Sahlins, "What Is Anthropological Enlightenment? Some Lessons of the Twentieth Century," *Annual Review of Anthropology* 28 (1999): 1–23.

49 James Clifford, *Routes: Travel and Translation in the Late Twentieth Century* (Cambridge: Harvard University Press, 1997), 10.

SELECTED BIBLIOGRAPHY

Abel, Richard. *French Cinema: The First Wave, 1915–1929*. Princeton, N.J.: Princeton University Press, 1984.

Appadurai, Arjun. *Modernity at Large: Cultural Dimensions of Globalization*. Minneapolis: University of Minnesota Press, 1996.

Badger, Reid. *A Life in Ragtime: A Biography of James Reese Europe*. New York: Oxford University Press, 1995.

Barber, Benjamin. *Jihad vs. McWorld: How Globalism and Tribalism Are Reshaping the World*. New York: Ballentine Books, 1996.

Barkan, Elazar, and Ronald Bush, eds. *Prehistories of the Future: The Primitivist Project and the Culture of Modernism*. Stanford, Calif.: Stanford University Press, 1995.

Barrot, Olivier, and Pascal Ory, eds. *Entre deux guerres: la création française entre 1919–1939*. Paris: Editions François Bourin, 1990.

Beale, Marjorie. *The Modernist Enterprise: French Elites and the Threat of Modernity, 1900–1940*. Stanford, Calif.: Stanford University Press, 1999.

Becker, Jean-Jacques, and Serge Bernstein. *Victoire et frustrations, 1914–1929*. Paris: Editions du Seuil, 1990.

Bertaut, Jules. *Paris: 1870–1935*. Translated by R. Millar. London: Eyre and Spottiswoode, 1936.

Blake, Jody. *Le Tumulte Noir: Modernist Art and Popular Entertainment in Jazz-Age Paris, 1900–1930*. University Park: Pennsylvania State University Press, 1999.

Blumenthal, Henry. *American and French Culture, 1800–1900: Interchanges in Art, Science, Literature, and Society*. Baton Rouge: Louisiana State University Press, 1975.

Brody, Elaine. *Paris: The Musical Kaleidoscope, 1870–1925*. New York: George Braziller, 1987.

Brubaker, Rogers. *Citizenship and Nationhood in France and Germany*. Cambridge: Harvard University Press, 1992.

Chevalier, Louis. *Montmartre du plaisir et du crime*. Paris: Editions Robert Laffont, 1980.

Clifford James. *The Predicament of Culture: Twentieth-Century Ethnography, Literature, and Art*. Cambridge: Harvard University Press, 1988.

——. *Routes: Travel and Translation in the Late Twentieth Century*. Cambridge: Harvard University Press, 1997.

Cohen, William B. *The French Encounter with Africans: White Response to Blacks, 1530–1880*. Bloomington: Indiana University Press, 1980.

Cohen-Portheim, Paul. *The Spirit of Paris*. Philadelphia, Pa.: J. B. Lippincott, 1937.

Collier, James Lincoln. *The Making of Jazz: A Comprehensive History*. New York: Dell Publishing Co., 1978.

——. *The Reception of Jazz in America: A New View*. New York: Institute for Studies in American Music, 1988.

Conklin, Alice L. *A Mission to Civilize: The Republican Idea of Empire in France and West Africa*. Stanford, Calif.: Stanford University Press, 1997.

Cross, Gary. *Immigrant Workers in Industrial France: The Making of a New Laboring Class*. Philadelphia, Pa.: Temple University Press, 1983.

de Grazia, Victoria. "Mass Culture and Sovereignty: The American Challenge to European Cinemas, 1920–1960." *Journal of Modern History* 61 (March 1989): 53–87.

Delaunay, Charles. *Hot Discography*. Paris: Jazz Hot, 1936.

——. *Django Reinhardt*. Translated by Michael James. New York: Da Capo Press, 1961.

——. *Delaunay's dilemma: de la peinture au jazz*. Mâcon: Editions W, 1985.

Dillaz, Serge. *La chanson sous la IIIe république (1870–1940)*. Paris: Tallandier, 1991.

Eksteins, Modris. *The Rites of Spring: The Great War and the Birth of the Modern Age*. New York: Anchor Books, 1989.

Fabre, Michel. *La Rive noire: de Harlem à la Seine*. Paris: Lieu Commun, 1985.

——. *From Harlem to Paris: Black American Writers in France, 1840–1980*. Urbana: University of Illinois Press, 1991.

Fulcher, Jane F. *French Cultural Politics and Music: From the Dreyfus Affair to the First World War*. New York: Oxford University Press, 1999.

Furlough, Ellen. "Selling the American Way in Interwar France: *Prix Uniques* and the Salons des Arts Menagers." *Journal of Social History* (spring 1993): 491–519.

Gagnon, Paul A. "French Views of the Second American Revolution." *French Historical Studies* 2 (1962): 430–49.

Gelatt, Roland. *The Fabulous Phonograph: From Tin Foil to High Fidelity*. Philadelphia, Pa.: J. B. Lippincott, 1955.

Gendron, Bernard. "Jamming at Le Bœuf: Jazz and the Paris Avant-Garde." *Discourse* 12 (fall/winter 1989–1990): 3–27.

——. "Fetishes and Motorcars: Negrophilia in French Modernism." *Cultural Studies* 4 (May 1990): 141–55.

——. *Between Montmartre and the Mudd Club: Popular Music and the Avant-Garde*. Chicago: University of Chicago Press, 2002.

Gioia, Ted. *The Imperfect Art: Reflections on Jazz and Modern Culture*. New York: Oxford University Press, 1988.

——. *The History of Jazz*. New York: Oxford University Press, 1997.

Godbolt, Jim. *A History of Jazz in Britain, 1919–1950*. London: Quartet Books, 1984.

Goddard, Chris. *Jazz away from Home*. New York: Paddington Press, 1979.

Goffin, Robert. *Aux frontières du jazz*. Paris: Editions du Sagittaire, 1932.

———. *Jazz: From the Congo to the Metropolitan*. Translated by Walter Schaap and Leonard G. Feather. Garden City, N.Y.: Doubleday, 1946.

Golan, Romy. *Modernity and Nostalgia: Art and Politics in France between the Wars*. New Haven, Conn.: Yale University Press, 1995.

Haggerty, Michael. "Quand la France découvre le jazz." Special issue of *Jazz Magazine* (January 1984).

Hargreaves, Alec G. *Immigration, "Race," and Ethnicity in Contemporary France*. London: Routledge, 1995.

Huddleston, Sisley. *Paris Salons, Cafés, Studios*. New York: Blue Ribbon Books, 1928.

Jackson, Jeffrey H. "Making Enemies: Jazz in Interwar Paris." *French Cultural Studies* 10 (June 1999): 179–99.

———. "Making Jazz French: The Reception of Jazz Music in Paris, 1927–1934." *French Historical Studies* 25 (winter 2002): 149–70.

Jordan, Matthew F. "Jazz Changes: A History of French Discourse on Jazz from Ragtime to Be-Bop." Ph.D. diss., Claremont Graduate School, 1998.

Kenney, William Howland, "Le Hot: The Assimilation of American Jazz in France, 1917–1940." *American Studies* (1984): 5–24.

———. *Chicago Jazz: A Cultural History, 1904–1930*. New York: Oxford University Press, 1993.

Kern, Steven. *The Culture of Time and Space, 1880–1918*. Cambridge: Harvard University Press, 1983.

Kuisel, Richard F. *Seducing the French: The Dilemma of Americanization*. Berkeley: University of California Press, 1993.

Laude, Jean. *La Peinture française (1905–1914) et l'art nègre*. Paris: Editions Klincksieck, 1968.

Lebovics, Herman. *True France: The Wars over Cultural Identity, 1900–1945*. Ithaca, N.Y.: Cornell University Press, 1992.

Leonard, Neil. *Jazz and the White Americans: The Acceptance of a New Art Form*. Chicago: University of Chicago Press, 1962.

Levenstein, Harvey. *Seductive Journey: American Tourists in France from Jefferson to the Jazz Age*. Chicago: University of Chicago Press, 1998.

Lloyd, Craig. *Eugene Bullard: Black Expatriate in Jazz-Age Paris*. Athens: University of Georgia Press, 2000.

Martin, Denis-Constant, and Olivier Roueff. *La France du jazz: musique, modernité, et identité dans la première moitié du XXe siècle*. Paris: Editions Parenthèses, 2002.

Mathy, Jean-Philippe. *Extrême-Occident: French Intellectuals and America*. Chicago: University of Chicago Press, 1993.

Matsuda, Matt K. *The Memory of the Modern*. New York: Oxford University Press, 1996.

Miller, Michael B. *Shanghai on the Metro: Spies, Intrigue, and the French between the Wars.* Berkeley: University of California Press, 1994.

Noiriel, Gérard. *The French Melting Pot: Immigration, Citizenship, and National Identity.* Translated by Geoffroy de Laforcade. Minneapolis: University of Minnesota Press, 1996.

Panassié, Hugues. *Hot Jazz: The Guide to Swing Music.* Translated by Lyle and Eleanor Dowling. New York: M. Witmark and Sons, 1936.

——. *The Real Jazz.* Translated by Anne Sorelle Williams. New York: Smith and Durrell, 1942.

——. *Douze années de jazz: (1927–1938), souvenirs.* Paris: Editions Corrêa, 1946.

——. *Cinq mois à New York.* Paris: Editions Corrêa, 1947.

——. *La Bataille du jazz.* Paris: Editions Albin Michel, 1965.

——. *Monsieur jazz: entretiens avec Pierre Casalta.* Paris: Stock, 1975.

Peer, Shanny. *France on Display: Peasants, Provincials, and Folklore in the 1937 Paris World's Fair.* Albany: State University of New York Press, 1998.

Pells, Richard. *Not Like Us: How Europeans Have Loved, Hated, and Transformed American Culture since World War II.* New York: Basic Books, 1997.

Perloff, Nancy. *Art and the Everyday: Popular Entertainment and the Circle of Erik Satie.* Oxford: Clarendon Press, 1991.

Rearick, Charles. *Pleasures of the Belle Epoque: Entertainment and Festivity in Turn-of-the-Century France.* New Haven, Conn.: Yale University Press, 1985.

——. "Song and Society in Turn-of-the-Century France." *Journal of Social History* 22 (fall 1988): 45–63.

——. *The French in Love and War: Popular Culture in the Era of the World Wars.* New Haven, Conn.: Yale University Press, 1997.

Roberts, Mary Louise. *Civilization without Sexes: Reconstructing Gender in Postwar France, 1917–1927.* Chicago: University of Chicago Press, 1994.

Rose, Phyllis. *Jazz Cleopatra: Josephine Baker in Her Time.* New York: Vintage, 1989.

Sahlins, Marshall. "What Is Anthropological Enlightenment? Some Lessons of the Twentieth Century." *Annual Review of Anthropology* 28 (1999).

Sanjek, Russell. *American Popular Music and Its Business: Volume III, from 1900–1984.* New York: Oxford University Press, 1988.

Schneider, William H. *An Empire for the Masses: The French Popular Image of Africa, 1870–1900.* Westport, Conn.: Greenwood Press, 1982.

——. *Quality and Quantity: The Quest for Biological Regeneration in Twentieth-Century France.* Cambridge: Cambridge University Press, 1990.

Schor, Ralph. *L'Opinion française et les étrangers en France, 1919–1939.* Paris: Publications de la Sorbonne, 1985.

Schulman, Seth. "The Celebrity Culture of Modern Nightlife: Music Hall, Dance, and Jazz in Interwar Paris, 1918–1930." Ph.D. diss., Brown University, 2000.

——. "Pleasures of the Primitive: A Cultural Genealogy of the Jazz-Band in Post–World War I Paris," *Proceedings of the Western Society for French History* 26 (1998): 354–61.

Seigel, Jerrold. *Bohemian Paris: Culture, Politics, and the Boundaries of Bourgeois Life, 1830–1930*. New York: Penguin, 1986.

Senn, Christian. *Hugues Panassié: fondateur président du Hot Club de France*. Lausanne, Switzerland, 1995.

Shack, William A. *Harlem in Montmartre: A Paris Jazz Story between the Great Wars*. Berkeley: University of California Press, 2001.

Southern, Eileen. *The Music of Black Americans: A History*. 2d ed. New York: W. W. Norton, 1983.

Smith, Geoffrey. *Stéphane Grappelli*. London: Pavilion, 1987.

Stearns, Marshall. *The Story of Jazz*. New York: Oxford University Press, 1956.

Stovall, Tyler. "Paris in the Age of Anxiety, 1919–39." In *Anxious Visions: Surrealist Art*, ed. Sidra Stich. New York: Abbeville Press, 1990.

——. "Colour-Blind France? Colonial Workers during the First World War." *Race and Class* 35 (October 1993): 35–55.

——. *Paris Noir: African Americans in the City of Light*. Boston: Houghton Mifflin, 1996.

——. "The Color Line behind the Lines: Racial Violence in France during the Great War." *American Historical Review* 103 (June 1998): 737–69.

Strauss, David. *Menace in the West: The Rise of French Anti-Americanism in Modern Times*. Westport, Conn.: Greenwood Press, 1978.

Taylor, Denise Pilmer. "La Musique pour tout le monde: Jean Wiéner and the Dawn of French Jazz." Ph.D. diss., University of Michigan, 1998.

Tournès, Ludovic. "L'Américanisation de la culture française, ou la rencontre d'un modèle conquérant et d'un pays au seuil de la modernité." *Historiens et géographes* (July/August 1997): 65–79.

——. *New Orleans sur Seine: histoire du jazz en France*. Paris: Fayard, 1999.

Vihlen, Elizabeth. "Jammin' on the Champs-Elysées: Jazz, France, and the 1950s." In *"Here, There, and Everywhere": The Foreign Politics of American Popular Culture*, edited by Reinhold Wagnleitner and Elaine Tyler May. Hanover, N.H.: University Press of New England, 2000.

——. "Sounding French: Jazz in Postwar France." Ph.D. diss., State University of New York at Stony Brook, 2000.

Watkins, Glenn. *Pyramids at the Louvre: Music, Culture, and Collage from Stravinsky to the Postmodernists*. Cambridge: Harvard University Press, 1994.

Weber, Eugen. *The Hollow Years: France in the 1930s*. New York: W. W. Norton, 1994.

Williams, Alan. *Republic of Images: A History of French Filmmaking*. Cambridge: Harvard University Press, 1992.

Wilson, Robert Forrest. *Paris on Parade*. Indianapolis, Ind.: Bobbs-Merrill, 1925.

Wohl, Robert. *The Generation of 1914*. Cambridge: Harvard University Press, 1979.

Woon, Basil. *The Paris That's Not in the Guide Books*. New York: Robert M. McBride, 1931.

Zeldin, Theodore. *France: 1848–1945, Volume 2: Intellect, Taste, and Anxiety*. Oxford: Oxford University Press, 1977.

INDEX

JEFFREY H. JACKSON

IS ASSISTANT PROFESSOR IN

THE DEPARTMENT OF HISTORY

AT RHODES COLLEGE.

Library of Congress Cataloging-in-Publication Data

Jackson, Jeffrey H.
Making jazz French : music and modern life
in interwar Paris / Jeffrey H. Jackson.
p. cm. — (American encounters/global
interactions)
Includes bibliographical references and index.
ISBN 0-8223-3137-3 (cloth : acid-free paper) —
ISBN 0-8223-3124-1 (paper : acid-free paper)
1. Jazz—Social aspects—France—Paris.
2. Paris (France)—Social conditions—20th
century. 3. French—Ethnic identity. I. Title.
II. Series.
ML3918.J39J33 2003
781.65'0944—dc21   2003001722